A KEY, A PADLOCK AND MILK OF MAGNESIA

A COLLECTION OF UNLIKELY, NONFICTION SHORT-SHORT STORIES TO WARM THE SOUL

A KEY, A PADLOCK AND MILK OF MAGNESIA

A COLLECTION OF UNLIKELY, NONFICTION SHORT-SHORT STORIES TO WARM THE SOUL

BY

FRANK BANCROFT WALKER

Bookstand Publishing

www.bookstandpublishing.com

Published by
Bookstand Publishing
Morgan Hill, CA 95037
3778_1

ISBN 978-1-61863-401-6

Printed in the United States of America

iv

ACKNOWLEDGEMENTS

My heart goes out to the following for their considerable help:
    Isabel Walker
    Frank Walker, Jr.
    Larry Villot,
    Allen Shields

INTRODUCTION

Biographies and memoirs can take many forms. For this book I have chosen the form of short, short stories, primarily events from my eight decades of planet earth living.

These stories, because of their brevity, are comfortably read before nodding off to sleep. Their widely varying content reflects my diverse life's experiences.

My selection of stories was designed to suit the intellectual choices and curiosities of most readers. Some stories are highly unusual, others gripping and some even controversial. All are interesting.

Each chapter deals with a specific theme and is accordingly titled. Thus "Latin America" speaks of adventures during my long residence and travel throughout most of those nations south of the border. The chapter on "Journalism" deals with a number of the fascinating if exciting activities of my father, Fred J. Walker, a long time Hearst editor. He constitutes the primary source of my writing inspiration.

In this book you will learn how close I came to being caught smuggling a shotgun into Brazil. Or how sinking ducks saved my company from a major lawsuit. Or how my father was almost fired by William Randolph Hearst at his San Simeon Castle because of Marion Davies' unwelcome flirtatious ways. Or my close encounter with Sir Winston Churchill. Or the time our dear little mountain hamlet's citizenry was frozen in horror only later to melt in helpless laughter and all because of a little old cigar humidor. Or how my father scooped the competition by getting an infamous murderess's full story while dancing with her at a San Francisco nightclub with her sheriff-captor looking on. Or how a close family friend, a German, who saved Hitler's life in WWI, became the Fuehrer's private secretary and personal envoy, only to turn on Hitler in a huge act of traitorism to the Nazi cause. Indeed, no less than Churchill himself credits such sedition as a key turning point in WWII. Our two families were to see much of each other. During this man's post war de-nazification trial he was declared a secret savior of the Jews.

So curl up in a comfortable chair, sip on your favorite drink and enjoy.

Note: My book title, *A Key, A Padlock and Milk of Magnesia*, refers to a story found at the end of Chapter 2. Front cover pictures can be found on "Photos" listings.

PREFACE TO CHAPTERS

Chapter 1. Humor: This subject was given prominence primarily because my father, a fine writer, always reminded me. "Son, never forget your "sansa youma." The Brazilian Santa Clause story is about a São Paulo shopping mall Santa that darn near blew our Christmas budget with his lavish promises to our little tots.

Chapter 2. Unusual: About remarkable times, like when I purchased a used filing cabinet only to find it loaded with super-secret files of a Fortune 500 corporation.

Chapter 3. High Drama: Speaks to exciting times, like the Los Angeles earthquake of 1994 I was caught in.

Chapter 4. Inspirational: Deals with such stories like bread on the waters when a good deed for a little old blind lady returned to me 100 fold.

Chapter 5. Latin America: Concerns an area I worked in for 21 years. "The Wretched Mess" story took place in Brazil. It was about the time I was elected to tie up lots of flies for my fishing buddies. Only problem was the rum they gave me that produced startling albeit surprising results.

Chapter 6. Famous People: My encounter with Winston Churchill is tantalizingly intriguing.

Chapter 7. Miracles: I define miracles as those occurrences which can only be explained by Divine intervention. "A Lost Cashier's Check" is a case in point.

Chapter 8. Journalism: These are experiences my father, a leading William Randolph Hearst editor, had, largely with prominent people.

Chapter 9. Non Latin America: "A Paris Hotel" speaks of a hotel erroneously booked by a relative for our family of eight which turned out to have been in a Paris red light district.

Chapter 10. <u>WW II</u>: "The General's Birthday Party" was supposed to prove how bad Clark Field food, during WW II in the Philippines, really was. That contention backfired in this story's astonishing ending.

Chapter 11. <u>Pathos</u>: "Silent Dialogs" speaks of dialogs between deaf mutes.

Chapter 12. <u>Tender</u>: "Glimpses of My Dad" tells of actions that proved my father's love for me.

Chapter 13. <u>Miscellaneous</u>: Varied but interesting stories.

Chapter 14. <u>Satisfying</u>: "Oh Really, A Riley" tells of a car that wasn't supposed to move very fast, but fooled everyone.

TABLE OF CONTENTS

CHAPTER 1

HUMOR

-----

* See photo

BRAZILIAN SANTA CLAUS

It was Christmas Eve in São Paulo, Brazil where our then young family was living. The phone rang. It was our dear friend, Lucho Gianoli. "Frank," he said excitedly, "Have your kids seen Santa yet?"

"No, Lucho, they haven't, although they are well-primed. Stockings are up and the children have already scoured the fireplace so Saint Nick won't get soot all over himself. At this very moment their ears are perked for the expectant clatter of hoofbeats on the roof."

"Great, Frank, can I bring Santa over?" Lucho asked. "I found one a couple of hours ago complete with beard and costume. He looked a bit the worse for wear at this bus stop where I first saw him. He'd been bouncing kids on his knee all day long at a local department store. So when we arrived at my house I poured him a few stiff belts. Right now he's in my living room, purring away, and seems ready to put on a good show."

Seizing what appeared to be a made-to-order windfall, I quickly agreed.

"I'll be right over," said Lucho.

It wasn't long before the doorbell rang. There was Lucho, beaming away, as he presented his North Pole visitor. Our little tots, already tipped off that Santa was coming, were bubbling with excitement and oozing good behavior.

Isabel and I greeted him in unison, "Please do come in, Santa."

As he climbed the stairs to our front door it was easy to see he was feeling no pain, because when he got to the threshold he tried to ascend a final stair that wasn't there.

Now, to enter our living room where our children were waiting it was necessary to pass through the foyer and by our bar. I saw Santa do a double take at our bottled array of Christmas cheer. (It will later be evident that his memory bank had carefully recorded in italics this fortuitous discovery as he laid plans for the kind of stellar performance he felt would merit a liquid award).

One by one our awed youngsters took turns on his lap enthusiastically pouring out their list of requests. To each wish dear Nick would nod while assuring, "Ah yes, you will get that and even more," (in between his furtive glances, that is, in the direction of our bar).

This unexpected goldmine of generosity did not pass unnoticed by our children as they quickly upward-revised their petition inventory.

With alarm Isabel and I observed this fast-escalating give-away program.

I whispered to Lucho out of the corner of my mouth, "How do we turn this guy off? He's already blown our budget and seems to be just warming up."

With supreme confidence Lucho smiled, "Hooch, Frank, hooch."

A word to the wise was sufficient and I made a beeline for the bar. Soon I caught our visitor's attention by slowly pendulating a bottle of Johnny Walker Black well within his angle of vision.

As if in a hypnotic trance, Santa rose, turned to his subjects to fling a final bank-breaking salvo of promises, and headed straight for the bar and the reward he figured he'd more than earned.

I poured liberally and handed him the glass. "Excuse me," he apologized, "but may I have a straw? I don't want the alcohol to dissolve the glue that holds my beard on."

Only seconds later I was astonished to hear slurpings signaling that his glass gauge read empty.

After Santa had downed a couple of refills, Lucho led him out the door and, amid gushings of eternal gratitude, Nick waved goodbye.

Isabel then turned to me and whispered "Whew!" to which I sighed in full agreement.

"Honey, *NOW* what do we do?" I moaned.

Then later I got called on the carpet by my better half for having contributed to the delinquency of a Santa. And, in retrospect, I guess she was right.

*   *   *

THE HAPLESS HUMIDOR

Heath Porter was known and admired by those who knew him, which was most of Mariposa.

For many years he had worked out of his barber shop just across from our town's only post office.

An imposing figure at 6 feet 7 inches, he was an excellent barber and hair stylist right up, that is, until his fatal car accident.

Mariposa County High School's auditorium was packed for Heath's memorial service where his widow, Mary Ann, asked me to read my story about Heath. It dealt with an event that rocked Mariposa, but, in a surprise ending, left our town rolling in helpless laughter.

Here is that story.

Heath just loved to smoke cigars and he knew the importance of keeping them moist. But humidors costing what they do, and Heath being a resourceful chap, it was not long before he designed a handy one of his own. He made it out of a short section of pvc pipe with a cap at either end.

Well, sir, one fine autumn day, right in front of our small town's busy post office, where all of us residents would go daily for our mail, Heath's home-made treasure fell unnoticed from his car.

Soon this innocent little item was mistaken for a pipe bomb by an over-zealous citizen who screamed, "It's a bomb, it's a bomb!" and all hell broke loose in this sedate, quiet mountain hamlet, where ordinarily an item like Aunt Mamie's new apple pie recipe is front page news.

Sirens whined and colored lights flashed as cop cars, fire trucks, ambulances, bomb squads, rubberneckers and the media all converged on this quizzical humidor that was lying there just minding its own business.

Up went the police department's emergency yellow cordoning tape while blaring megaphones warned the excited crowd to move back.

Heath poked his head out of his nearby barbershop door to see what all this commotion was about. What he saw were oodles of scared eyes all riveted to his missing humidor as if it were a king cobra ready to strike.

The solution seemed quite simple to Heath. He strode up to the yellow tape, ducked under it, preparatory to scooping up his humidor when suddenly four no-nonsense lawmen tackled, manacled and shackled poor, unlucky Heath.

"Hey, what's goin' on?" Heath cried in surprise.

"Obstruction of justice," they shot back while whisking him off to the cooler.

En route to the lock up, befuddled Heath sounded like a broken record as he kept pleading, "But fellas, honest, that isn't a pipe bomb. It's only my cigar humidor."

Undaunted by what Heath insisted was but his beloved, inoffensive cigar humidor, the bomb squad, fearing another potential Oklahoma City bombing disaster, blasted to smithereens Heath's whimpering humidor and its prized contents.

Later Heath and his accusers stood before the judge who knew he was on the horns of a dilemma. On the one hand he realized the amusing truth of this incident, yet on the other hand he was confronted with a save face problem due to an over-reaction to the rash panic shout of a jittery, misinformed citizen.

Down banged the gavel, "$200 fine, Mr. Porter," ordered his honor while doing his best to keep from bursting out laughing, while Heath wiped his brow in relief.

Now the problem facing Heath was this: What would be the design of his next humidor?

But for those of us who knew Heath, we were not at all surprised to learn that just when everyone thought this whole hilarious episode had finally been laid to rest by his honor's gavel, up comes Heath with a law suit against the county for the loss of his humidor and cigars.

*　*　*

Butch Skinner, a fellow senior citizen, once lived across the street from us right here in Mariposa. He was a kindly soul. One day he approached me, "Frank, I just have to tell you a story about your little grandson."

(You see, Nick, a loveable seven-year-old ball of non-stop energy was living with us at the time.)

Then with a smile Butch said, "The other day your little Nick came over while I was holding a very stiff metal rod that had a reflector on top of it. It had fallen over and I was getting ready to poke it back in the ground. This rod I put at the edge of my lawn as a warning so cars will stay off the grass.

"So with Nick looking on, I told him that sometimes this rod gets pushed over and I merely jam it back in the grass the way it was."

Well, Nick was listening attentively and sort of sounding me out, I was to learn, for the next thing I knew he volunteered, "Mr. Skinner, did you know that the other day a little boy knocked over your reflector," as his eyes searched for my reaction.

"Oh, no problem at all, Nick, it is so easy to put back, just like I'm doing right now."

With re-enforced courage Nick then bowed his head, and I heard him quietly say, "Would you please forgive me?"

*   *   *

My "X"

The other day at a check-out stand I handed the girl my Visa card. Soon she gave me a pen and a charge slip to sign.

To inject a bit of humor I asked her if she would mind witnessing my "X".

With a twinkle she replied, "Sure, where is she?"

*   *   *

I was a San Francisco high schooler when America's involvement in WW II erupted onto the world scene immediately following Japan's December 7, 1941 sneak attack on Pearl Harbor.

In 1942, during my school's summer break, I joined the pipe fitter's union as a helper. Henry J. Kaiser was cranking out a slew of liberty transport ships from his San Francisco Bay Area shipyards and much finishing work, to include extensive piping, was still required after each hull was launched to prepare it for wartime service.

So I enrolled in a souped up trade indoctrination course sponsored by the severely undermanned pipe fitter's union, emerging two weeks later as an official pipe fitter's helper.

With my course completed, my pipe fitter's union certificate declared that I knew how to thread pipe, take measurements, differentiate between such items as a coupling and a one quarter bend and that I was able to use the basic tools of the trade.

Apprentice pipe fitter Walker, credentials in hand, then reported for work aboard a liberty ship tied, as so many other ships were, alongside a Bay Area pier while undergoing their myriad finishing operations.

An educational experience it was for me in many ways. For example, I quickly learned the existence of more four letter words than I thought even Noah Webster was aware of.

The pipe fitter I was assigned to really knew his stuff and my skills were honed perhaps a bit faster than normal since I was trying hard to avoid having to cringe from his spicy epithets every time I cross-threaded a brass pipe or handed him the wrong tool.

That work place was terribly noisy as dozens of full-leather-clad welders constantly banged away with their chipping hammers to loosen slag from their sizzling welds before laying on their next bead. The din of reverberating metal striking metal was oftentimes deafening.

And, of course, there was always the practical joker. One noontime, while sitting against a bulkhead enjoying my Mom's brown bag goodies, my attention was drawn to a nearby group of fellow workers slapping their knees while roaring with laughter.

It seems that one of them had been relating a recent experience. (Parenthetically, it should be said that all of us, for security reasons, were obliged to wear i.d. tags with our fotos in plain view.)

Well, our prankster, to test the efficacy of the i.d. tag inspection system, had substituted his picture for that of a monkey and his by then ten-day-long charade had still gone undetected.

Our toilet facilities were off the ship at the pier's face where a six-holer was cantilevered out over the water.

It would get pretty windy out there and not infrequently the used tissue on its way to the water would be caught in an updraft.

Picture, if you will, the privy's occupants weaving and dodging those bits of used paper that had successfully made their way back up through one of the vacant holes with our nervous sedentary friends trying desperately to avoid being part of an ecru collage.

Ours was an industrious plumbing team and we had soon gained the dubious reputation as "eager beavers."

"Hey, slow down," the other crews would shout at us, "you're making the rest of us look bad. Besides, we're all on t and m (time and materials) and we want this job to last."

Then one day while walking down a familiar passageway I looked up at the extensive piping network we had labored so long and hard over and which had been thoroughly inspected and passed by higher powers. I was unprepared, however, for what I saw. Nothing was there. Not an inch of our pipe remained. All of our painstaking work had been torn out.

"So that's how t and m works," I mused.

There was a fellow I would always see, pencil behind his ear, clipboard in hand, drawings tucked under his arm as he walked importantly to wherever he was going. But as it turned out he never had any particular destination. He just walked around impressively all day long and that's all he did, walk around. One day his ruse came to light and he got his final walking papers.

Yet despite all this muddling, I am pleased to report that America actually won the war.

*   *   *

MY DISASTROUS BARBECUE

The Iraqi war had just ended, Kuwaiti oil fields were ablaze because of madman Sadam Hussein's scorched earth policy, and our family was finally becoming unglued from the TV and CNN's constant coverage of that conflict.

We decided to take a break, leave Mariposa and spend the day up at spectacular Tuolumne Meadows in Yosemite National Park.

So we all piled into the car with Bandit, our Labrador Retriever, licking everyone in his delight over being included in the outing.

When eating time rolled around, yours truly was elected (by default) to wear the chef's hat. When all the votes were in at our meal's conclusion, I was generously awarded a C-.

You see, it was windy and really hard to light the briquettes, so I sloshed on the starter fluid like it was going out of style. Presently, I had flames and smoke that would have made a Kuwaiti emir sit up and take notice.

One couple at a table down wind from us started gasping and fanning the air. To make light of my growing disaster, I shouted over, "And I'll bet you came up here precisely to get away from big city smog!"

Well, they flashed me the weakest of smiles, picked up their blackened sandwiches, and stomped off.

Back home that night Isabel came up to me and, while gingerly holding the last remaining evidence of my culinary flop well in front of her, sighed, "This smells like an oil derrick. May I throw it out?"

*　　*　　*

ONE MOSQUITO AND A TOILET SEAT

For a number of years I suffered from a constantly recurring slipped disc problem. I recall one afternoon our twin sons, then six years old, approaching me at the club swimming pool with a joint request which, because of its enthusiasm and insistent tenor, demanded my immediate attention.

They wanted me, an admitted mediocre belly flopper, to show them how to dive off the high platform.

So, with one son pulling me while the other pushed, I reluctantly started the long climb. Once at the summit I timidly peered down and could see no difference

8

between the distance to the water there and when I used to look over the Golden Gate Bridge rail at the San Francisco Bay far below.

Even though my paternal honor was now at stake, still I found myself chickening out each time my toes got to the platform's edge.

After about the third unsuccessful foray to the brink, my sons, by then a bit exasperated, said "Look, Dad, it's easy." Whereupon they soared out over the pool. "It's fun!" they yelled up at me from the water. "Jump, Dad."

My fatherly reputation now on the line and with no loopholes left to escape through, I gulped and jumped. Partway down I must have subconsciously twisted my body for I felt a crack in my lower back. When I surfaced it was all I could do to dog paddle to the pool's edge. My back was out.

For a week I hobbled around like a man twice my age. Then one morning I found myself attending to the call of nature. From my enthroned position I noticed a mosquito eyeing me. He seemed quite excited over the size of his exposed target.

On one of his whining passes, I twisted around and clapped the bugger into oblivion. It was then that I heard that familiar crack only this time my back pain was gone. The disc was now back in place.

Ever since then I have heartily given my Rx to all slipped disc sufferers who care to listen, that for a sure fire cure all they need is a toilet seat and a mosquito.

*　*　*

You're Out!

Tee ball is a sport designed to get little grammar schoolers into baseball. To ease the kids into the art of hitting, the ball is placed atop a low, flexible post at home plate from where each batter has a turn at whacking it and, if successful, then running to first base, then second and so on.

This being the debut for many of the little tykes aspiring to future greatness, lots of swings either fanned the air or else hit the post well below the ball with the ball then dropping to the ground untouched. Those lads who took an extra healthy cut but missed, often found themselves spinning and falling.

Our little grandson, Nick, was up at the plate in Mariposa, his uniform cap way too big and all but blocking his vision. His proud grandparents were there watching.

He connected but then, a bit confused, lit out for third base. Part way there he caught his error, stopped and then headed for first.

But the ball got there before he did and the gloating first baseman was standing there, just itching to tag Nick out.

Nick saw his predicament and chose to deny his rival the satisfaction of tagging him. So he pulled up just short of first, put his hands on his hips, and stuck his tongue out at his would-be-tagger.

Everyone roared with laughter.

*   *   *

THE "WIFE" RULE-OF-THUMB

Having lived in big cities most of my life, when my wife and I finally moved to the small mountain community of Mariposa, it was necessary to adjust to a new life style, to include learning the art of burning wood in a fireplace.

So I asked my neighbor, Joe Emerson, what rule-of-thumb he used in order to tell when a log was big enough to require splitting.

"Very simple," he replied with a twinkle in his eyes. "When it's too heavy for my wife to carry in."

*   *   *

WORMS FOR THE MADAM

We were about to pull stakes and head for Mariposa. Our Woodland Hills, California home was up for sale. But since we had done a major face-lift to this property to include a regulation size tennis court, we were asking a pretty penny. There were lots of lookers. This story is about one of them.

A very business-like woman came to the door. She was stocky, sharp and seemed to know what she wanted. From her belt hung a huge assortment of keys.

We began showing her around. When we got to the tennis court, she waved the back of her hand at it and declared, "Well, here I would plan to raise worms."

"Raise worms on top of a tennis court," I gasped, my incredulity clearly showing.

"Why of course," she brazenly replied.

When she left I was still muttering to myself. "Worms on a tennis court. She's got to be nuts."

Later I spoke of this strange woman to my neighbor across the street who had seen this person come to our place and recognized her.

Chuckling she said. "She no more wants to grow worms on your tennis court than I do. That woman is a notorious madam, well-known in these parts. Her cock-and-bull story was merely a preposterous attempt to hide her cat house plans for your property."

So we wound up selling our home to a more legitimate buyer, since I would not have wished such a legacy onto my neighborhood friends, who might have then responded by burning my likeness in effigy on my front lawn.

*   *   *

HOPPING WORMS

Back in the fifties I experienced a humdinger of a nervous breakdown.

So I was hospitalized for ninety days where my treatment consisted of daily injections of insulin followed immediately by electro-shock which, of course, would always knock me out. At the time this was the state-of-the-art medical procedure.

Each day I was revived with a massive injection of glucose, administered with a huge syringe and needle. My arm, from so many punctures, soon became a brilliant rainbow of black, blue and yellow. And every morning as I would come to I felt the premonition of death. It was quite scary but, thank goodness, that feeling would last only for a minute or so.

I got to know some of my fellow patients. In the hospital wing where I was were those with problems similar to mine but all of us (presumably) still dealt with a full deck. Other wings, however, housed the less fortunate, the padded cell set.

One of my hospital colleagues there was an American Redemptorist missionary priest who had lived in the Amazonian jungle and this life of great privation and solitude had finally gotten to him.

But he did have a delightful sense of humor. I recall the time we decided to team up to play a prank on a brand new nurse since she thought every patient in the hospital was nuts, including the residents of our annex.

Our tongue-in-cheek ploy was to re-enforce her errant assessment of our mental state.

So one afternoon as this sweet little thing was marching toward us, her jittery eyes darting every whichway, we went into our act.

"Say, Frank," he said loud enough for her nervous ears to pick up, "do you know how you can find an invisible frog?"

(And it is superfluous to say that from that very instant we had assured ourselves of her undivided attention.)

Dutifully I replied "Gosh, no, Joe, how can I find an invisible frog?"

"Very simple," he retorted with supreme smugness, "just sprinkle a few worms on the ground and then wait for them to hop."

Well, I don't have to tell you what happened. Our white-clad audience of one gasped, quickly covered her mouth, and, letting out a muffled shriek, did a 180 and fled back down the hall.

When my hospital time was up, my employer wanted to be sure I had completely recovered before sending me to head up their South American operations out of São Paulo, Brazil.

So, I was asked to see what I could do to develop a market for one of the company's new and highly profitable agricultural chemicals.

Within a year I had the fortune of breaking the national sales record and our family then moved to Brazil, leaving behind all hopping worms, real or imagined, while spending an event-filled eight years in that delightful part of the world.

*　*　*

ELSIE

It was during my senior year of high school. My mother had sent me over to her mother's to deliver some things in Oakland.

"Hi, Grandmother," I greeted her in her Mills College office where, as M.D., she was the campus physician of this at the time, an all girls' college.

My business taken care of, I proceeded to look at her framed certificates, photographs and college calendar of coming events.

Then something caught my eye. It was the announcement of an upcoming prom, so I casually commented on it.

"Oh, would you like to go?" Grandmother Nell eagerly asked.

"I might, Grandmother. Why, do you have someone in mind?"

"Well, as a matter of fact I do. Her name is Elsie."

A short time later Elsie called to invite me and I accepted, in faith and sight unseen.

It was now the day of the long-awaited prom. I proudly stepped into my rented tuxedo and took a second peek into the box and tissue that cradled Elsie's orchid corsage, just to be sure all was in order.

The next thing I knew I was on the house phone in the reception area of Elsie's dormitory. "I'll be right down," her lilting voice caressed my phone's ear-piece. With the moment of our first encounter but minutes away, my expectations had now built to a high pitch. My heart was pounding so hard I was almost self-conscious.

Then it suddenly happened. There she stood, all 5'-11" of her (plus high heels) as I looked up at her from my full 5'-9" of stretched stature. Her smile greeted me through buck teeth. Her hair was red with freckles to match. And her gown, oh well, it really doesn't matter.

My countenance had taken an uncontrollable nose dive, though I hoped it wasn't too obvious. It really wasn't her fault and besides Mother always insisted that we be charitable.

As I danced across the ballroom floor with Elsie in tow, girls, and some of them real lookers, kept smiling at me. So during intermission, I approached several to inquire whether we had met before.

"Not exactly, but we know you from your picture on Dr. Bancroft's desk," they cooed.

"Grandmother," I muttered to myself, "with all these dazzling beauties why did you have to pick a Sadie Hawkins for me?"

Back home late that same night, I removed my shoes so as not to awaken anyone. But half way up the stairs old elephant ears himself, my dad, yells out, "Is that you, Son? Come on in and tell your mom and me all about it."

So as I poured out my tale of woe, Mom chuckled but Dad's roars of laughter aroused my five brothers and sisters who poured in to find out what was going on.

Next morning Dad was on the phone with the errant matchmaker. While straining to hold back a belly laugh, he sternly inquired, "Nell, how could you do this to my son?"

*　*　*

My 60th high school reunion dinner was coming up in September of 2003 and I planned on wearing the same suit I wore for my 50th reunion. So the other day I tried it on just to be sure all systems were still go. Well, they weren't. I couldn't button the pants. "Honey," I said to my wife, "will you please loan me your tape measure?"

With the facts now in hand, I gulped while concluding that either I had to buy a new suit or else go on a diet because my pants had "shrunk" three-and-a-half inches.

Then to make matters worse, a friend chimed in, "And don't forget you also have to exercise."

"Chabuca," (my wife's nickname), "from here on in it's rabbit food for me," said I. For a month I'd been a good boy, munching lettuce, doing sit-ups and trying (oftentimes unsuccessfully) to hit a tennis ball. Then I struck on a novel idea.

"Why," I mused, "don't I start punching my belly? After all, boxers condition themselves by having a heavy medicine ball thrown at their mid-section, so I can use my fist instead of a medicine ball."

No sooner had I begun pounding my belly when I noticed that a swelling had suddenly appeared just above my midriff, in the area of my solar plexus. It was sort of like squashing one end of a long balloon only to find the other end with a new bulge. My son Will, an ex EMTer, examined me. "Dad, I think you just gave yourself a hernia."

Jokingly I addressed my dear daughter-in-law, "Renda, have I shown you my HIMnia since HERnias are for ladies?" To which, with her sharp wit fully engaged and a twinkle in her eye, she retorted, "Did it HIMt you much when it happened?" Ah, yes, where would we be without the well-timed pun?

* * *

ICE CREAM AHOY!

Nipannawasee resident Bob Fish was a close friend and fishing buddy.

In fact it was thanks to Bob that my wife and I wound up settling in Mariposa, California.

Bob had an abiding love affair with ice cream, one that approached the legendary.

He told my wife Isabel and me a hilarious story on himself which began after I kidded Bob over his favorite dessert.

So, ignoring my teases, he fairly radiated (actually, "drooled" might be a better word) as he described with utmost reverence and in lavish detail the root beer float he had concocted earlier in the day.

Then he spoke of a book he had started to read whose author was an ice cream hater.

One entire chapter was devoted to the dire consequences that await all ice cream addicts.

Stoutly declaring that this writer was on very shaky ground, Bob put the book face down and flat out refused to finish it.

I think he felt that to have reacted any differently might easily have bordered on traitorism to the ice cream cause and, Lord forbid, might even have been interpreted as endorsing that writer's anti-ice cream crusade.

On another occasion, to repay Bob and Edith for their many kindnesses, I asked Bob to pick a restaurant they both liked. "It will be on Isabel and me," I told him.

The appointed time came and Bob led us to the Oakhurst dining place of his choice.

Now to get to the dining area, guests were first required to pass through the buffet section with all its enticing dishes and aromas, surely designed to whet the appetite.

Suddenly Bob stopped and, in mock surprise, followed by an ear-to-ear smile, queried, "My, what DO we have here?"

There before him was an absolutely massive mound of ice cream challenging even the most resolute of ice cream shunners (of whom Bob clearly was anything but one) to put all dietary intentions on temporary hold.

Do I think Bob knew beforehand of that calorie-loaded Matterhorn awaiting all of us? You'd better believe it!

*　*　*

Our family was visiting London on vacation. We were five strong to include a staircase of three little ones.

During our tour of this world-famous city, our twin sons kept clamoring to see Madame Tussaud's Wax Museum and Chamber of Horrors.

So, amid nervous gulps, my wife and I finally relented. As we passed by life-like replicas of Jack the Ripper attacking a victim and other equally hair-raising scenes, Isabel and I wanted out, but fast.

Not the kids, however. They were just getting warmed up by the time we had reached the exit.

"Hey, Dad, hey, Mom, can we go through again?" they clamored. "Not on your life, I've had it," I snapped, my frightened eyes still wide as platters and smarting from dripping sweat. "Aw, golly, we never have any fun," they nagged through pouting lips. "Sorry about that kids, but we're off to visit a very famous department store known as Harrods," said I, bent on shifting our tourist focus away from gore to something more sedate. "Honey, I'll take the twins if you'll ride herd on Peter," I suggested. So, with Frankie and Willy in tow, I asked my way to Harrods' sporting goods section, while Isabel left in another direction.

When time came for us to meet the rest of the family for lunch, I took a short cut to the elevator through the crystal ware and cut glass department. The boys were skipping as we went, and out of the corner of my eye I noticed a salesman twitching nervously.

Figuring to make light of what this clerk envisioned as his elegant display on the verge of being reduced to shards, I innocently inquired, "Would you mind if my sons played baseball here?"

I was secretly testing his sense of humor since I had been under the impression (erroneously, I was to learn), that the British were slow to fathom a joke. Consequently, I was unprepared for his witty rejoinder.

"Oh not at all, my good man. I assume you have a credit card!"

*   *   *

TOILET GEYSER

My dad was a great humorist, loved the practical joke and was forever saying, "Son, never forget your sansa youma."

All of which brings me to the time I heard my sainted father laugh so hard that I honestly thought he would rupture something.

The rain was coming down in sheets that day when Dad and I ducked into a public building in downtown Washington D.C. and made our way down to a subterranean rest room.

Dad's reason for being there was more transitory than mine.

So there I was, enthroned and heavily concentrating, when my toilet contents decided to play "Old Faithful."

A geyser suddenly shot out of the toilet bowl, knocking me off the seat. I scrambled out of the stall like a scared rabbit, sopping wet, bare-fannied and on all fours.

When I looked up there was Dad, his peals of helpless laughter having momentarily caused him to lose his breath. Tears of merriment were streaming down his cheeks. It seemed like minutes before he was able to speak and when he did it was in between uncontrollable sobs and howls of absolute hilarity.

Years later I became a licensed plumber and when I reflect back on that incident I was able to conclude that during that building's construction phase, building inspectors who should have been "code over-seeing" were guilty of "code over-sighting."

By code, in order to avoid precisely what had happened to me, street surface run-off drains must never be tied into sewer lines. For if a downstream obstruction should ever occur, then toilet geyser, here we come.

But plumbing goof or not, this incident was truly a side-splitter and even today I find myself chuckling. However at the time I frankly thought it anything but funny.

*   *   *

JUST HUM SOFTLY

While living in Los Angeles during the depths of the Great Depression a number of my grammar school classmates and I sang in a choir. Bob Mitchell was our gifted choirmaster, organist and pianist. All of us sopranos could hit high "C". We had a wide repertoire of songs both church and secular. Our performances were often broadcast over the radio.

When we sang at church we were called St. Brendan's Choir and elsewhere we were known as the Bob Mitchell Boys' Choir.

After I left, this choir became famous and appeared in many movies. Twice Bob Mitchell was featured on the nationally televised show, "This Is Your Life."

Years later my wife Isabel and I were walking through a shopping mall. Barbershop quarteters were harmonizing on a stage there and nearby was a sign-up table.

Nudging me, Isabel smiled, "Why don't you try out? You used to sing a lot."

With a tone of finality I replied, "Honey, that was 40 years ago. I'd be a disaster today."

Not to be swayed she bugged me into action. So, grumbling, I made my way over to the recruiting table.

The appointed day arrived for my audition. I walked into the hall where clusters of skilled quarteters were practicing and immediately I felt intimidated. Presently I was led to a small room. The door closed behind us. The tester pulled out his pitch pipe, blew a note, pointed to me and barked, "Okay, hit it!'

Gulping, I inhaled and nervously gave it my best which turned out to be weak and flat.

His brow furrowed.

Thinking he may have heard wrong, he chose another note and, hoping for the best, blew again.

My response was even worse than the first. Disastrous would best describe it.

He looked at me with compassionate eyes and gently said, "Look, you can join our group, but do you think you could just hum softly in the background?"

Later as I walked into our home I yelled, "Honey, I just flunked." *(See photo.)*

Saint Brendan's Choir, 1933

*   *   *

SEVEN DIAMOND EARRINGS

We were both waiting for this copy house to open up. The other person was a girl in her early twenties. I noticed she had seven pierced diamond earrings on one ear running in a line from the lobe all the way up her ear.

So I commented on how unusual I thought this was. She then told me the following story.

She was recently going with this guy. When she first met him she only wore two diamond earrings on that ear. But he happened to be the demanding type and told her that he didn't want to see her with any more earrings than just those two.

"Or else?" she inquired.

"Or else we're all through," was his firm reply.

At their next meeting he did a double take when he noticed not two but seven earrings.

"I thought I told you," he declared indignantly, "that if you wore any more than two earrings we would be all through."

She smiled and replied, "Now you're catching on. Bye bye."

*　*　*

PINEAPPLE JUICE

W.C. Fields' love for alcohol was legendary and, for any skeptics, the color of his nose quickly dispelled all doubt.

He oftentimes would bring a small suitcase with him to the movie set.

It contained bottles innocuously labeled, "pineapple juice, grape juice, etc." And in between takes he would walk over to take a few snorts.

That he would customarily be a bit wobbly by mid-morning suggests that his labeling might have been a bit misleading.

One day a joker decided to have a little fun. Surreptitiously he replaced the "2,000 proof" vodka in his bottle labeled "Pineapple Juice" with a liquid that more accurately reflected what the label said.

During a pause in the filming, Mr. Rednose, true to form, made a beeline for his portable refreshment center.

He poured himself a healthy belt from his bottle labeled "Pineapple Juice." No sooner was the expected fortifying tonic in his mouth when he made a horrible face, spewed it out in a misty cloud while bellowing, "Who poured pineapple juice into my pineapple juice?"

*　*　*

BOB'S GOAT

My friend, Bob, lived in the small mountain hamlet of Nipinnawasee, California. He had a neighbor who would loan his goat out for brush control.

So Bob borrowed the nanny, tied it to a tree that was surrounded by lots of poison oak, those itch-producing plants that goats adore but people don't. He then told the beast to have at it.

Now it seems that this critter was only programmed to walk in one direction around anything it was tethered to. Poor Bob, thus, found himself on constant call to unwind the goat before it did itself harm.

Once Bob ran out when he noticed the hapless critter had spiraled itself so tightly around its mooring that it lay unconscious. He quickly administered artificial respiration and the poison-oak lover finally came to.

When he told the story to his grandson about how he had revived the goat, the lad worriedly gasped, "Gosh, Grandpa, I sure hope you didn't use mouth-to-mouth!"

*   *   *

THE DECEPTIVE WALLET

In 1964 we traveled from Brazil to Europe on vacation. In Paris our young sons were being entertained by their older teenage, fun-loving French cousin, Jean Michel.

It was Sunday morning and the church service up the street from Jean Michel and his family's third story apartment was just letting out. In anticipation of that event, and to test the effect the priest's message had had on the faithful, Jean Michel unfolded an ingenious plan.

He had taken a wallet and tied to it a thin, virtually invisible fishing line which he let down with his rod and reel to the sidewalk far below.

As passersby would spot this potential windfall, their assorted reactions kept us all literally in stitches of laughter.

One well-dressed woman, prayer missal under her arm, spied the billfold out of the corner of her eye. While looking straight ahead, posture erect, she bent her knees and without breaking stride lowered her hand preparatory to scooping up her discovery.

With split second timing, Jean Michel lifted his rod and up soared the wallet just as she was about to grab it.

Tilting her head upward, she saw a window full of giggling faces, and hurried on hoping her crimson face was not too noticeable.

Another human fish soon bit but, like the first, wasn't fast enough. In mock anger he shook his fist up at the other end of the nylon tether.

And while all this was transpiring, a nearby bench was filling up with spectators, most of whom had already bitten on this ruse and hence were anxious to see others share in their chagrin.

Next was a woman who also was a second too slow. However as it developed, this gal had a sly plan. She ditched into a doorway just below Jean Michel and out of his sight.

Unaware of her lingering presence, Jean Michel prepared for his next victim and once again lowered his bait.

Suddenly from the shadows a figure pounced on the wallet. Then with her prize firmly clutched in her hand, she raised her arms in triumph with a victorious grin spread across her face. Fishermen and the numerous fish then all laughed heartily over this delightful interlude.

*　*　*

RED-FACED AT THE AUXERRE CATHEDRAL

During my first trip to Europe I traveled with my family from our temporary home in Brazil. My wife Isabel's sister and French brother-in-law lived in Paris and they took us on a tour of some of France's historic landmarks.

One of these was the famous Auxerre Cathedral, noted for its exquisite stained glass windows.

Once inside this ancient and marvelously crafted church, I was soon totally engrossed in photographing its windows from every conceivable angle.

So carelessly oblivious was I to anything and everything not related to my picture-taking that I had not noticed that partway through my photographic project a high Mass had begun. There were gorgeous windows to one side of the altar crying for my attention and I was responding in obedient concentration.

Suddenly one of the three priests officiating at this people-packed ceremony left the altar, walked over to where I was crouched behind my tripoded camera, and with nostrils flaring began to rake me up one side and down the other. Crimson-faced, I listened attentively, and though barely understanding a word of French, I discovered that this man-of-the-cloth had made his point crystal clear. I had been thoroughly chastised.

Those pictures by the way, turned out well and during the subsequent slide shows I have given of that trip, this priestly encounter I usually allude to, much to my audience's delight (and my renewed chagrin).

*   *   *

BEER BARREL POLKA AT JAIL

My good friend, Ron Sexton, was conducting a Bible study at his church. My wife and I were there.

He began by telling of a recent incident at our local Mariposa jail where he and I both serve as chaplains. Ron indicated that while I was playing harmonica in one of the rooms for a group of inmates, he was conducting a service elsewhere for a second group.

Usually I will play church songs, either on my harmonica or accordion, and that particular evening was no different. What I did not know then, however, was an event that Ron took special delight in recounting.

It seems that in the jail's central control booth, a switch had inadvertently been flicked, and my music was being piped into the room where Ron was holding his service.

After the titters from Ron's church audience had subsided, I spoke up, "You know, Ron, on one occasion a guard put in a request for Beer Barrel Polka."

*   *   *

BINGO BEANS

Dad loved humor and had been a practitioner of the harmless joke all his life.

While growing up in San Francisco I remember dad, oftentimes upon returning home from work, laughing to the point of tears as he recounted to mom and all six of us kids the details of his latest escapade at the office.

He was the steady customer of a store that sold items suitable for perpetrating his crimes of merriment.

One time he purchased a book entitled, "Secrets of an Arabian Harem," jacketed with drawings designed to arouse the curiosity of the browser. He would casually leave it on a desk in the large press room in plain view.

Victim after victim bit on this ruse for, while surreptitiously attempting to steal a peek at the contents, they would trigger a loud explosion that brought guffaws from the roomful of newsmen and women.

Dad's prime target was one of his cub reporters, a young lady whose longer term aspiration was to become a religious nun. And so as she would pass by this piece of literary temptation, all heads in the room, although bent over their respective typewriters in mock concentration, would have their eyes rolled in expectation toward this pretty little quarry.

But to her credit (and the chagrin of the perpetrator and his accomplices), not once did she so much as glance at that book's cover.

His bingo bean trick was, however, quite another story.

This bingo bean is about the size of a bean. However it is actually a mild percussion cap which explodes whenever pressure is exerted on it. So dad, armed with a pocketful of the little gems, would quietly enter the men's room and look around to be sure he was alone. Then he would place one of his bingo beans under each of the two rubber pads that cushion the toilet seat and then gingerly lower the seat.

Each time nature called an innocent to the throne room, smirks would light the expectant faces of all who were privy to dad's scheme. The explosion, occurring as it did in such a confined space, was quite a startling event and usually was quickly followed by the victim bolting through the door in the act of pulling his britches back on, only to be greeted by helpless snortings and deafening squeals of uncontrollable laughter.

Then one evening close to quitting time dad tipped off everyone that the big boss was to be his next victim the following morning. So dad's reporters, rewritemen and cameramen made a point of being there extra early for the show.

Sure enough, like clockwork into the little room marched the guy who signed the paychecks, newspaper tucked under his arm in anticipation of a relaxing half-hour.

The noisy sequel was every bit as funny as that which had befallen his predecessors.

At first blush one would think this a rather risky bit of humor to engage in, the need for paychecks being what it is. However, everyone (including the boss) knew that dad, as city editor of San Francisco's largest newspaper, was the brains behind this daily's great success and its recent award, the coveted William Randolph Hearst certificate for America's best illustrated newspaper. So no one lost his job.

*   *   *

Hair Today, Gone Tomorrow

My wife and I had just gone into retirement and we were exploring the possibility of relocating to northern California, with Mariposa winding up being our ultimate if happy choice.

While our search was in progress, we found ourselves attending a Sunday church service in Penn Valley not far from Sacramento.

During the pastor's sermon he quoted from Matthew 10:30, *"But the very hairs of your head are all numbered,"* while referring to Our Creator's all-knowing attribute.

Then he asked, "Does any one of you know how many hairs you have on your head because God knows exactly?"

He looked around but no one replied.

Finally I, who sport a Yul Brynner hairdo, slowly raised my hand.

Doing a double take on my billiard ball scalp, the preacher began to laugh and the congregation soon joined in during this light-hearted moment.

*   *   *

The Leak

The other day it rained pretty good, so I went out back to the workshop to see if my ancient roof had held up okay.

Soon I was able to home in on a problem area and found myself removing damp, do-it-yourself books from a box I had unfortunately stored below a leak in the roof.

The book that was in the worst shape of all (it was sopping wet) was entitled, "Weatherproofing."

*   *   *

HUMMERS

I noticed the level of sugar water was low in our hummingbird feeder, so I began to fill it.

Dainty, diminutive Isabel reminded me, "Don't forget, honey, it's four parts water to one of sugar, and if they don't like it that way, they can shove it."

*   *   *

MEXICO'S FLYING SAUCERS

Back in the fifties flying saucers were the rage and new sightings were constantly being reported.

At the time I was living in Hermosillo, Mexico with my family.

One evening my wife, brimming with excitement, shouted, "Come quickly, I see a flying saucer!"

Sure enough, through the bedroom window, our eyes bugging out, we both witnessed an eery green flashing light streaking across the heavens at a speed I calculated at several thousand miles per hour.

While hurtling through space it suddenly changed direction and headed toward us. Our thrill mounted the closer it got.

Presently we were able to make it out very clearly.

It was a firefly.

*   *   *

THE MOVE

My son was being discharged from the army and had applied for free moving of his personal effects.

"Sorry," said the sergeant manning the scales, "your load weight is below the required minimum to qualify for a free move."

Grumbling, he then mustered the resourcefulness he had been trained to use. Soon he returned to the scales and easily passed the weight requirement.

Around the corner he stopped and opened his van's rear door. Out stumbled oodles of giddy, extra-weight-producing army buddies clutching the beer cans provided as a reward. *(See photo.)*

The Move

*   *   *

WHAT NICE PLANTS YOU HAVE

The home where we once lived in Port Hueneme, California, had a back patio abutting our neighbor's patio and the two were separated by a common six-foot high wooden privacy fence.

One morning my dear wife's curiosity could no longer be contained. She just had to see what was on the other side.

So, stepping up on a chair, she peered over. There she noticed many potted plants.

A bedroom was at the opposite end. The drapes were open as was the sliding glass door. Isabel saw a person in bed.

Suddenly the reclining figure turned over and their eyes met. "Yes, may I help you?" the voice asked.

After ever so slight a pause Isabel smiled sheepishly and answered, "My, what lovely plants you have."

*　*　*

PIERRE THE PORTRAITIST

Once while vacationing in Paris our family used the home of my wife's sister, Mariana, and her artist husband, Pierre, as our home base.

It was late one morning when I approached their door just as Pierre was saying goodbye to a woman of stunning beauty.

After she had left, and I had regained my breath, I said, "Wow, Pierre, who was that?"

"Oh," he replied, "I am painting her portrait."

"Tell me, Pierre," I then asked, "how many sittings do you normally require to complete a portrait?"

"Well, Frank, I am usually quite fast," he admitted, "and can often complete a work in two or three sittings. But," he added with a twinkle to his eye, "in the case of the lady you just saw. I have been on her portrait now for eight sittings and I'm not even half done."

*　*　*

Jack and I were very close friends. We went to high school together and were roommates in college.

Oftentimes we'd go out on double-dates.

In those years Jack was a devoted practitioner of the prank and worked hard at refining that avocation. On more than one occasion he sucked me in as an accomplice. And sometimes I was even the brunt of his machinations.

This story recounts two instances when the worm turned and Jack found himself on the receiving end.

Still smarting from being the victim of his latest prank, I approached his celestial navigation instructor. After providing that professor with background on Jack, I noted his immediate willingness to participate in my plot of retribution.

"Leave everything to me," he said gleefully while rubbing his hands in anticipation.

Later that day I was engrossed in one of my college study assignments, when in walked Jack, muttering and mumbling.

Feigning saintly ignorance and with my halo fairly glistening above my head, I asked, "Hey Jack, what seems to be the problem?"

"That darned navigation instructor, the nerve of him," groused Jack

"Frank, get a load of this," Jack went on, clearly eliciting my sympathetic indignation.

"No sooner had our class begun when the Prof said, 'Students, today we are going to study the star, Betelgeuse, that comes out in the early evening, oh, roughly at the same time Jack Unsinn starts on his regular nightly prowl.'"

"Why, Jack, the very nerve!" said I oozing exaggerated shock and profound compassion while fighting to keep a straight face.

- - - - - - - - - - - -

During WW II Jack was the U.S. Navy's chief local disbursements officer on the Pacific island of Peleliu where his reputation of being a practical joker had been rightfully earned.

It was pay day and on Jack's desk were stacks of currency he was counting when nature called and he responded, leaving all that money in plain view.

Upon returning, he resumed his counting, humming all the while for Jack was a very happy soul and always upbeat.

Suddenly his brow creased and he began whipping through the bills much faster than before. Finally he let out an audible groan while recounting even faster all the money before him.

Unable to contain his shock, he stood and with quavering voice addressed everyone in the large room, "Has anyone seen $10,000?"

After the screams of laughter had subsided, the missing $10,000 was handed to the red-faced officer who mumbled something that could easily have been mistaken for "touché."

*　　*　　*

RECYCLED URINE

My brother, Mike, loves humor as well as the harmless practical joke. And during one of his hospital stays he once had the opportunity to have some fun with his nurse.

She had given him a container into which he had been asked to leave a urine sample.

A while later the nurse returned to retrieve Mike's liquid deposit. What she did not know was that Mike had secretly poured apple juice into the urine bottle.

Noticing the different-than-normal color, she commented, "My, what have *we* here? *Our* color is lighter than normal."

Mike, reaching for the flask, remarked, "Oh, don't worry, I'll correct the problem by just recycling it." He then gulped down its contents while observing with delight her gasps of absolute horror.

*　　*　　*

THE RIGHT ANGLE

Dad had just had a cancerous tumor removed from his brain and was recovering on the neurological floor of the U.C. Medical Center in San Francisco.

He introduced me to a patient friend whose arm was in a sling and later told us the story of why that friend was in the hospital.

30

A bulldozer operator (or "cat skinner" as they are known by in the profession), this man had climbed down from the cockpit without noticing that a boy had clambered up into the seat he had vacated moments earlier.

The lad began tinkering with the control levers when suddenly the massive dozer blade dropped and severed the operator's arm at the elbow.

Soon a fellow worker was rushing him to the hospital, his upper arm blood flow stemmed by a makeshift tourniquet and his loose forearm in a bucket of ice.

Before the anesthesiologist put him under, the surgeon said, "Your bones at the elbow cannot be repaired. They were too badly crushed. This means that while we are reattaching your arm it will be necessary to lock your elbow permanently at some angle. You may choose what angle you wish."

"Well, Doctor, when I belly up to the bar I lean on it (while demonstrating with his good arm) about like this, so this angle would be just fine."

As a postscript, this man regained the use of his hand, thanks to the great skills of a medical team that had labored many hours during that highly complex reattachment procedure.

*　　*　　*

TUCUMAN'S HORSES

My work in South America primarily involved developing farm chemical markets. So I was required to service our numerous distributors on that continent through frequent visits.

On one of my trips to Argentina, our national distributor and I were chatting when he told me what I thought was a highly amusing story.

In the province of Tucuman in northwestern Argentina much sugar cane is grown. Not only is Tucuman's cane used to make sugar but it is also an excellent source for one of the country's strongest and most popular rums.

And that beverage's easy availability was understandably responsible for the addiction of many of Tucuman's cane growers.

Oftentimes a grower would emerge from his favorite watering hole so soused that it was all he could do to clamber into the saddle of his horse that was hitched outside.

But that was only half his problem. He then had to try to stay aboard until his hay burner got him home.

Well, during the ride our tipsy friend would oftentimes begin to doze and in the process start to lean rather precariously.

His horse, well-trained for such predictable episodes, would catch his rider from falling by a timely side-step that would right his master.

*   *   *

A Tahiti Experience

My brother Jim and his wife Shirl had longed to vacation in Tahiti. So one day, following up on an advertised plane/ship package deal, they bought their tickets.

But when it was close to departure time, the travel agent phoned to say there had been over-bookings and space was no longer available.

"That was the bad news," the agent reported. "But the good news is that if you and your wife would be willing to accept an alternate booking date we, to show our earnest desire to please, will only charge you one dollar for the entire trip."

It would be superfluous to state what Jim's reply was.

So they flew to Tahiti where they boarded a luxury liner that was to be their floating hotel.

At one of the ports of call, Jim was making his way toward what he thought was the bar that someone had told him about.

"My, this IS a fancy place," Jim mused as he climbed the marbled steps and walked past the vaulted pillars that flanked the stately entrance.

Once inside he headed for the refreshment center tucked in the corner of a spacious living room. To the gentleman behind the bar he said, "I'll have a scotch and soda please."

The reply came back, "I would be most pleased to serve you what you asked for, but are you aware that this is a private residence?"

*   *   *

No Dead Weevils?

Years ago I worked for a farm chemical manufacturer. One of its executives related a hilarious incident that occurred at a sales meeting.

It seems that another producer of insecticides was interested in having my company handle one of its products, a weevilicide, used in killing granary weevils.

Since his chemical did not compete with ours and could help round out our product line, it was agreed to allow this man a few minutes at that sales meeting to extol the virtues of his weevilicide.

So he stood up, thanked our company for the opportunity to demonstrate his chemical's efficacy, and then began his spiel.

"I have here three clear glass jars. Each has grain in it. And into each has been introduced the same number of live weevils.

"You will note that in Jar #1, which has no chemical added, that the weevils are active, fat and sassy." With that he passed the jar around the table for all to inspect. After everyone nodded, he then continued.

"Now we can look at Jar #2. Its contents were sprayed with a competitor's weevilicide. You will notice that the weevils are likewise as healthy as in the first jar." More nods as it was sent around the table.

"And now, gentlemen, Jar #3 with our product... oh, whoops, something's wrong here!"

All eyes were riveted to that jar which showed weevils every bit as active as in the other two.

After this salesman had slunk out, the room erupted in laughter and the moderator then remarked, "You know if I'd been that guy, I would have smacked each weevil dead before I put them in his Jar #3."

*　*　*

THE WRONG ADDRESS

This true story was recently told me by a very dear pastor friend.

He was asked to pray over a grave where a casket had recently been buried, but was given the wrong address.

When he arrived he saw two men, one with a shovel and the other on a back hoe, completing their burial assignment at what, for all the world, seemed like the correct burial plot. So, out came his Bible and he read an appropriate passage.

Closing his Bible he prepared to leave when he heard the worker on the backhoe say to his partner, "Hey pal, I've buried many a septic tank, but this is the very first time I've had one prayed over."

CHAPTER 2

UNUSUAL

A.S.A. RATING

During the early stages of my tennis teaching career I had as a student a man named Fred Krug. He was, at the time, Walt Disney's chief wildlife cinematographer and would spend months on end in Africa. Later he went on to become a successful movie director.

He once told me the following story. During a filming sequence out in the wilds of Tanzania, he saw a loin clothed native brandishing a spear as he darted behind a nearby clump of bushes.

Quite unnerved, Fred did not know what to expect next and feared for the worst.

Presently that native approached him and in impeccable queen's English inquired, "I say, old man, could you tell me what A.S.A. rating your film is?"

* * *

Bob Daniels is my friend and next door neighbor. He had just returned from an extremely serious operation and called me over to recount that experience.

I, of course, had remembered the constant prior pain Bob had been suffering in his legs, excruciating pain that had been giving him absolute fits.

Earlier visits to local orthopedists had accurately diagnosed his pain as coming from nerve difficulties within his spinal column and would require surgery in the hope of correcting the problem.

Bob knew that for a surgeon to perform in such a delicate (indeed dangerous) area as the spinal column surely is, he had to be a top drawer specialist with an outstanding track record.

Fortune smiled and Bob found just the man, one Dr. Judd Alamin.

So it was that he wound up going under the knife at Stanford Hospital in Palo Alto with Dr. Alamin, assisted by Dr. Richard Thunder.

In preparation for that highly demanding medical procedure, the anesthesiologist approached Bob with needle poised to send him into happy land.

Bob held up his hand, "Doctor, I don't believe that will be necessary. I can put myself under," whereupon Bob, drawing upon a recently-acquired skill of self-hypnosis, put himself into a pain-free trance.

The doctors, once convinced that Bob was indeed "out," opened up his back and did what had to be done. In the process, they found that the offending nerves had somehow become snarled like the line in a back-lashed fishing reel. They corrected the snarl and sewed Bob back up.

He was then wheeled into the recovery room amidst gentle protests from Bob who insisted that his recovery was unnecessary and that he felt just fine. So he was taken back to his room.

Shortly thereafter Bob was sitting up enjoying his meal to the wide-eyed amazement of Dr. Alamin who had popped in to check on him.

When Bob's account ended, the writer, just as astounded as everyone else, left his grinning, pain-free neighbor so he could rush home, sit down at his keyboard, and bang out this eye-opener, this unique story of great surgical AND self-hypnotic skills.

*   *   *

The following is a letter of thanks I wrote to friends who had prayed for me during one of my kidney stone hospitalizations:

Dear Friends:

This letter is to fill you in on my latest kidney stone episode in which, I must say, you all, through your prayers, played a major and a beautiful role whether you realize it or not.

Early last Saturday Isabel rushed me to Kaiser Hospital because I was having a kidney stone attack. I remained hospitalized for six days, constantly being given shots for pain while I waited for the stone to pass.

On Thursday, when it appeared that to wait any longer might cause permanent kidney damage, I was scheduled for surgery the following morning at ten.

However, much was still to happen that same Thursday. The doctors paraded into my room and scared me half to death as they explained the surgical procedure they were planning for me. I signed the consent-to-operate form but did so with great reluctance since I had heard that the success of kidney stone operations was notoriously "iffy".

In the early afternoon the nurse rushed up to me and excitedly displayed the small stone fragment which had been collected in the sieve I had been using. Incidentally, all of the nurses were pulling for my stone to pass since they were well aware of the riskiness of kidney operations.

So I urgently called for the doctor. He came, inspected the sieve contents and then said it was not significant.

Still clutching the dwindling hope that the stone would pass before my scheduled surgery, I asked the doctor how possible it might be that the kidney stone could have already dislodged and dropped into my bladder. "Highly unlikely," he replied.

Later I got to thinking, "What if, due to my bedridden inactivity, the doctor was wrong?" So I got out of bed, jumped up and down to get my bladder contents all churned up and then found to my delight that the sieve I had just put into action now had many more bits of kidney stone in it. The nurses rejoiced with me.

Later still that same Thursday I was ready to make another liquid deposit but my privacy had been invaded by my roommate's many visitors who blocked the way to our semi-private bathroom.

So, getting out of bed, and with my trusty I.V. and antibiotic bottles in tow on the rickety dolly they provided me with, I made my way down the hall to a public restroom.

Soon I found myself doing a series of incredulous double-takes, as large pieces of stone began to collect in the toilet bowl. I dashed out of the bathroom. Nearby were several well-dressed men talking. I said to one of them, "Would you mind terribly making sure no one enters the men's room until I return?" (I sure didn't want anyone accidentally flushing down the commode this kidney stone passport out of the hospital before my knife-happy surgeon started cutting me open.)

Whereupon I rushed down the corridor to the nurses station, my hospital gown fluttering in the breeze while my I.V. companion waved and sloshed from its precarious mooring I was pushing ahead of me.

I screeched to a halt before a nurse and breathlessly said, "Please come quick! I've got to show you something important!"

So, back again I raced with sloshing I.V. and one nurse bringing up the rear. Moments later I was down on my knees at the toilet bowl saying to her, "Can you see what I see, all those pieces of kidney stones there on the bottom?"

"Yes," she said, "but how can I record their size?" So we agreed on a plan. With her pen she drew on the palm of her hand the size of each stone she saw. These sketches she later transferred to a more permanent record. (Dumb me, I should have ignored the yucky yellow water, reached down and grabbed these precious stones, but I wasn't thinking.)

Needless to say, all kidney stone pain had left me by then.

The doctor ordered new x-rays. Subsequent analysis of these pictures showed my kidney no longer had a stone.

Despite all these developments of Thursday, by early Friday morning the doctor had still not cancelled my scheduled 10 a.m. surgery. A blood sample, in preparation for that operation was drawn at 7 a.m. One of my team of two surgeons saw me at 8 and said they'd be coming for me at 10. To which I responded that there were interesting developments he should first apprise himself of by checking my records at the nurses' station. Amazingly, he responded, "Regardless, I feel we should still go ahead."

By then I was thinking, "Over my dead body!"

At 9:30 a.m. my doctor approached me and said that the x-ray evidence now justified his cancelling my surgery.

Whew! Talk about high drama!

Clearly the hand of the Lord was involved as far as I was concerned, and just as clearly was the effectiveness of your prayers. Thank you all!!

Sincerely, Frank B. Walker

*   *   *

KIDNEY STONES – PART II

Over the past 20 years I have been a virtual kidney stone factory with attacks which have easily numbered in the dozens. These attacks have always been signaled by intense pain and often accompanied by a premonition of death.

During that period I developed my own system frequently successful, for dislodging the stone. It consisted of quickly gulping down prodigious volumes of water. Then, while standing stiff-legged, knees locked, I would rise repeatedly on my toes and allow the full weight of my body to suddenly drop onto my heels. Those bone-rattling thuds, coupled with simultaneous hard whacks by my fist to the offending kidney area oftentimes would dislodge the stone and all pain would abruptly stop.

However my self-help formula did not always work, which necessitated my being hospitalized on four separate occasions.

My last hospital stay for kidney stones happened in Butterworth, northern Malaysia in 1990. To this day I am convinced that the diligent prayers of my missionary companions caused that particular attack to be amazingly short-lived, far shorter than normal.

A few weeks later while still in Malaysia I was riding on a train north-bound out of Kuala Lumpur. The person seated across the aisle from me was an English-speaking Moslem civil engineer.

After he learned of my kidney stone difficulties, he said, "Say, there is an ancient Chinese remedy that is supposed to combat that problem very effectively."

Seconds later a man of Chinese extraction seated directly behind the engineer remarked, "Excuse me, but I could not help but overhear your conversation. There is indeed an excellent remedy for kidney stones and I will write you out the name of it. Most any Chinese pharmacy in Malaysia will carry it." Armed with the name of the remedy, I later purchased a whole case (some 1,000 pills) which cost me the equivalent of 12 U.S. dollars.

In subsequent years I have had the need to grab for these pills. In each instance they have stopped the kidney stone attack dead in its tracks.

And now for an interesting sequel to this story. Months following my wife's and my return to California from Malaysia I was walking our Labrador Retriever, "Bandit," in the woods of Midpines, a small mountain hamlet near Yosemite National Park, when the dog decided to roll in some weeds, doing so with the abandon of a cat frolicking in catnip.

As a consequence he smelled to high heaven. Once Bandit and I had returned home, my wife commented on a familiar odor our dog had just brought in. Going to our medicine cabinet she reached for my Chinese pills. She uncorked the bottle and exclaimed, "Just as I thought. Same smell!"

Could it be that China for the past millennium has been secretly importing weeds from Midpines to make those very same kidney stone pills I had bought back in Malaysia?

*   *   *

The Case of the Sinking Ducks

It was back in the 60s; I was living in Brazil.

One morning I learned from my U.S. employer's nationwide Brazilian distributor, Agrobras, and on whose board I sat, that a large cattle rancher from the southern state of Rio Grande do Sul was planning to launch a substantial lawsuit against our company.

It seems that one of our tickicides, which he had used as a dip to kill the ticks on his cattle, was allegedly responsible for the deaths of many of his animals, and this rancher was fighting mad.

We immediately dispatched a team of investigators. Their penetrating study stands out in my mind as the greatest single example of truly superlative sleuthing that I ever experienced in my many years of servicing farm chemical complaints.

This team, headed by a marvelous agronomist named Sebastiao Torres, whom I had pirated from Geigy Chemical Co., determined that our chemical known as Garrathion unfortunately had killed this man's cattle just as was claimed.

However, this very same Garrathion had been used by neighboring ranchers who were highly satisfied.

Intensive questioning and alert attention to even the remotest of clues by our men produced some startling discoveries.

By chance there was a pond close to the dip vat in question where migratory ducks would land to rest. These birds were mysteriously drowning, a phenomenon virtually unheard of.

Upon deep probing my men learned that a sack of a product called Vedacit had been carelessly dumped into this pond. It had been used earlier by this cattleman to repair the cracks in his concrete dip vat just prior to his using our tickicide.

40

Now Vedacit, when allowed sufficient time to set up, would effectively seal cracks in cement vats.

If, however, label instructions were not followed and the vat was filled with water and chemical too soon after application of Vedacit, that substance would wash out of the cement cracks and into the vat dip solution. And that was precisely what had happened in this case. Interestingly one of the ingredients of Vedacit was sodium tri-poly phosphate which is a detergent recognized for its degreasing properties. This was why the ducks were sinking and drowning. Vedacit was washing the oil from the ducks' feathers which destroyed the fowls' buoyancy.

Armed with this incredibly fortuitous find, Torres and his men were able to prove that this same Vedacit, which the claimant himself had earlier used improperly, had dissolved the protective oils from the hide surface of his cattle, thereby permitting our toxic chemical to penetrate through the animal's hide and into its bloodstream.

Confronted with these hard facts, the rancher was left with no choice but to drop his law suit against us.

* * *

A SHATTERED GLASS

During one of my business visits to Bogota, Colombia, I had occasion to dine at a restaurant in a fashionable residential district.

Converted from what had once been an upper class home, this eating establishment, known as the Balalaika, was run by a Russian and his wife. Her earlier career had been that of a New Orleans dancer, while he had sung opera in Japan before both emigrated to Columbia. Their son was the bartender.

That evening, after a few drinks to take the edge off what had been a busy day for us both, Rick, a business associate, and I were shown to our candle-lit table.

The atmosphere was quite cordial and cuisine clearly Michelin four star. A wandering gypsy violinist made his way from table to table, playing requests. After the evening had progressed through the salad and entrée to dessert and liqueur, our host then began to sing to the accompaniment of his violinist. It was at once apparent that we were being treated to a very special talent.

This accomplished baritone filled the room with one favorite aria after another. At one point, while standing close to where we were seated, he struck a high note and held it. I noticed my wine glass beginning to vibrate. Suddenly it burst.

So impressed was I by such superb singing that I hardly noticed the spilled wine that my shattered glass had once held.

*　*　*

SPIDERS AND ME

In my grammar school days I was deeply attracted to spiders, frogs and snakes. I also raised a lot of white rats but that's another story.

During one period I collected a number of large frogs which I kept in a tub that Mother had lent me. Feeling, I suppose, that my pets needed also to socialize outside of their own genus, I dumped several live water snakes into the tub.

This stirred up much activity, the tub arena being as confined as it was, and frankly I was unsure of how well my frogs and snakes would get along.

The next morning I bounced out of bed and made a beeline for the tub. Off came the lid. Gaping, I saw my frogs fat and sassy but nary a snake.

For me that was one for the books, frogs that dined on snakes.

My next adventure involved black widows, LOTS of black widows, although it didn't start out that way. After all, I began with just two, a big shiny black one with a bright red hourglass on its belly and a much smaller spider that my mommy told me was the daddy. I kept them in a large, clear bell jar and fed them flies and bees and other bugs.

It wasn't long before little cotton balls started to appear, suspended on the mixed-up web that had been spun. Mommy said that soon a whole lot of little spiders would be crawling out of those white balls.

One day I was looking and peering and searching, but nowhere could the smaller spider be found; only the big, shiny black one that was hanging from the web near the white balls.

When I told my mommy, she said, "Well, you see, Frankie, the reason why that big spider is called the black widow is because after she and her small husband make baby spiders, she then feels hungry so she eats him all up."

Boy, that was a real eye opener. I was so surprised I could hardly believe such a thing could happen. It made me wonder whether I wanted to marry when I grew up.

Then one afternoon Daddy surprised me when he handed me a gift. It was a box. Inside I saw a huge, hairy spider. It was a tarantula, Daddy said. He had seen it crossing the road so he had caught it for me. It was so nice of Daddy to remember me with such a nice spider.

Well, just like my frogs and snakes, I wanted to experiment all over again, so I put my mommy black widow in with the tarantula.

At first the black widow tried to stop the tarantula from walking by webbing the tarantula's legs to the bottom of the jar, but the big spider kept walking around because he didn't want his legs stuck down.

Well, I watched the two spiders for the longest time until my mommy said it was time for bed.

Bright and early the next morning I dashed over to the jar but do you know what? There was the tarantula flat on his back with his legs all curled up. He was dead. Then I looked and looked for the black widow, but she was gone.

So I yelled for Mommy. When she came I said, "Mommy, last night there were two live spiders in my jar and now I only have one dead tarantula and my black widow isn't there."

"Son," she confided soothingly as she stroked my head, "the tarantula ate the black widow but then died from its poison. This is why you must be so very careful with your black widows because if they bite your legs they might curl up too."

I decided to get rid of all my black widows after that.

*   *   *

AN AMAZING FIND

Back in the years when I was a Los Angeles building contractor I had need for two additional filing cabinets for my office. So I went hunting.

It was not long before I spotted two horizontal type cabinets in a used furniture place. The price seemed reasonable until, that is, I asked for the proprietor to open them for me so I could see how well the drawers worked.

"Oh, I am so sorry," he said, "but the drawers are jammed and I haven't been able to open them. But I will reduce the price if you would like to buy them as is."

Figuring I might be able to tinker enough to lick the problem, I gambled and made the purchase.

Once back at my office, I fiddled using thin tools and a flashlight and my persistence rewarded me with success, but I was not at all prepared for what I found inside.

The drawers of both cabinets were chock full of files, many of which were labeled "top secret." Cursory inspection soon told me that these files belonged to a subsidiary of a well-known, multi-billion dollar, international petroleum conglomerate.

So I call that subsidiary and informed them of my find. Surprisingly their reaction was ho-hum, virtually bordering on disinterest with gratitude for my call strangely absent. At one point they casually suggested I could drop them off at their office.

Ignoring their flippant delivery instructions, I carted several boxes of files to my pick-up and headed for the conglomerate's world headquarters. I asked my way to the suite of the chairman of the board. He was out of town, but I was shown into the office of another board member. As he leafed through the files I had placed on his desk, his eyes bugged out and he let out a low whistle.

Then reaching into his desk drawer, he withdrew a gold-plated pen and pencil set, handed it to me while thanking me profusely.

Although I left before he called the subsidiary owners of those files, it did not take a rocket scientist to surmise what must have hit the fan during the inquest that surely followed.

That gold pen and pencil, by the way, wrote quite well.

*   *   *

MICROFILM TO GELATIN

Returning to my home in São Paulo, Brazil after a particularly grueling business trip around South America, I decided to take my wife on an R and R. So we hopped the shuttle plane from São Paulo's Congonhas airport and landed at the Santos Dumont airdrome in Rio fifty minutes later. Soon our taxi deposited us at the door of the small but charming Ouro Verde hotel that fronted on world-famous Copacabana Beach. Having stayed there before, we were attracted to its superb service and cuisine as well as to its congenial family atmosphere.

The surf looked most inviting and in no time we were out the door, onto the beach, picked a spot, put up the umbrella, stowed our stuff and raced out into the gentle breakers. I had read about Rio's notorious theft rings, so from the water I kept an eye on our isolated beach location that we'd purposely chosen, believing that to be an adequate precautionary measure. But during one of my glances beach-ward I suddenly noticed a man walking away from where our things were. He had a dark blanket draped over his arm.

I raced back to our spot on the sand only to find all my prize camera gear missing. Unquestionably it had been hidden under the thief's blanket as he retreated and subsequently melted into the crowd.

The police were polite but of no help. They merely confirmed that, "Yes, there was an active gang preying on bathers along that beach whose m.o. was to hide their loot," precisely as I had witnessed. "So what else is new," I mumbled to myself.

Then I phoned my insurance agent, reported this loss and arranged to meet with him upon my return to São Paulo. Over lunch, surprisingly on that agent's nickel, I poured out my tale of woe. The upshot was that he granted me total reimbursement for the loss, no questions asked. Was I ever relieved.

Then he said, "You know, Frank, the same day you reported your theft I received the oddest claim. It was from a Tulane University professor who was on assignment in Brazil researching what had become of the many post Civil War discontents who had moved to Brazil to start new lives. His travels took him on many journeys all over the country. Laboriously he was following lead after lead, ferreting out key information and photographing it.

"Each time he returned to his home base in São Paulo he would deposit in his bank's safe deposit box all the microfilm representing his copious findings. But on his most recent visit to the bank to store yet another batch of microfilm he noticed, to his absolute horror, that every last roll of microfilm had turned to gelatin! Two years of painstaking work down the drain! So he brought his claim to us and we began our investigation. What we uncovered, much to that professor's chagrin, exonerated both the bank and ourselves. The problem wound up being inadvertently caused by the claimant himself.

"It was found that the stored microfilm had not been thoroughly washed after it was developed. Some of the residual acid had then reacted with the metal coins he was keeping in the same box, turning all his coveted research microfilm to gelatin. I felt sorry that we had to reject his claim. And I was doubly pained for him when I reflected on the chewing out that surely awaited him by his boss, Tulane University's president!"

*   *   *

It was late afternoon. My car slowed down at the stop sign and then I turned right. Immediately I was greeted by an officer waving me to the shoulder for failure to come to a complete stop. So I parked behind a long line of cars this officer of the law had already rounded up, and then waited my turn to receive a ticket.

The day of my court appearance came. I was one of several hundred fellow traffic offenders who had been ticketed by the same policeman.

His honor was becoming increasingly upset over hearing victim after victim complain about the ticketing officer's poor bedside manner.

The person appearing before the judge just prior to me was a smart alecky kid flanked, as no one else present was, by his lawyer on one side and his daddy on the other. His offense had been speeding.

Unfortunately, the pursing officer had been going in the opposite direction when he spotted the teenager's car traveling at high speed. By the time the police car had stopped and done a 180 so he could confirm the speed infraction, the alert kid had slowed down to a legal speed.

The boy's lawyer smugly observed that speeding proof was missing. Then, adding insult to injury, he made a few choice remarks about how nasty the officer had been.

The judge was no dummy. He knew full well that the lad had broken the law. For that reason and because of all the grumblings against the officer he had been subjected to all morning, he was fuming mad.

Biting his lip, however, his honor was forced, albeit with great reluctance, to acquit for lack of evidence.

The veins in his honor's neck were still standing out when my turn came.

He snapped, "Frank Walker, failure to come to a complete stop, how do you plead?"

"Guilty with explanation, your honor," I answered.

"Let's have it," he ordered.

"First off, your honor, I wish to state that this officer treated me with courtesy."

Doing an astonished double take, the judge then stammered, "Wo, wou, would you be willing to write a letter to the officer's superior stating what you just told me?"

"Yes, your honor," I quickly answered.

"Case dismissed," as his gavel banged down while I exhaled in relief, grateful for the inadvertent opening this Peck's Bad Boy had provided me.

*　*　*

THE PIGEONS OF VICTORIA STATION

Isabel and I once found ourselves spending several hours at London's venerable and historic Victoria Railroad Station waiting to catch our train to Dover.

As we sat inside on one of the many benches illuminated by massive overhead skylights, we commented on the gripping stories this huge building's walls might tell us, if only they could speak.

Presently one pigeon, then another, followed by still more, all lit close by. Their eyes fixed on ours as they tilted their heads in expectation of a handout, for we were in their territory and clearly they wanted to collect from us a toll for our presence.

We were soon to learn that the nutritional content of our offering made little difference since over the years these feathered residents of Victoria Station had grown quite accustomed to a varied diet. As we looked around us we observed other travelers tossing bits of sandwiches, popcorn, peanuts, candy and assorted non-descript foods. All morsels quickly found their way into many a hungry gullet. But before long Isabel turned to me, and with sadness in her voice, made an observation which perked my attention. Many of these cooing visitors were walking around with no feet. It was only then that I began to marvel at their ability to keep their balance while moving about on mere stumps.

Then the pathos of it all finally hit me. Here at Victoria Station generation after generation of pigeons were constantly being born, living and then dying. This was their home and its many transients provided their food source.

And so it was that these plumed mendicants would constantly land on the station's sand-paper-textured pavement to elicit donations from the countless visitors in this, one of London's busiest railroad stations.

With so many landings and takeoffs, their feet would slowly wear away. First a talon would disappear, then a toe and before long a deformed stubby bottom to each leg would be the only reminder that a whole, intact foot had once been there.

My wife wiped away a tear while my brow creased in concern as we rose to answer the loudspeaker announcing our train's departure, leaving behind our footless friends.

Several of these uncomplaining pigeons, resigned to but perhaps oblivious over their deformities, waddled on their stilts to a couple now occupying the bench we had vacated moments earlier. With eyes riveted to their newly-adopted meal tickets, they once again tilted their heads in expectation. This was the only life they knew.

* * *

GARLIC FLAVORED MILK

One day in my São Paulo, Brazil office I received an urgent call from Santiago, Chile. On the line was our company's Chilean representative, Duncan Fox, requesting my immediate presence.

A major agricultural problem had developed and our help in finding a solution was being desperately sought.

It seems that garlic-flavored milk was mysteriously reaching the market place and important segments of the farm and dairy communities were understandably in deep trouble.

Investigators soon discovered the contaminant. Dairy cattle were historically fed oats, but serious infestations of wild garlic had invaded a number of oat fields.

Unfortunately wild garlic matures at the same time as oats and hence is unavoidably harvested with the oats. How to separate the two different seeds following harvest baffled the granary technicians. They tried colorometric separation to little avail because the contaminating seeds were too close in color to the oat.

Chile then invited herbicide producers from all over the world to come up with a selective chemical herbicide that would kill the wild garlic without hurting oats.

The only product we had that might have stood a chance was a temporary soil sterilant. But it was tricky to use. Following surface application of this product, its immediate incorporation into the soil was mandatory otherwise its active ingredient would turn to a gas and escape harmlessly to the atmosphere before it could kill the wild garlic.

We arranged for a field test at a farm in southern Chile. Everything was ready to go when I arrived. But as luck would have it, this host farmer's only tractor broke down just before our scheduled test.

So we tried to improvise by using oxen to pull the plow, however these plodding animals did not move fast enough so our experiment flopped. (As an aside: Once, while giving a Latin American slide show at Mariposa County's jail, I told the above story. When I got to the part of the unacceptably slow oxen being used to pull the plow, one of the prisoners called out, "I could have got those oxen to move in a hurry. I would have kicked 'em you know where." The laughter that erupted was a show-stopper.)

Later when a full economic feasibility study was made, all realized that our product was simply too expensive anyway for such a use. So we did not bother to repeat the experiment.

And since none of our competitors could produce an effective solution either, those poor afflicted oat producers had to switch to other crops (like garlic for example).

Chile's consumers simply were not ready for garlic-flavored milk!

*　*　*

MY EXPERIENCE WITH CURARE

This is about a deadly poison I once was given.

My family and I were living in São Paulo, Brazil when one morning I felt sharp pains in the lower right quadrant of my abdomen.

Over the phone I described my symptoms to our family doctor. "Probably not your appendix," he opined, "since rarely is the pain from an appendicitis felt right where the appendix itself is located, unless in very advanced cases of attack when danger of rupture is imminent. Nonetheless, let's not take any chances. Please get right over to the hospital so we can diagnose the problem."

Then with the lab test results in hand, I heard my physician pronounce, "Your appendix is ready to burst. We must operate at once."

I was wheeled to the pre-op room where the anesthesiologist was waiting. He pulled out a shelf from beneath my gurney and instructed me to lay my arm across it. "I will be giving you a shot of sodium pentothal which will knock you out quickly," he pronounced.

As he was inserting the needle, I recall asking him, "Doctor, roughly how long does it take this anesthetic to work?" and that was the very last thing I remember because I went out like a light.

When I awoke it was to the words of my surgeon as he stood over my bed. "The operation went well. Although, it was not without its moments of suspense. We made our initial incision, which was small as is customary, but could not find your appendix where it was supposed to be. Se we had to widen our cut and then to inspect your intestine inch-by-inch, much the way cinematographers analyze the film they're editing.

"In the process, your stomach muscles began to tighten up which further complicated our surgical procedure. So we administered curare which is a muscle relaxer. But since curare also adversely affects the normal function of your lung muscles, we were forced to perform artificial respiration using a ventilator until the effects of the curare had worn off."

All the while I was musing, "Hmmm, curare – isn't that the poison the Amazonian Indians use on the tips of their blowgun darts?" And my memory did serve me rightly, for the doctor then nodded his agreement in reply to my question of curare's alternate use on poison darts.

I'm so glad it was he who administered that curare and not the dart of an Amazonian Indian.

Epilog. My wife brought me a book to the hospital. Written by H. Allen Smith, this book on humor was so hilarious, I couldn't put it down. Yet, every time I laughed, which was often, my side killed me, a credit to H. Allen Smith.

*　*　*

A KEY, A PADLOCK AND MILK OF MAGNESIA

When I was still in grammar school my four siblings and I had to drink a weird hot chocolate mix every Saturday morning. Mother would have prepared it by stirring milk of magnesia into each of our cups of chocolate. "Keeps the body working right," she would smilingly address our unsmiling faces, while standing over us to be sure we drank it.

And in retrospect I'll just bet I knew where Mom's penchant for that yucky cocktail came from. Her mom was a medical doctor. Grandma Nell, as we called her, an erstwhile surgeon, in her later years had become campus physician at Mills College, a lady's institution of higher learning in Oakland.

How well I recall my visits with her, sent on errands by my mom, during my high school years, only invariably to be asked, "My dear, how are your bowels today?"

"Oh, grandma!" I would squirm in reply, uneasy over her plumbing fixation. And when I shared with mother her mom's embarrassing question, I recall with sadness my mother's comments on why Grandma Nell was so intent on how my innards were functioning. Poor grandmother had had most of her intestines and stomach removed because of cancer.

And now back to my chocolate milkshake story. None of us liked that drink one bit and we would endlessly stall and dawdle while our awful drinks grew stone cold.

On one of those occasions mother hit on an idea to encourage our compliance. She enthused, "Kids, I found this key in the backyard.

"Whoever finishes his drink first gets the key."

Now it so happened that I loved to rummage through the neighborhood trash cans each time that they were set out at the curb for the trash man to empty. I used to find all sorts of treasures that way. Once I acquired a fine padlock. It didn't have a key, but oh how I cherished that padlock.

So, remembering my keyless trash can treasure, I quickly gulped down my laxative-laced chocolate and then proudly held out my hand for the key.

Racing upstairs, I soon was pawing through my toy box until I suddenly gave a triumphant, "Aha!" while holding that special padlock high in the air.

Into its keyhole I excitedly inserted my recently-won prize. And, with a quick turn…..presto, the padlock sprung open!

When I told mother, incredulity filled her face. She gasped, "Oh, my heavens!"

As for me, I was not a bit surprised. I just knew that the key would work.

CHAPTER 3

HIGH DRAMA

The Green Berets of Dogdom
My 6.6 Experience
Communist Take-Over in Brazil Thwarted
Leave or Die
* The Amazing Fritz
Making Artificial Horse Manure
W, X, Y and Zock
Scorpions
Jim's Bodyguard
The Accident
Don't Ask
The Elephants Foot
My Gosh, it Shrunk!
Murder of a Teacher
Mycorrhizae
* Steelhead Woes
The Apazauca
A Relative in Australia
The Black Eye
Black Widow Venom
The Cat and the Catfish
Charley and the Trees
Concrete Collapse
The Condor
My, He's Late This Morning
Our Neighbor, Gil
The Overcoat
It's Raining Bears
Sequel to Spaz
A Varig Flight
The Embalmer

-----

* See photo

In the years I lived in Brazil, my business frequently took me to Argentina, a country I got to know and like.

Well to Argentina's south in the wind-swept Patagonian steppes is located the Rio Negro Valley, a major apple-producing region. My U.S. employer manufactured pesticides needed by the apple grower and I was responsible for developing those markets.

It was in the late afternoon on one of my business visits to the Rio Negro Valley.

I was standing in front of my hotel in the dusty town of General Rocca.

With me was a local agronomist.

We were chatting when I noticed a pick-up truck headed in our direction. Something very large and black and dead was lashed to the roof of the cab. As the vehicle approached I saw that this dark hulk was an absolutely massive boar whose hairy face displayed fearsome tusks. Several enormous and muscular dogs were riding in the truck bed.

My companion then launched into one of the most fascinating stories I had ever heard.

It seems the driver of that pick-up was a local legend and man of considerable valor. He was an apple grower by trade, however his all-consuming hobby was hunting wild boar on horseback with his specially bred and trained dogs, Mastiff-Great-Dane hybrids, as his only weapon.

At the beck and call of sheep ranchers far and near, he would rush to the aid of anyone sending him an SOS announcing wild boars were ravaging his sheep.

The victimized rancher would have a horse ready and saddled for the hunter's arrival.

Upon approaching the scene of devastation, signaled by sheep carcasses littering the landscape, the dogs after picking up the scent would then bound off howling, in fast pursuit as the hunter brought up the rear.

Once run down and cornered by these dogs, the boar would wheel, lunge and slash.

The horseman, invariably one of the targets of the boar's fury, would stave off its vicious charges with a padded pole, a more benign version of the instrument used by the picador of bullfight fame.

These dogs, oftentimes bloodied in such fights-to-the-death, usually won. Much careful preparation was needed for these St-George-and-the-dragon forays, centering primarily on breeding, rearing and training the dogs.

A high-walled ring was used into which a mountain lion would be introduced to do battle with these hunting dogs. Being extremely quick and dangerous, the lion was a highly effective training tool in fine-tuning these canines for their mission in life.

Not all dogs survived this boot camp, but the ones that did were the Green Berets of Dogdom.

*　　*　　*

MY 6.6 RICHTER EXPERIENCE

At 4:31 a.m. on Monday, Jan. 17, 1994, I was jolted awake by what sounded like a freight train bearing down on me. The entire house was shaking as if in the clutches of an angry King Kong bent on tearing it apart.

Seismologists later would pinpoint the epicenter of this quake as a scant six blocks north of my sleeping bag.

Instinctively I knew I should rush to the relative safety of a doorway but the house was moving so violently that I could not even stand up. So I scrambled on all fours.

Pictures were crashing from walls. Bookcases were toppling. Glass was breaking everywhere. Water gushed from pipes that a scared water heater had left behind. My host, Dick Oswald bolted from his bedroom yelling, "Praise the Lord, Praise the Lord!!"

No one had to tell me that I was in the middle of something really major.

Those incredible 15 seconds seemed like an eternity before a pall of eery, uncertain silence settled over the home.

That silence was soon replaced with a cacophony of sirens and barking dogs which was to last until my departure for northern California four days later.

The three of us, Dick and Joan Oswald and I, after surveying the immediate damage, started walking the neighborhood. Masonry garden walls were flattened all over the place. I don't think I saw a single chimney intact. Some chimneys before toppling had pulled away from the walls where they once stood leaving huge gaping holes behind as grim reminders.

All power, of course, was out (and stayed out for days) and my notebook, containing my log of these events is still splattered with candlewax.

Because of the severity of this earthquake and its too numerous to count aftershocks, front lawns and parks soon became one huge campground. Tents were everywhere. Victims either had no home to return to or else were too frightened to go back.

Acts of heroism and the milk of human kindness abounded as souls, once introverted and anti-social, reached out to help their fellow sufferers.

The Van Nuys Department of Building Safety was immediately swamped with frantic calls from literally thousands of dwellers needing to know if their buildings were safe enough to permit their returning.

Because I used to be a builder and also had my own building inspection company, I volunteered my inspection services. Soon Building and Safety teamed me up with a Public Works engineer and the two of us, joined by hundreds more, fanned out to survey the damage.

In the process, a number of structures we had to red tag as being flat out unsafe. Others were but cosmetically defaced.

One swank, four story office building on Ventura Blvd. in Encino had huge, floor to ceiling plate glass windows many of which had already crashed to the sidewalk below. Marble slabs, once neatly adorning the building's façade, now had either fallen or were dangerously hanging out, ready to break loose and crush anything in their path.

Although this particular building had been vacated, the power was surprisingly still on and the elevator operational. I went to the top floor where I made my way past once plush desks, now in shambles, to where a frightened glazier was struggling to pull in a badly bent window frame. He admitted he was scared to death, especially because of the constant aftershocks, heightened by the thought of having to remove the loose marble.

As I was leaving the building I heard a deafening crash right behind me. I wheeled around to see the shards of what had been a plate glass window spraying in all directions.

With freeways knocked out, my route home to Mariposa had to be circuitous and gerrymander-like.

During one of the Building and Safety briefings I attended, we heard pronounced a figure of at least "two years" before some semblance of normality would return to much of shattered Los Angeles.

56

The outpouring of compassion and aid has been truly heartwarming but much, much help is still badly needed in this earthquake-convulsed part of California.

And in retrospect, I felt pangs of guilt over returning to the comforts of my unscathed home in Mariposa.

*   *   *

COMMUNIST TAKE-OVER IN BRAZIL THWARTED

Brazil at one point in its history came dangerously close to becoming a satellite of Communist China. That Asian country, we were later to learn, had plans to carry out a major blood bath as part and parcel of their intentions to swallow up Brazil and make it a political captive. I knew this all too well because at the time I was living with my family in São Paulo, a city where much of this drama was playing out and where the air was literally charged with excitement and apprehension.

The whole problem began in 1960 when Janio Quardros was elected president of Brazil following his highly successful governorship of Brazil's economic crown jewel, the state of São Paulo.

Frustrated over crippling opposition to his plans for sorely needed sweeping change, O Janio, as he was called, resigned in a pique of disgust after but seven months into his presidency.

Because of his popularity, Quadros fully expected the people to refuse to accept his resignation and, instead, to carry him back on their shoulders with a new and sweeping reform mandate.

But his strategy failed. Instead, Quadros' vice president, one Joao Goulart, assumed the presidency and he ushered in changes of the very worst kind.

Goulart was the rumored illegitimate son of former dictator, Getulio Vargas yet, and as a surprise to most, his ideology was soon-to-be-revealed as strongly Marxist.

Joao Goulart had great oratorical skills. Frequently we would hear him on the radio, at rallies and on television speaking to the nation and he had the same charisma that Hitler had, that innate ability to hypnotize the masses. "Povo do Brasil," (People of Brazil) his voice would quiver over the airwaves while his audience would sway and cheer as if in a trance. We even heard him pronounce, "We're headed for a blood bath (banho de sangue)!" which words came very close to becoming prophetic.

But while Goulart, the spellbinder, was hoodwinking his people with flattery and platitudes, behind the scenes he was giving the green light to Maoist communists from China who quietly slipped into Brazil and began setting up small but highly organized and initially secret Marxist cells in each city and town in the nation.

Thinking people realized what was happening and soon became highly alarmed.

The military also were aware of the growing danger and were itching for justification to step in. But they had to be careful since Goulart had been duly elected and the military were sworn to uphold Brazil's democracy.

Happily that chance came. It was April of 1964 that we, along with millions more, watched a march which made history. Called "A marcha do silencio" (the silent march), thousands of citizens, men and women, while fingering their rosary beads, marched soundlessly from Praca da Se to Praca da Republica, two public squares in downtown São Paulo. This massive, peaceful demonstration constituted what the military, thankfully for the good of Brazil, chose to interpret as a plebiscite.

In no time soldiers invaded the presidential palace and spirited Brazil's traitorous president, Joao Goulart, out of the country and into exile in neighboring Uruguay.

A benevolent military dictatorship was ushered in and we all learned over the ensuing months just how close Brazil had actually come to enslavement by communist China.

Tons and tons of communist literature were discovered in warehouses just waiting to be distributed at the take-over signal.

One Sunday at church in São Paulo we heard an important prelate speak from the pulpit. In his hand he held high for all to see a list he had discovered of names of people to be summarily executed by the Communists immediately following the planned capture of Brazil by Communist China.

Astoundingly, this very same man-of-the-cloth's name was on that list!

I recall vividly our friend, Ernesto Guaderrama, an attaché with the American Consulate in São Paulo, calling to warn us to get our passports in order fast since it might well be necessary to flee Brazil at a moment's notice.

Those were indeed action-packed times in Brazil.

*   *   *

Back in the sixties my family and I were vacationing at a small hotel in the highlands of Brazil's interior, a half day's drive from our São Paulo home.

The graying hotel manager, an Italian immigrant whom we had befriended, approached our table in the dining room one evening. He was a kindly man, old for his years and suffering from a bad liver.

We motioned for him to join us and it was not long before he had launched into a fascinating phase of his life's story.

While still a young man, one of his earliest jobs in Brazil was as a coffee plantation foreman. The wealthy plantation owner who hired him gave him carte blanche, the only stipulation being that he increase profits.

It is important that the reader understand that in parts of Brazil semi-feudal systems still exist and include oftentimes the way a coffee farm is run. Larger plantations are operated like a small town with the owner much like a mayor. The workers live in small homes rented to them by the owner. They buy their food in markets likewise operated by the same owner and go to movies shown, for a price, right on the plantation.

Many, if not most, of these coffee barons added insult to injury by charging their already overworked but underpaid laborers exorbitant prices for home rent, food and movies. Hence very little take-home pay would be left from their paycheck.

Obviously disgruntled, these laborers worked at the barest acceptable pace.

And that was precisely the condition our Italian narrator found when he took over as foreman.

So he instituted major changes. Home rent was slashed, food was sold at cost, movies were free and wages were tied to performance.

Worker esprit de corps soared, along with coffee production and profits.

The owner was tickled pink.

Farm hands from neighboring plantations soon learned of this model farm and were clamoring to join this Italian's work force.

And then, oh yes, and then, our friend received a visit from several nearby irate plantation owners. One of them had a gun which he pointed at the Italian while warning, "You have twenty-four hours to leave."

So he left.

*   *   *

The year was 1939. I was a San Francisco high school freshman. It was after school this particular day in May when I was playing throw and catch with a friend in front of my house. A sleek convertible Mercedes Benz sedan pulled up to our home. Dad emerged as did the driver, a tall, monocled gentleman.

Soon I was introduced to this man. "Son, I would like you to meet Capt. Fritz Wiedemann, Germany's new Consul General for San Francisco." At the time father was city editor of the San Francisco Call Bulletin, our city's leading daily newspaper. It was my dad's custom to bring home important people making the news. Wiedemann had just been appointed by Adolph Hitler to that position. And as this story unfolds it will soon become quite evident that Fritz Wiedemann was indeed a personage.

After that first meeting many more were to follow to include picnic outings together with our two families. Father's friendship with Fritz Wiedemann would continue for many years thereafter. My father, who had the uncanny ability of quickly and accurately sizing a person up, labeled Wiedemann an honorable man, as history ultimately proved him to be.

Wiedemann had been Hitler's superior officer during WW I, during which period he was credited with saving Hitler's life. Hitler, Wiedemann's message runner at the time, had developed a hero-worship complex over Wiedemann. Indeed, Hitler's dedication as a Corporal earned him the Iron Cross from none other than Lt. Fritz Wiedemann.

Therefore it was little wonder when later Fuehrer Hitler sought Wiedemann out and named him his private secretary and personal envoy. Wiedemann only later was to learn, with surprise, as many others did, that his boss had developed into one of history's greatest despots and mass murderers or surely such clairvoyance would have caused him to think twice about rescuing Hitler back during their WW I days together.

When Hitler finally deduced that Wiedemann was a Nazi in name only and one who never bought into what Nazism stood for, he fired him and offered him the conciliatory post in San Francisco. Why Hitler did not have him killed as a traitor probably resides in his lingering esteem and gratitude carrying over from WW I.

Many years later I was to undertake exhaustive research into Wiedemann's exciting life which uncovered facts proving he not only was involved in an unsuccessful plot to assassinate Hitler (the famous Stauffenburg led July 1944

Rastenburg, East Prussia attempt on Hitler's life, code word "Valkerie") but even more importantly, provided top secret information to the Allies which Sir Winston Churchill credited in a major way with Hitler's ultimate defeat. Jews even called Wiedemann their secret savior!

You see, in November of 1940 while still Germany's Consul General in San Francisco Wiedemann met with a top British secret service agent at the Mark Hopkins Hotel in San Francisco. For over five hours, with the FBI taping everything, Wiedemann gave away the store – Hitler's ultra secret war plans and time tables, Hitler's personal weaknesses, etc., etc., in a word, "everything." The reader may be sure that had Hitler ever gotten wind of this traitorism, Wiedemann's life would not have been worth a plugged nickel.

Hence it was understandable when Winston Churchill subsequently credited the information gleaned from Wiedemann as providing the turning point in WWII.

A movie script detailing my findings on Wiedemann's exciting life, little known to the world, is now in the mill. *(See photo of Wiedemann with Hitler and others.)*

At Berchtesgaden

* * *

After a four year stint commercially fishing for broadbill swordfish in Peru, South America, I found myself looking for greener pastures. I soon landed a job with a San Francisco-based chemical company that had an opening in Mexico.

It seems that one of their farm chemical super distributors for Western Mexico was dipping into the till, but he was covering his tracks so cleverly that the company had been unable to catch him.

Because of my business background and Spanish fluency I was hired by high-ups in that company. My employer's master plan was to train me sufficiently to where I could pass as an entomologist. Then with that as my cover I was to move to Mexico. Ostensibly my job was to entail working closely with a network of Mexican sub-distributors and their entomologists to insure that our pesticides were being properly used. Surreptitiously, however, I was to sniff out how the thefts were being pulled off.

From the very outset I knew absolutely nothing about entomology, my formal schooling having been engineering and international trade.

Thus my first year with that company was a training period at its agricultural chemical research laboratory where I studied under entomologists, plant pathologists, soil scientists, chemists and agronomists.

As an ego deflator, my apprentice kick-off assignment was learning how to prepare artificial horse manure. You see, many thousands of common house flies were raised at the laboratory for use in initial screening work of candidate chemical compounds. In nature, adult flies usually seek out animal dung on which to lay their eggs because the heat generated by fermenting dung presents an ideal environment for the hatching of fly eggs.

And by following a recipe of molasses, oats and other ingredients to produce artificial horse manure the company was able to avoid contaminants that might otherwise produce false readings during the chemical screening process.

So it was that "chef" Walker became a four star Michelin artificial horse manure concocter.

For twelve intensive months I soaked in more knowledge than I thought possible on all key aspects of my up-coming assignment.

When they figured I could tell the difference between coleops and lepidops and whatever else was needed to pull off the great deception, I was handed a box of calling cards that said, "Frank B. Walker, Entomólogo." And off I went to live in

Hermosillo, Sonora, where my territory comprised the Mexican states of Sonora, Sinaloa and Baja California.

En route to Hermosillo, I looked up the friend of a friend in Los Angeles. He was a retired movie director whose Solomonic wisdom was to prove invaluable to me. After explaining to him what my mission was he said, "Frank, that super distributor will try to discredit you right from the word go (prophetic words), since he will be smart enough to see through your ruse. So early on you must establish solid credibility. One way to accomplish this is to go on the lecture circuit. Get yourself a projector, a collection of slides depicting the insect pests that your chemicals are designed to kill and start speaking before anyone who will listen."

I followed his advice to a tee, especially since my predecessor had left because of a nervous breakdown produced by the very same sly super-distributor I was destined to work with. In the process I established a solid reputation while speaking before farm coops, chambers of commerce, etc., to the point where newspapers and radio stations gave me good play and helped entrench my reputation as an authority. Much to my amusement, I became known as *Doctor* Walker, if you please.

Indeed, at one point the Dean of the University of Sonora asked me to lecture before the agronomy students and that University even wound up using as one of their texts a pest control guide I had written.

All was not milk and honey, however, just as my movie director mentor had predicted. My nemesis did indeed attempt to smear my name on numerous occasions. One such instance occurred during a lecture I was giving to a farm group in Guaymas. As was my custom, at the end of each lecture I would throw the session open to questions from the floor. That evening in the lecture hall was a man jumping up and down and waving his hands for my attention. He was holding a jar full of insects which I suspected (rightfully I later learned) were not common at all to that area and which he wanted me to "fail" to identify. Clearly this man was a plant.

I feigned poor eyesight and recognized the safer questions from others while studiously avoiding his.

Then, glancing at my watch, I excused myself. As I headed for the exit I could not help but notice out of the corner of my eye that my intended detractor, clearly frustrated, was pogo sticking from his seat while brandishing his jar of exotic insects desperately clamoring for recognition.

Throughout my entomological work in Mexico I was simultaneously uncovering enough confidential information to enable our company ultimately to blow the whistle on that super-distributor, thereby ending his pilferings.

Toward the end of my assignment in Mexico I came down with a major nervous breakdown. It required three months in the hospital with daily electro-shock and injections of insulin. And the main reason for the breakdown, I was later to learn, was because the stateside boss I had been placed under was in cahoots with the crooked super-distributor. That boss constantly discouraged me from reporting my findings of irregularities to him, but especially to his superiors. But I, albeit nervously, ignored his orders. Later the whole truth came out.

Soon after that I was transferred out from under my difficult boss. So, from concocting artificial horse manure years earlier in a Mountain View, California, laboratory, I now found my career had blossomed into a new and exciting phase, that of chemicals market development throughout the 13 countries of South America with base in São Paulo, Brazil.

*   *   *

W, X, Y AND ZOCK

George Zoch and I, roommates back during W.W.II, were midshipmen studying at Cornell University for our U.S. Navy ensign stripes. Customarily, while lining up for roll call, George could always be heard muttering under his breath, "I know, I know, line up alphabetically, W, X, Y and Zoch. I'm always last."

When we graduated, George and I were sent in different directions. I wound up at North Carolina State University in Raleigh where the Navy had an officer's diesel engineering school. Upon completion of those studies (and in defiance of all logic) I was then ordered to the Port Director's office in Manila where I found myself loading and unloading Navy ships.

George, on the other hand, pulled duty aboard a Navy training vessel, a destroyer escort (D.E.) based on Chesapeake Bay, and this is where our story takes place.

This particular day his D.E. was tied at the face of a pier. As a junior officer, George was ordered to take over while the commanding officer and his first lieutenant went ashore on leave.

Shortly thereafter, down in the engine room, one of the neophyte grease monkeys accidentally opened the wrong valve and the hull began to fill with water. He panicked, and before he could shut the darn thing off, he found himself beating a hasty retreat topside.

So poor George, with great reluctance, had to order all hands to abandon ship as it slowly sank, gently coming to rest on the floor of the Chesapeake Bay.

With wavelets lightly lapping the ship's superstructure (the only visible part of George's D.E.), there on the pier beside his warship stood George, forlornly awaiting certain doom from his approaching stunned, wide-eyed, jaw sagging and thoroughly incredulous superior officers.

*   *   *

SCORPIONS

Early in my professional career I was heavily involved in entomology, a science that went hand in glove with my duties in Mexico of promoting the sale of my stateside employer's farm pesticides.

Our family established residence in Hermosillo, capital of Mexico's northwestern state of Sonora. It was an extremely hot and dry area and we were soon to learn that poisonous scorpions abounded there. At the time we were a small family which included infant twin boys.

My wife, Isabel, to her horror, began to find scorpions in our small duplex apartment which, because of my frequent absences on business, forced her to be the one having to kill them to protect our young ones.

Our babies' crib legs I swathed with a tangle of fibrous hemp to discourage that arachnid's dark intentions of climbing up and doing harm to the twins.

In researching through my entomology books, I located the various kinds of scorpions found in Mexico. One medical account detailed the excruciating pain and convulsions one victim of a Durango scorpion sting underwent before expiring. I was unnerved to say the least.

At one point I drew a picture of a scorpion on the top of a piece of paper to leave room below for my wife to tally the scorpions she killed in our home. During our two years of residence there Isabel had squashed 66 scorpions.

So obsessed had she become with those dangerous intruders that she exclaimed to me one day, "Frank, that lump on the wall covered with paint. I think it hides a scorpion!" To humor her I went over to it but the laugh was on me. As I flicked the bulging paint, to my amazement and chagrin, it was indeed a dead scorpion that had been painted over, just as Isabel had feared. Talk about the protective instincts of a mother!

My work often took me to farms, cotton farms mostly. There I found that the scorpion, being the democratic bug that he was, had not just singled out the Walkers for his visits. No siree, he was in the local farm houses as well.

Those cotton growers I knew had discovered a unique and highly effective system for minimizing the harmful effects of poison from a scorpion sting. Once stung, the victim would immediately freeze the area using a CO_2 fire extinguisher (when, that is, he wasn't using it to cool his beer).

As thawing took place, the poison would gradually find its way to the blood stream but in the process would have become highly diluted to where its otherwise injurious effect of pain, shock or worse would instead have been rendered quite tolerable. Those not utilizing such a practice would suffer greatly because the poison would travel through the body in a far more concentrated form.

In fact, such a counteractive procedure was also used to downgrade pain and physical damage from black widow bites.

Ellen Long was a friend of ours who also lived in Hermosillo. She once told us of putting on her dress without realizing that a scorpion was inside. It promptly stung her. Fortunately the poison was from a far more benign species of scorpion. She felt pain, great dizziness and her mouth became terribly dry but within a few days she was back to normal.

Lizards, snakes and roadrunners love scorpions. But Isabel and I prefer limiting our scorpion relationship to what we can glean from books.

* * *

JIM'S BODYGUARD

There are stories I enjoy remembering and chuckling over. This one involves an incident at a San Francisco Chevron gasoline station that my brother, Jim, ran for many years.

Jim always had a knack with people and his own men were fiercely loyal to him, no doubt because Jim always stood up for them. It was a trait our own father had followed all his life and then passed down as an abiding legacy.

This one particular day Jim was near one of the pump islands when a car screeched up. Jim had to fall back to avoid being hit.

"Hey, watch it," Jim yelled, "You almost ran over me!"

The driver, clearly bent on impressing his bevy of giggling lady passengers, got out and, after unfolding himself upward, looked way down at Jim, who himself stood six feet.

"Want to make something out of it?" he bellowed at Jim.

Sensing danger, one of Jim's mechanics, a Japanese American, short in stature but a seventh degree black belt, ran up wiping grease from his hands and, with his loyalty clearly showing, quickly positioned himself between the two adversaries.

"Stand to one side, boss, I'll take care of this guy," the Japanese American said with quiet confidence.

The bully looked way down at this shrimp in the karate crouch, glanced at his car and accurately concluded he was probably but seconds away from sporting two broken knee caps.

So into his convertible he swung and, with tires smoking, roared off.

Was it Jim's unquestioned loyalty to his men that provoked this story's ending?

You'd better believe it!!

*　*　*

THE ACCIDENT

It was dark that Christmas Eve except for the headlights of cars mostly on the way home, many with last minute purchases. Others were party bound.

William, our son, was on his heavy Honda Goldwing motorcycle going with the flow of traffic. Holiday gifts were bungied to the rack behind him.

Suddenly from out of nowhere and right in the middle of the block a young girl on her bike darted in front of William. He smoked his tires but to little avail. The collision was inevitable. Both went down.

Will rushed to her unconscious body and immediately began to administer mouth-to-mouth resuscitation.

The police and an ambulance arrived.

Shortly my wife and I received a call from the hospital. In no time we were striding down the hall of the emergency wing as the nurse led us to where William lay in shock.

Before we entered his room, we noticed in the adjoining room several aides and a doctor working feverishly over a young girl. Repeatedly they would shoot electrical jolts through the pads they held above her heart. Each time her little body would convulse and then lapse into quiet inertness. We watched, transfixed, realizing, because of the look on the face of the nurse accompanying us, that this was the same girl involved in the accident with William.

Time after time her little body heaved and collapsed, heaved and collapsed.

Finally we saw the doctor shake his head and an attendant then gently pulled a sheet over her lifeless body.

Isabel and I tiptoed into where William lay. He was awake. His eyes were scared. He had heard what had transpired in the room next to his. Looking at us searchingly he quietly inquired, "She didn't make it, did she?"

The three of us wept.

Later we spoke with one of the investigative officers who comforted us with the words, "There was absolutely nothing your son could have done to avoid what happened. Had I been on that motorcycle instead of William, the outcome would have been the same."

William went into severe depression and was too devastated to attend the funeral. So Isabel and I went in his place.

The girl's father approached us during the burial. We hugged and sobbed.

He asked where William was. We replied that he was simply too broken up to be present.

Later that day our doorbell rang. It was the little girl's daddy. He wanted to see William.

The two were alone for the longest time, crying and embracing.

That visit of love was what William needed to begin his long emotional healing process.

And while the lass did not make it, in another sense William too almost didn't make it, save for the timely visit of a grief-stricken but compassionate father.

*   *   *

DON'T ASK

Our little grandson, Nick, is an absolute ball of non-stop energy, at home, at school, at our place or anywhere else.

Finally came that much anticipated day. Nick was now old enough for preschool. With a tremendous sigh his mom saw him off on the bus and then collapsed into her chair.

By the time this first day of school was over Nick had left his indelible mark, for in his wake lay the strewn bodies of an exhausted teacher, a frayed principal and bewildered classmates.

His smiling mother was awaiting his arrival at the bus stop. As Nick alighted she enthused, "Hi, Nick, how did it go?

With head bowed, the glum reply came back, "Don't ask!"

*   *   *

THE ELEPHANT'S FOOT

Puoppy was a family friend. She lived in Santiago, Chile.

On one of my frequent business trips to Chile I recall visiting her at her home.

As I stepped across the threshold I noticed a hollowed-out elephant's foot she used for canes and umbrellas, so I commented on it.

"Oh, that," she sighed, "It was a gift from my ex-husband. He said I was always putting my foot in it!"

I suppressed an urge to ask who initiated the divorce proceedings.

*   *   *

MY GOSH, IT SHRUNK!

Mauricio and his family were close friends during our Brazilian residency. On a number of occasions we were guests at their mountain ranch near São Paulo.

During one such visit Mauricio had a suckling pig killed and dressed out which he then presented to us as a gift. He recommended that we have it roasted at one of São Paulo's bakeries as was the custom.

So my wife followed his instructions and left the piglet off at a bakery near our home. The proprietor said it would be ready that afternoon.

When Isabel returned to claim her roasted pig she could not help but notice that one of the two large hind legs was totally missing.

She called her observation to the attention of the baker who, with surprise (real or mock) written all over his face, exclaimed, "Well what do you know? It must have shrunk!"

*   *   *

MURDER OF A TEACHER

Back in the seventies I was an assistant professor at California State University at Northridge, California, where I taught advanced tennis.

The chairman of the P.E. Department had called a staff meeting in anticipation of the upcoming semester.

Conspicuous by her absence was the tenured coach of the ladies tennis team and genuine concern was expressed over her whereabouts, since she had a reputation for reliability and punctuality.

I was approached and asked if I would be interested in replacing her if, for some reason, she was unable to continue.

My reply was that I would first like to see what the job entailed and the remuneration it provided.

So the next day I was introduced to the ladies team. I spoke with the number one racket and arranged to have her meet me the following morning to help me bring the practice balls to the court.

But she never showed up. Instead, the day of our planned practice session, her picture, under banner headlines, was on page one of the area's largest daily. She had been picked up by the police, questioned and jailed but a few hours after I had first spoken with her.

It seems she had been wandering aimlessly along a north San Fernando Valley street with her two hands inexplicably tied together in front of her. Stopped by the police, she promptly led them to a shallow grave where the body of the missing tennis teacher was buried.

She was tried, convicted and sent to prison for murder. The media reported this as a crime of passion arising from a lesbian triangle.

70

That vacated teaching position I ultimately declined for economic reasons, since $1.75 per hour simply wouldn't cut it.

*   *   *

MYCORRHIZAE

While winding up my three year assignment in Mexico, I came down with a humdinger of a nervous breakdown which required three months of hospitalization in New Orleans where my daily treatments consisted of electro-shock. Anything less than complete recovery would have greatly jeopardized my big impending promotion to manage my company's market development program throughout South America.

Finally leaving the hospital, I was given an interim job while management's eyes were closely monitoring my performance. I had been asked to promote sales in Louisiana for one of our company's newest and most profitable proprietary pesticides. Called Vapam, it was a temporary soil sterilant.

My biggest initial hurdle was this chemical's high cost in one of the nation's least affluent farm communities, so I had to seek out those very limited markets that would justify such an expense.

At the time, Louisiana, among numerous other southern states, was engaged in a full-blown, government-sponsored reforestation program. Vast acreages were being planted to pine, primarily Loblolly, Slash, Short Leaf and Long Leaf.

Government-run nurseries were busily engaged in growing many millions of seedlings for subsequent transplanting in the field. This was a very costly operation and one which happily could support the expense of Vapam, providing this sterilant lived up to our claims.

So I targeted the pine tree nurseries for much of my market development efforts. This involved putting out numerous test plots aimed at demonstrating that our product could improve production.

When the test results were in, I had amply proven my initial claim of greatly increased yields attributable to the use of our product.

But just before numerous nursery managers were to sign very large purchase orders for Vapam a huge fly dropped into the ointment. One of the government's top silviculturalists, whose word was gospel among all government-sponsored pine tree nurseries in the south, decreed that Vapam was not to be used. His contention was that it destroyed the beneficial, nitrogen fixing fungi known as mycorrhizae and, therefore, would unavoidably result in lowering crop yields.

So I flew to Atlanta to see this big time stumbling block to my future plans for South America. I was armed with test results proving that our chemical boosted production significantly, alleged mycorrhizae damage to the contrary notwithstanding.

To his eternal credit that man did not allow pride to stand in the way of reason. His intellectual honesty won out and he countermanded his earlier interdiction, thereby permitting my ensuing national record-breaking sales of Vapam.

Convinced now that I had indeed recovered following my hospital bout, my boss transferred me to São Paulo to head up market development activities on that continent.

And all because of a mycorrhizae incident.

*   *   *

STEELHEAD WOES

Our family lived for many years in Brazil, during which time I traveled heavily all over South America.

Argentina I had to visit with great frequency. And being a lover of trout fishing, I soon succumbed to the beckoning of Patagonia's trout-rich waters, particularly in the picturesque lake region of Nahuel Huapi well to the south of Buenos Aires.

So my artificial flies would strike frequent pay dirt on Lake Nahuel Huapi, its main outlet, the Limay River, plus a number of equally productive tributaries of that lake. It would not be at all unusual for me to pull in and then release on a given week-end of fishing, 100 or more trout, steelhead and land-locked salmon averaging some four pounds each. Yet my most exciting encounter was with a Sebago salmon that surely would have tipped the scales at 15 pounds because he often broke water close to me where I had a good look at him. His gallantry ultimately won him his freedom when, after our furious, thirty minute fight, my line suddenly went slack.

During one of his visits in South America, my boss encouraged me to take my wife along occasionally when I traveled. He reasoned, and accurately so, that Isabel, being Latin, fluent in Spanish and not without considerable charm, would be a valuable asset. I happily obliged.

72

Thus Isabel and I combined one of my business trips with a one-week fishing vacation in southern Argentina, precisely where I had wet a line with such success on prior trips.

It was in San Carlos de Bariloche on the shore of Lake Nahuel Huapi that we met our fishing guide, Sam Wagner. Soon after America's bloody Civil War had concluded, his father emigrated from the U.S. seeking a better life and wound up a professional fence builder for many of the large sheep ranchers of Patagonia, well to the south of Argentina's hub, Buenos Aires.

Sam was born in Argentina and in later years had acquired considerable fame as a fishing guide.

This one morning while Sam was rowing us to one of his favorite hot spots, he commented to Isabel, "Ma'am, I'd like you to know that that there sheepskin you're a settin' on President Eisenhower sat on." Sensing his fees about to take a quantum leap I quickly chimed in, "Sam, Ike may be a good guy, but I do not always agree with his political views." Happily he got the message.

While waiting for a strike, Sam would often urge us encouragingly. "Let's hear some of that Wagner music." By that he referred to the high-pitched buzz of a whirring reel produced by a hooked steelhead's fast stripping of line in its desperate race for liberty.

Being the fly-fishing addict that I was, I dutifully sniffed at all bait and hardware slingers with the disdain of a nobleman sighting down his nose at the peasantry. I was really going to show my inexperienced wife a thing or two about how a real pro does it.

Thus while Isabel was splashing her flatfish off one side of our boat, I was gracefully arcing my fly line off the other side.

Well, sir, she began pulling in one steelhead after another after another. All the while my flies were being totally ignored by Nahuel Huapi's finned denizens, as indignant smoke billowed from my ears and my lower lip uncontrollably extended in a massive pout.

In fact it got to the point, Isabel later confessed, where she purposely created snarls in her line just so she would not have to continue hauling in fish, thereby averting the addition of any more fuel to the considerable fire already burning within me, the self-styled fishing expert.

Then the climax came when she turned to me and pleaded, "Frank, could you please help me? My line is snagged."

I took her rod and soon determined that her snag was a very large fish. Indeed, that steelhead tipped the scales at 13.5 pounds and its image, alongside that of my wife, now graces a photo album for all posterity to exclaim over, while I ponder the imponderable, "What do Argentina's steelhead have against my flies?" *(See photo.)*

Steelhead

* * *

74

Col. Percy Fawcett was an English surveyor, hired jointly by the Bolivian and Peruvian governments, to establish once and for all the definitive border between those two countries. Such was designed in theory at least, to finally put an end to the historic bickering between those two countries, bickerings which were fanned every time a river, common to both nations, would change its course.

Shouldering his transit, Fawcett would spend two or three years at a crack away from his family while sloshing through Amazonian swamps.

The numerous letters he wrote to his wife back in England were, unfortunately, only posthumously published in a fascinating book entitled, *Lost Trails, Lost Cities,* since on his final trip to South America he disappeared, never to be heard from again.

One of his stories dealt with a notorious inn he purposely avoided staying at. That inn was beside a road he was taking in Bolivia's highlands en route to his destination, the steaming jungle below.

It seems that the proprietor of that inn had had the very unpleasant experience of continuously finding the guests in one of his rooms dead the next morning. Strangely, their bodies overnight would have turned an eery black.

After repeated investigations, the cause was finally discovered. A large spider known as the Apazauca was found hiding in the straw roof above the open rafters. At night it would drop from its lair onto a sleeping body and, without provocation, bite it. Since that arachnid's venom was deadly, the victim would have little or no chance of survival.

The Apazauca is described as being so big that a large dinner plate cannot cover it.

During the twenty-one years I spent travelling throughout Latin America and living there for extended periods, I never personally saw an Apazauca. However, while residing in Mexico during the infancy period of our first born, twin sons, my wife's protective instincts resulted in her squashing into oblivion over sixty poisonous scorpions inside our home.

And I do recall a conversation I had with Chile's chief entomologist, one Ing. Gregorio Rosenburg, with whom I had business dealings. He related an assignment he once had in Bolivia while on loan by the Chilean government.

As he was threading his way along a trail in the jungle near the Beni River, a tributary to the mighty Amazon, he came across spiders so large that when alarmed would stand on stiffened legs some 12" off the ground, a defense reaction designed to make themselves appear more menacing to an enemy.

*   *   *

A Relative in Australia

My nephew, Peter Huttlinger, was lead guitar in John Denver's band right up to Denver's tragic death. He would travel constantly with Denver both domestically and in foreign countries. Later he was to appear at Carnegie Hall on several occasions.

Pete has lots of relatives sprinkled across the United States and frequently he would invite them backstage to meet John Denver.

It got to the point where John Denver once smilingly said to Pete (while thinking, "I'll sure as heck get him on this one!"), "Boy, Pete, you sure have a lot of relatives. Tell you what. We travel next to Australia. Let's see what relative you can come up with there."

Now, Fred Walker is one of Pete's California cousins. When he heard of John Denver's challenge, he concocted a plan with Pete. "Pete," he chuckled, "I have a large credit of frequent flyer miles, plus plenty of unused vacation. What do you say to my taking a plane to Australia for Denver's upcoming gig there?"

Our story now shifts to Australia. It was intermission time Down Under. In the green room back stage Pete turned to John Denver and with a broad grin volunteered, "Say, John, I'd like to introduce my cousin, Fred."

While shaking his head in amazement, Denver laughed, "Touché, Pete!"

Subsequently Pete went on to win our nation's top honor as a guitarist and on three occasions was featured at Carnegie Hall.

*   *   *

The Black Eye

Our family was homeward bound on the passenger liner, Giulio Cesare, to Brazil following an eventful three months of vacation in Europe.

As we crossed the equator, organized hazings were the order of the day and people in droves were being chucked into the swimming pool to the enormous delight of all, but especially to the main thrower-inner who was ecstatic.

Then it was his turn to get dunked. When he saw the tables reversed and his role of perpetrator being suddenly changed to that of victim, he began to yell and swing out at his captors.

I happened to be one of the guys who held a part of him. As we approached the pool I forgot to duck and one of his flailings caught me square in the eye.

In no time I had a shiner bright enough to read by. For several days I wore dark glasses to hide my battle wound.

One noon our family was seated as usual at the table assigned us. Carelessly I had forgotten to wear my sunglasses. Our steward, the personification of decorum and diplomacy, looked me right in my pulsating eye without so much as blinking as he took my luncheon order.

Later back in our stateroom I gazed into the mirror, only to realize to my horror that I did not have my sunglasses on. How our waiter contained himself without bursting out laughing I'll never know.

Needless to say his admirable diplomacy earned him a generous tip.

*   *   *

BLACK WIDOW VENOM

While our family resided in São Paulo, Brazil, our dentist was one Dr. Shigelski and a finer dental craftsman it would be hard to imagine. Our subsequent dentists all gave him very high marks.

This Polish immigrant told us that many years ago he came to a crossroads in life and had to decide whether he wished to become a concert violinist or a dentist. Music lovers were poorer for his decision.

Over the years he plied his trade, oftentimes in severe physical distress due to shingles. There were days when he had to cancel our dental appointments because of his shingles flare-ups. He confessed that the suffering was at times almost unbearable. As he worked on our teeth we would be saddened to see him wincing as he moved about.

Drawing him out on how he had gone about seeking relief, I was intrigued by what he said.

Initially he traveled to Europe for treatment by a series of specialists but always with negative results.

Next he began seeing an East Indian fakir. He hoped he might learn the secret of how mentally to block out pain. He reasoned that if the fakir could rest on a bed of nails without discomfort, why could he not employ the same technique and be freed from his suffering.

Again, he met with no success.

Finally out of sheer desperation, Shigelski allowed a scientist friend talk him into being a guinea pig in the laboratory where that researcher worked at São Palo's world-renown snake institute, O Instituto Butanta. (One of Butanta's claims to fame is in the manufacture of antivenins which they ship all over the world. These remedies were, and still are, used to save countless lives of those bitten by venomous snakes, spiders and scorpions.)

This friend wanted to experiment on Shigelski using undiluted venom from the black widow spider. He theorized that this poison, which attacks the body's nervous system, might somehow work on the very nerves affected by his shingles condition and hopeful cancel out the pain.

The dentist was warned that this test would involve substantial suffering for seven days before the results were known. Already in severe discomfort, Shigelski figured he had nothing to lose so he readily agreed.

For one week he writhed in agony while the black widow venom was working in his system.

I then asked, "Doctor, did it work?" He shook his head and stoically went on living with his cross of anguish.

* * *

THE CAT AND THE CATFISH

It was back in the depths of the Big Depression when I was a child living in the town of Pittsburg, California.

Located on the San Joaquin River, Pittsburg's piers attracted many fishermen.

One Saturday morning I tried my luck and was rewarded with a nice catfish. After landing him I excitedly threw my newly baited hook back in, anticipating another catch.

Totally absorbed in the task at hand, I did not see the hungry cat that was creeping up until it was too late to do anything but yell as he made off with my catfish.

My next blunder was in not keeping all this to myself. Instead I had to blab it to my neighbor across the street, Phil Grant, a steel worker.

Well, he literally laughed himself to tears and by the end of the day everybody on the block was guffawing.

This much I now know. If ever a cat were to steal my catfish again, you can be sure it will remain a secret between the cat and me.

*　　*　　*

CHARLEY AND THE TREES

For a time, Dr. Charley Persing was my boss. He was an outstanding farm chemical research and development executive. Subtle humor was one of his strong suits.

One day I was over at his home. While showing me his garden, Charley pointed to a cluster of eucalyptus trees growing on his neighbor's property, dangerously close to Charley's house. The strong prevailing winds really worried Charley because they always blew from his neighbor's property, through these trees and then across his home. He feared that one day these monstrous trees could come crashing down on his roof.

Figuring he had a reasonable solution Charley walked over to his neighbor and asked for permission to cut the menacing trees down and explained his reason.

"Certainly not!" snapped the neighbor, so Charley went home and started scheming.

Now one of our company's proprietary chemicals happened to be a temporary soil sterilant. You apply it to the soil. It kills what's there and then dissipates without a trace.

The night was dark when Charley stealthily approached these trees. His job did not take long.

About two weeks later when the eucalyptuses had turned, what for Charley was a pleasant brown, Charley once again rang his uncooperative neighbor's bell. "I've noticed that your trees have died. Would you mind if I removed them?" he politely asked.

After confirming the demise of his row of stately shade trees, the now grateful neighbor replied, "Be my guest."

*   *   *

CONCRETE COLLAPSE

Just before my retirement as a general contractor I built two apartment house complexes in greater Los Angeles. The first was a 16 unit and the second a 41 unit.

We broke ground on the second complex two months after starting construction on the first thereby enabling me to use a number of the same sub-contractors on both jobs.

This story is about one of the sub-contractors who did my concrete work.

As a preliminary step before he could pour a twelve-inch-thick slab of steel re-enforced concrete as a deck ten feet above the ground-level parking area, he first had to rent and then position temporary support posts to hold up what were to be thousands of tons of wet concrete. Then after the concrete dried, aged and gathered sufficient strength, those supports could be removed.

Well, to save a buck on post rentals, that contractor purposely skimped on the number of post supports he was using. He was about to begin his concrete pour when I called him on it so he grumblingly made up for the post shortfall and the pour then proceeded with no hitches.

Now forewarned, and with me bird-dogging, he made sure on the second apartment complex project that he used ample posts.

His foreman was his son-in-law, married to his daughter.

From our job he and his crew moved on to others.

Then one day on the six o'clock TV news a terrible tragedy was announced. That very same foreman I had grown to know so well was literally crushed to a pulp when a concrete deck he had been working on collapsed on top of him.

Back to his old post-support short-changing tricks once again, that concrete contractor clearly wound up involved in the tragic loss of his foreman son-in-law.

My lingering hope is that not only that that man's daughter never learned of her father's criminal negligence in the death of her husband, but, of equal importance, that he mended his ways on future jobs.

THE CONDOR

While living and working in Peru during the early stages of my professional career I began to get into photography as a hobby. Once I rented a 4 x 5 Speed Graphic from a friend who was an American professional photographer who freelanced a lot. And over the months we developed a nice friendship.

We were visiting one day just after he had returned from an assignment high in the Andes and he was relating his experiences during that trip.

It seems that some of the highlanders, or "serranos" as they are called, used the condor as the protagonist in sporting events that bordered on the macabre, and my friend was taking pictures of those practices for a U.S. magazine.

One of these events entailed lashing the feet of a condor to the neck of a bull, and then letting the bull run berserk through the village, scattering villagers in a scene reminiscent of the running of the bulls of San Fermin. The condor all the while would be using his powerful beak to tear huge chunks from the neck of its hapless four legged vehicle.

Another pastime would find a group of highlanders sitting in a circle, passing the bottle and getting more and more soused with each round. In the center was a condor hanging upside down from his feet which were lashed to a rafter.

Directly below this huge bird was a growing pot of money. For, you see, the sport here was to ante up, which then gave each participant the right to take one swing at the fowl with his fist.

The one who dealt the lethal blow got the pot. But in the process, lots of blood flowed with ears, noses and fingers badly lacerated or torn off altogether as the feathered monarch fought for its life.

There are indeed primitive customs still alive and well in certain backward areas (and sometimes in not so backward areas, as witness the illegal dog and cockfights that proliferate here in America).

*   *   *

MY, HE'S LATE THIS MORNING

A construction project I once superintended was a 41 unit apartment house complex in Panorama City, California. Unfortunately this job was located in a high crime area where drug dealing, theft and killings were rampant.

Tool stealing at our job site was a constant problem since the fencing of such booty helped to finance the purchase of drugs.

Indeed a number of our sub contractors would wryly joke about brazenly being offered to buy back their own previously stolen tools from the suspected thieves themselves.

One day my man Friday, Porfirio Hernandez, reported that a drifter in broad daylight had climbed the scaffolding to gain access to our apartments and was caught in the act of making off with an armload of tools. With loot retrieved, the boys worked the culprit over pretty good.

We warned him that the police would be summoned the very next time he was caught trespassing. His comment? "I hope you do call the cops. I need a bed and three squares."

Actually, we did call the police but unfortunately they showed but mild concern. Oddly enough this same thief was later to return, often at predictable hours.

Then one morning my plumber glanced at his watch and, with tongue in cheek, remarked, "My, he's late this morning."

*   *   *

OUR NEIGHBOR, GIL

Gil used to be our neighbor and was a family friend. He was also chief surgeon of an important hospital not far from where we lived in San Francisco.

Many stories could be told about Gil. Two in particular I remember.

The first is about Gil and his close friend, Gene Belwamani, a dedicated prankster.

Once while Gil's house guest, Gene, proposed that Gil introduce him during one of his operations as a distinguished visiting surgeon from back East. They both were aware that Gene knew absolutely nothing about medicine.

Gil liked the idea. So the next day in the operating room Gil gave Gene a big build up and his staff of nurses and doctors was dutifully impressed.

Then Gil proceeded with an appendectomy while Gene, standing beside him, acted out his part of a renown surgeon to the hilt while assuming his most condescending air.

After Gil had excised the appendix he turned to Gene, dangled it under his nose and asked, "Doctor, what is your opinion of this appendix?"

Gene fainted.

- - - - - - - - - -

The second narrative finds Gil steaming mad after learning of his wife's unfaithfulness.

Gil tracked her to their house trailer where a tryst was in progress. Stealthily Gil locked the trailer door, hitched the trailer to his car and drove his two prisoners to a lonely road out in the desert.

There he unhitched the trailer and drove off.

* * *

THE OVERCOAT

My second job out of college was with a large chemical firm. Part of my training entailed going on the road with the company's top salesman, Doc, an ebullient extrovert.

After one particularly long day of visiting with farmers we pulled up to a motel. Trudging into our room, Doc hung up his expensive overcoat.

The next morning we checked out and ten minutes down the highway Doc suddenly gasped, "Gosh, I forgot my overcoat!"

So back we sped and as luck would have it he emerged from our old room smiling, his prize coat thrown over his shoulder.

No sooner had he fired up the car when he turned to me and remarked, "Frank, it's timely that we discuss expense accounts.

"Several years ago I lost another overcoat under similar circumstances and never did find it. So when I submitted my next expense account, I listed my food as so much, motels so much and one overcoat at $150.

"My boss called me into his office and told me I could not charge the company for the lost overcoat. I asked him why not. 'I was on a business trip, wasn't I?'

"'Sorry,' the boss snorted. 'Company policy does not allow for such expenses.'

"'Oh,' I said.

"When time came for turning in the next expense account I walked into my boss' office and handed it to him.

"'Boss,' I said with a smile, 'the overcoat is in there. You find it.'"

Because he was the company's star salesman he got away with it.

Happily my subsequent work took me to tropical climates where an overcoat was unnecessary, obviating the temptation of testing Doc's expense account procedures.

*　*　*

IT'S RAINING BEARS

Back in my college I roomed in a Georgetown (greater Washington D.C.) home whose owner told me the following story.

She was visiting a national park and wanted to see the bears. Her car was a convertible, a rag top, which she parked beside the road in the same long line of cars belonging to other visitors. Her car top she left up in case it rained.

When she returned, much to her consternation she found her car canvas top in tatters. It was as if someone had ripped it open.

Then she noted that the row of vehicles both ahead of her as well as the rear likewise had their roofs caved in.

It seems that a bear had decided to use that same line of vehicles my landlady was in as its walkway. So it dented in the metal roofs of many cars until, that is, it got to hers when it promptly fell through.

So she submitted her claim to the insurance company. Answering the standard question posed on the insurance form, "Cause of Accident," she dutifully put, "Bear fell through roof."

I can just imagine the chuckles this must have caused the claim processor as he brought her claim to his manager. "Hey, boss, here's a new one for you. Just look at this!"

Her claim, by the way, was honored.

*　*　*

SEQUEL TO SPAZ

And now for the sequel to Spaz, the frozen cat, and its owner, Marc.

So a couple days ago Marc, sans shoes and socks, steps out onto his patio only to be greeted by a real live rattler boasting eight rattles.

Clearly Marc's chickens were a target for this slithering intruder. What does Marc do? Well, he kills it. What was his weapon? Now isn't that a silly question. He used his bare heel of course.

Later that day he presented his parents (That's us) with his latest conquest, one dead rattler all coiled up in an oversize sandwich bag.

"What do you propose doing with that snake?" we inquired simultaneously in a strident blend of soprano and tenor designed to convey adequate repugnance to even the mere suggestion that his serpentine buddy be lodged in our fridge.

"I'm going to freeze him. Dad, mom, don't you know that rattler meat is a delicacy?"

We'll take his word but not his snake. He already has a dead cat in his freezer.

Thus ends our ongoing saga, "Flippantly Facing the Future of Fried Fauna" (fried rattlesnake with a side order of loin of cat).

May all of your meals find your gastric juices flowing in happy expectation.

*　*　*

A VARIG FLIGHT

Back in the sixties I was on a regular milk run from my base in Brazil. My destination that particular day was Montevideo, Uruguay.

Frequently I would choose by preference Varig Airlines because I had learned form experience that this Brazilian company was extremely well managed. Its schedule was reliable, its equipment well-maintained and its flight crews very competent.

The brains behind Varig's success was its president, a man of German extraction named Ruben Berta. He was a highly qualified, no-nonsense executive who had built his company from scratch to where it was, at the time, Brazil's premier airline. Berta really made his men toe the mark.

And so it was, surprisingly, on that almost fateful day that I lined up at the Porto Alegre airport's departing gate to board my Varig flight for Uruguay.

Outside I saw heavy storm clouds brewing so I queried Varig's boarding agent, "Say, that's some pretty nasty weather up there, isn't it?"

"Oh, it won't be a problem. The captain knows just what to do. Have a good trip."

Well, sir, we were not more than ten minutes aloft when our craft began to be tossed about like a cork on a monsoon swept sea. By then I had logged hundreds of thousands of air miles, but *never* had I experienced until that day as frightening an ordeal as that flight turned out to be.

Instead of skirting around the many thunderheads, our captain in his wisdom seemed to be going right through them as I constantly shook my head in disbelief. We would hit one down-draft after another with the sensation each time that my heart and stomach were simultaneously vying for occupancy in my mouth. It was the same feeling, I was convinced, one would get if on an elevator whose cable had just snapped.

Each time our craft came to a shuddering stop from its downward plummet, the loud creak of twisting metal caused the eyes of scared passengers to grow to platter size.

Two seats ahead of me a man was having a heart attack. His groans brought a stewardess to his side but she had to crawl to him on all fours because the severe jostling and lurching of the aircraft made walking impossible.

Outside lightning was constantly flashing.

Rain beat so hard against the outer window that it was clearly audible despite a sound insulating airspace between it and the inner window.

Looking around me I could only see white knuckles and faces. One man of the cloth had whipped out his rosary beads and was zipping through them so fast they almost smoked.

Because I am writing this eye witness account, it can be surmised that our plane ultimately made it to our destination in one piece.

But I was greatly upset over the substantial rashness of the pilot who had clearly chosen to put all of us passengers through such an ordeal. He could have opted to delay the flight or he might have skirted around the storm.

But no, he went right through the seething tempest, for all I knew because he did not want to be late for a date.

So after our plane came to a stop at the tarmac, I asked my way to the cockpit, the veins in my neck red and swollen. "How dare you put at risk your passengers because of your reckless decision to fly through such a man-killer storm?" I leveled at him.

His response, in essence, was that I should go fly a kite.

"You, sir, have not heard the last of this," I snapped and then strode my way to the exit door.

Not long after that I wrote Varig's president and C.E.O., a letter in which I provided every detail of that terrifying experience. I recommended that he take that plane out of service and carefully check it for metal fatigue.

In no time at all I received a response from Berta himself. He said he had immediately investigated the matter, suspended the pilot, withdrawn the plane from service, and he thanked me profusely for bringing the matter to his attention.

Mollified, I continued flying Varig without even a hint thereafter of the recklessness that had characterized that unfortunate experience.

* * *

THE EMBALMER

It was during one of my many business visits to Argentina. I was seated in Buenos Aires' Hotel Claridge dining room when I struck up a conversation with a gentleman eating at an adjacent table.

He was an embalmer and told me the following story.

After Evita Peron died, Dictator Juan Domingo Peron asked him to embalm his wife's remains in such a way as to make her look alive but asleep, much the way I understand Lenin was made to appear after his death.

In order to accomplish this it was necessary to dismember Evita, chemically treat her body parts, and then sew her back up. It was a lengthy procedure and one day as he was busily at work in his laboratory with sections of her body clipped to a line to dry, in walked Juan Domingo to check on the progress.

Gasping over what he saw, he ordered the embalmer to halt his work at once and place his dismantled former first lady back in the coffin.

Where her remains were finally laid to rest became a mystery. Peron wanted it that way.

CHAPTER 4

INSPIRATIONAL

A Little, Old Blind Lady
Nick at the Cemetery
Pa Stanton
Practice Makes Penmanship
Mothers…Our Great Blessing
Fred's Hotel
Manna House – A Mariposa Beacon of Love
Bandit
A Valuable Slip
A Death in Hermosillo
A Model Detention Center
Honesty a Treasure
Inspiration
Love in Action
* Manolete
Martha
A Refreshing Encounter
Thanks for the Speeding Ticket
This is My Answer
Joe Feeney

-----

* See photo

A LITTLE, OLD BLIND LADY

I was covering South America out of São Paulo, Brazil for a U.S. based, fortune 500 company. I was on the board of two subsidiaries. My salary and perks were quite acceptable. Thus we had a cook and a maid plus a governess for our children, a three month vacation every three years in the U.S. or abroad at my option, besides two weeks per year of local vacation. Our children's private schooling was also part of my benefits package as was the rent for our lovely home.

So one day I up and quit. Ostensibly this seemed like a pretty dumb thing to do. But I had my reasons.

Add to that the eroding effect on one's morals that the business world's temptations all too frequently can offer, and something just had to happen, and happen it did.

One morning from my hotel bed in Santiago, Chile, I looked up at the ceiling and found myself saying, "Lord, I'm not going to make it. I am headed for Hell."

Little did I realize that by such an admission I was setting wheels in motion for future major changes in my life.

Not long after that Santiago experience a superior asked me, as he had done before, to engage in a highly illegal business act which, had it occurred earlier, would not have caused me to bat an eye.

But somehow things were now different. God was tugging at my heart strings. "No," I replied. "I cannot do that. It is wrong and it will jeopardize all that we have been trying to achieve. I know of others who have tried it, been caught and paid dearly."

"There, there Frankie boy. We know what is best. You are not to question our decisions. Just keep quiet and don't rock the boat," I was smugly told.

Then I was amazed when I heard myself respond, "If you insist on taking that course of action I will resign from the company." This was no small thing for me to say, what with well-established job security, great perks, eight mouths to feed, a cushy job and a bright future.

But my boss had not taken me seriously, for weeks later I learned that our company's attorneys had set the wheels in motion to carry out that very same dangerously unlawful plan. So I shot off a cable to our New York City corporate headquarters which said, "Effective at once I am quitting the company."

The next day my manager, director of international marketing, plus the financial director of our multi-billion dollar corporate conglomerate flew down from the states.

"Frank," they said appeasingly, "We want you to stay. We are prepared to purchase an expensive home as our gift to you; just don't question our decision on this matter."

"Gentlemen," said I, "I've made my position quite clear. I cannot nor will not budge. Since you obviously have made up your minds, you leave me no option but to repeat myself. I herewith tender my resignation effective immediately. If it would help I will give you two months to find a replacement, then I'm outa here."

Later, leaving my family behind, I flew to New York to begin my arduous task of finding another employer.

90

It was to be six long months of pavement pounding, with many doors slamming in my face, before I would find suitable employment. But those six months seemed like six years. New York City can be a very cold and inhospitable city under those conditions, regardless of the season of the year.

My base of operations I set up in a small seedy hotel in downtown New York, since anything fancier would have done serious harm to my financial nest egg.

So it went… day after day, week after week, month after month, in and out of my hotel. Sometimes flying to other cities to follow up on job leads. All the while my poor dear wife was holding down the fort back in Brazil managing our household of seven.

Now it so happened that in an alcove just inside my hotel's main entrance was a small news stand run by a single mom, a kindly, poor, blind old lady whom, over the months of my residency, I had befriended. I recall one time learning that the hotel management was planning to kick her out so I raised a stink…… and she stayed.

Another time while in my hotel's cafeteria, I found myself slipping this blind lady's demented son some money which he clearly needed, but which my fast shrinking bank savings by then could ill afford to part with.

Then one evening my little old lady friend, white cane in hand, was crossing the street when a car struck her. Learning of her mishap, I bought a box of candy and traveled for the longest time before reaching the run-down government hospital where she was.

As I handed her my small gift she wept and said, "Oh, Mr. Walker, here I am, just a nobody, and you have come to visit me."

It was my turn to shed a tear over her exemplary humility. I thought to myself, "My, how Our Lord must love such a person, one who has not an ounce of pride and there I was, so terribly proud by comparison."

Upon returning that evening to my hotel I had a message to call Gulf Oil Corporation. It was an offer to head up its Latin American chemicals operation, a territory embracing 21 countries, and I accepted. My prayers and the prayers of many around me had indeed been answered.

To this day I have not the slightest doubt that I owe that job windfall to the Alter Ego of a little old blind lady… for in Christ's own words, "Whatever you do to one of the least of these my brethren you do to me."

Epilog: As it turned out, that job was merely a stepping stone toward the ultimate plan which God had mapped out for me.

And so it was that after an eventful time with Gulf Oil, I finally gave my life over to Jesus Christ, left Latin America and my heavy travel behind, drew closer to Him and to my family, first as a professional tennis teacher, and later as a general contractor.

The Lord was of immense help to me in both professions. For example where tennis was concerned I was literally flabbergasted with the success Jesus bestowed. From international sales management to teaching tennis was for me a huge step of faith, particularly given my relatively advanced age of 47 as well as the fact I had never been on a tennis team, never won a trophy and never taught tennis. But the idea appealed to me especially because it would mean I would see my family every night instead of every several weeks.

So I bought 150 books on tennis and began to devour them, went to tennis clinics to learn state-of-the-art teaching techniques and built a regulation size tennis court on my Los Angeles property.

Then I hung out my shingle and began instructing, all the while learning as I went and, of course, praying. After a year and a half I applied for membership in America's most prestigious tennis teaching organization, the U.S. Professional Tennis Association. Passing three days of testing was required for membership. I passed, and within two years I was elected to their California Board of Directors where I chaired their Instruction Committee.

From teaching on my own court I went successively to two tennis clubs as resident pro. Following that I taught nights at Santa Monica College and days as the lead pro among a staff of eight tennis instructors at California State University Northridge.

I found myself writing articles on teaching techniques which were published in national tennis magazines. During that period I got heavily into kinesiology, the science of body motion and gave lectures on the subject to include to my fellow members of the U.S.P.T.A.

I recall preparing for a particularly important lecture before all members of the U.S.P.T.A. which dealt with the cannonball serve, a study which included a mathematical equation for the perfect fast serve which my astrophysicist brother-in-law and I had worked out. To insure that my study was not basically flawed I enlisted the help of the head of USC's kinesiology department. He agreed to listen to my dress rehearsal for that event and offer his critique to include any and all corrections. When

I finished he said, "Don't change a thing!" Later that same professor offered me a position on his staff.

The only reason I have gone into so much tennis detail is to brag a bit about Jesus and the way He can make a silk purse from a sow's ear as He surely did in my case. Jesus knew full well that I had stepped out in a giant leap of faith to follow Him. He knew I had deep-sixed my international career which my degree from Georgetown University's School of Foreign Service had amply prepared me for, my fluency in Spanish and Portuguese, etc. This modern day miracle in my life I owe strictly to Him to whom I give my thanks and praise.

For brevity I will not go into my experience as a licensed general building contractor other than to say that Jesus was equally helpful. He led me from simple remodels to second story additions to apartment house complexes.

Upon my retirement, my wife and I went through Youth With a Missions' Discipleship Training School with subsequent missionary outreach in Malaysia.

Then for a number of years my wife and I became Manna House staffers in Mariposa distributing food to the poor. Concurrently I joined Gideons where I spoke at churches to raise money for Bibles to leave at motels, etc. And for the past 18 years I have been privileged to conduct church services and bring the Good News inside prison walls where, as chaplain, I have witnessed many, many hundreds of inmates give their hearts to Jesus.

By worldly standards I am not wealthy, living on a fixed income as I do. But by eternal standards my wealth is boundless.

And all because of a little old blind lady and the Cross.

*　*　*

NICK AT THE CEMETERY

Our then-5-year-old grandson, Nicholas, stood among the crowd at Mariposa's tiny cemetery.

Mamena, our beloved friend, at age 99, was being laid to rest.

One by one, eulogies would float out across her grave.

Presently, little Nicholas spontaneously stepped forward and began to orate. Words flowed as freely and as delightfully as a sparkling mountain brook. They were filled with feeling, but were profound in their simplicity and meaning.

Complete with gestures, Nicholas' eulogy went on and on, as the lad clearly was just getting warmed up.

Finally, I saw the pastor glance worriedly at his watch and then pounce on an instant when he noticed Nick pause to inhale, and with a smile he gently pronounced the word, "Amen."

During one of our subsequent visits to Mamena's grave, we were once again with Nicholas. After praying at her burial site, we began wandering by the tombstones of this tiny, comforting and historic graveyard, frequently stopping to read inscriptions.

Suddenly Isabel turned to me startled and gasped, "Where is Nicholas?" and the hunt was on.

Presently our eyes fixed on a tiny figure standing by a grave, head bowed, hands together, praying for the unknown occupant of that grave.

It was Nicholas.

*　　*　　*

PA STANTON

My college engineering studies were interrupted one year shy of graduation by WWII when the U.S. Navy abruptly sent me for duty to the Philippines. By then, however, the fierce battles that once raged across that entire Asian archipelago had drawn silent.

Hundreds of war ships, laying strewn and rusting, had become popular havens for aquatic life on Leyte Gulf's ocean floor, as well as along many other submerged Pacific graveyards.

Manila was largely in ruins and General MacArthur had already made good on his now famous, I shall return, resolve.

That Philippine chapter in my life gave me pause to reflect on my career plans. And so it was that I abandoned engineering to embark on international trade studies.

This narrative focuses on a stateside friendship with Pa Stanton, which I developed while a post-war university student in Washington, D.C. During that period of higher learning, the G.I. Bill was to prove a true God-send, for it absorbed my full, heavy college tuition and book fees right through graduation.

Living expenses were a different story, however. Those were on my nickel.

So my first part-time job had me working as a clerk typist for the federal government. I enjoyed the work and became proficient and quite fast on my Underwood mechanical keyboard. I was once clocked at 127 words per minute. But was it ever a hassle to correct a mistake, what with having to erase seven or more carbon copies each time, weighty government bureaucracy being what it was.

As time wore on it became increasingly apparent that my grades would suffer unless I reduced my extracurricular work load.

That was how I got to know Ma and Pa Stanton. Ma Stanton hired me to care for her ailing husband whose stroke had left him partially paralyzed.

Ma probably could have attended to Pa herself had it not been for her many commitments both as a Quaker and as an active member of the WCTU (Women's Christian Temperance Union) known for their active crusade against alcoholic beverage consumption.

I recall one afternoon during the Christmas season. Ma was having a big WCTU meeting in her living room. The doorbell rang. It was a college friend of mine, Carlos von der Becke. He was holding a Christmas present for me, a bottle of wine, whose tissue paper was a total flop in masking its identity.

Carlos walked right by this array of shocked platter-size eyes as these ladies clucked away sounding for all the world like a hen house that was being raided by a fox.

But back to Pa Stanton. Among my duties, I bathed and dressed him, put his leg brace on, fed him and took him for walks, pushing him along on his wheelchair. Pa's brain worked just fine, but his words, because of his stroke, came out quite slurred. However, I soon got the hang of his unique mumblings. At that point I was to spend many an hour captivated by vignettes from Pa's rich life's experiences.

Early in his career while on staff with the U.S. Coast and Geodetic Survey, Pa Stanton, weaving his way in and out of mosquito-infested mangroves, surveyed from a rowboat much of Central America's Caribbean coastline.

Later, while working for the National Archives, he invented a document-restoring machine which, the last time I heard, was still in use. This complicated piece of machinery was 60 feet long. A valuable document, creased and dirty with the grime of time, would be fed in at one end. Out the far end would emerge a spiffy sheet of paper almost unrecognizable from its earlier self.

Once at Pa's insistence, I helped him down the steps leading to the basement. "Frank," his muffled words pronounced while his eyes danced and sparkled excitedly, "I want to show you something I built just before my stroke."

I gasped in amazement. For there before me on a large workbench I beheld our entire solar system in miniature. Each planet was motorized and rotated about its own axis while simultaneously journeying on its separate orbit around the sun. Pa's mathematical calculations that helped make possible this astounding accomplishment filled the many clipboards I saw hanging on nearby hooks.

Then Pa took a turn for the worse.

I remember him clutching my hand almost desperately, a hand that had been at his beck and call for those many months, as I walked beside the gurney that a paramedic was pushing toward an awaiting ambulance. Those same happy eyes I had grown used to were now darting and frightened. Clearly Pa was sensing his sands of time about to run out.

Later, with head bowed during the grave side ceremony, I reflected on my friend, this once entrancing, gentle soul and the rewarding if fleeting interlude it had been for me to know Pa Stanton.

* * *

PRACTICE MAKES PENMANSHIP

Penmanship, I'm told, is largely an acquired art, except in those rare cases where one is born with an innate handwriting skill. My father fell into the latter category.

At the age of 14, he was given a teacher's certificate in the Palmer Method, and samples of his marvelously free-flowing penmanship were on exhibit at the San Diego World's Fair of 1915.

Not so with me.

However, my atrociously illegible handwriting finally did come to an abrupt halt, but that was late in life, at age sixty to be precise.

It all began, strangely enough, with a dream. I had awakened in the early hours of a San Fernando Valley morning when I found myself then dozing off only to see, in my mind's eye, a freshly plowed field. Up through that rich brown loam appeared fresh green shoots.

This picture meant nothing to me when all of a sudden, I sensed a meaning. It was a message that said, "I will make all things new."

Not long after that I found myself screwing up sufficient courage to say, "Enough is enough. It's time to quit acting the doctor your ain't!" Up to then, so

96

horrible were my hen scratches that if I'd been smart back during WW II when our military was clamoring for unbreakable codes, I could have volunteered and earned who knows, maybe a presidential citation, for my undecipherable handwriting.

Up till then, I was constantly being embarrassed over mistakes my terrible penmanship was causing.

Yet here I am, 87 years young. For the past 25 years I've been able to claim writing legibility without too many detractors yelling, "fraud!"

The penmanship style I have chosen is called "Copperplate Calligraphy," which I have used in all sorts of ways to include, as a SPICE volunteer, inscribing graduation certificates.

How, you may ask, did I accomplish this?

The answer is really quite simple. All you need is a sample of the writing style that attracts you and enough time to practice it.

Like myself, you do visit your doctor, do you not? And your doctor has a waiting room, right? And believe me, they don't call it a waiting room for nothing.

In fact, doctors' waiting rooms, more often than not, are a true test of patience, with spiders having a field day of webbing down the languishing, the seemingly inert, the forgotten.

And so it was over the years, while waiting and waiting to be seen by my physician for various and sundry ailments, I would spend many an hour on alphabet drills, both upper and lower case. Over and over and over, my pen would course across my pad of paper, A,A,A,B,B,B and so on.

With my efforts finally bearing fruit, I remember one day walking into my bank and up to the teller.

"Ma'am, I'd like to register my new signature with your bank," said I.

With heart-warming courtesy to include a cheerful smile, she responded, "But of course. I'll get your signature card."

In no time she was back and pointing to where I was to sign.

Soon, with sudden incredulity written all over her ashen face as she compared my unlikely calligraphy alongside the old hieroglyphics, I heard her gasp, "Please don't do that. You're giving me a heart attack!"

So, while most doctors' signatures may irrevocably, if justifiably, be compared with cuneiform simply because professional courtesy does not require, nor permit, your doctor sufficient waiting time to practice penmanship in his own personal doctor's reception area, your own waiting room time on the other hand, dear reader, can pay off handsomely.

Believe me, if I did it, ANYBODY can!

*　*　*

MOTHERS . . . OUR GREAT BLESSING

How wonderful that America sets aside a very special day each year when mothers can be honored. Much has been written about mothers down through the ages and much should be written here and now, were it not for the constraints of time and space.

So this article will focus on a few vignettes designed to provide something of the flavor for why mothers merit being placed on a pedestal.

Rita Finn is one of Mariposa's justifiably proud mothers who has imparted to her firefighter daughter, Diane, many admirable qualities.

One of these is bravery in the line of fire to which Diane has added an ability to summon extraordinary adrenaline flows enabling her diminutive frame to perform surprising feats of strength.

The world witnessed such qualities last September during Ground Zero rescue operations and we see it daily among fire fighters all across our nation. Some make it and some perish but all are genuine heroes.

In Diane's case, she and her Fresno City Fire Department fellow crew members answered a call. A residence was ablaze. They were able to knock down enough of the flames to enable entry.

During their ensuing search for potentially trapped occupants, they finally found an unconscious victim in a back bedroom.

Carrying the inert body, Diane and her partner, on their way out, found themselves blocked by a huge and weighty bookcase. How Diane alone was able to move such a bookcase, one that a muscular man would have had great difficulty with, is still a mystery. But she did.

Had that victim received less devotion to duty from Diane and her partner than was actually the case, he could easily have become an obituary statistic.

But he survived. Diane and her crew were awarded medals at Fresno's City Hall for an act that fire fighters consider "all in a day's work" but which we, the laity, rightfully recognize as high valor.

Our next two mothers worthy of praise have adult children soon to depart on foreign missionary assignments.

Karren Striplin's son, Mike is headed for Brazil's remote, upper reaches of the Amazon River in July. He will be with one of his church's three teams whose multi-faceted plan is to assist in the physical and spiritual wellbeing of some of that nation's most backward Indians.

The specific assignment of Mike's team is as intercessory prayer warriors. This means they are to be in constant prayer to Our Lord for the protection and success of the overall mission.

Steve Striplin, Mike's older brother, is not new to the mission field. He has passed on his considerable construction skills to the needy both in Romania (two tours) and in Chile.

Kathy Olson's daughter, Susan, is headed back to an orphanage of toddlers in Hong Kong for a second tour of duty, this time for a full year.

Many Mariposans help Mike and Susan's money-raising efforts. An important funding source came from a large yard sale with all proceeds helping defray their heavy travel costs.

Susan and Mike have mothers whose love for The Lord they have inherited through example.

God-fearing Clarice Schoff is the spry 92 year-young mother of Stephen who, as an accomplished electrical engineer, was with General Electric up to his retirement.

To him Clarice provided a good education while imparting the admirable qualities of diligence and dependability. Her 93rd birthday, coincidentally, falls this year on Mother's Day.

Yes, Rita, Karren, Kathy and Clarice and mothers everywhere – you are indeed to be feted for the admirable qualities you weave into the very fabric of your progeny, selfless traits that place the well-being of others far above your own comfort.

Our hats go off to you!

*   *   *

WWII was finally over and I had just returned from my Navy stint in the Philippines. Dad and my five younger brothers and sisters had been waiting for me so that we could pull stakes, depart our long-time home in San Francisco and, as a family, relocate to Washington, D.C.

All of us needed that change since our dear mother had died tragically three years earlier leaving behind us children ranging from ages two to nineteen.

So, with house trailer hooked to our Chevy sedan, off we trekked on our 9,000 mile odyssey. We zigzagged across America and even included a side excursion deep into Mexico.

It was an incident south of the border (and a sequel to it) that is the focal point of this narrative.

We entered Mexico from Laredo, Texas. Our destination was Mexico City which rests on a high plateau well to the south. Everyone had warned us to take along plenty of extra radiator water because the climb was tough and would be even more so due to the extra weight we were towing.

Despite our precautions, we still ran out of water during our long ascent to Mexico City.

That was how we met this Mexican angel of mercy.

Our car and trailer were beside the road, hood was up and a geyser of steam was shooting from our radiator.

A huge semi truck headed downhill saw our plight and stopped. Out jumped its short, feisty Mexican driver who walked briskly over to us carrying his canvas bag of drinking water. He only spoke Spanish.

And at the time our Spanish was limited to a few select words like "bueno, magnífico and estupendo." So we had to rely largely on gestures, facial expressions (and erroneously thinking we had to speak loud English) to communicate.

We certainly did not want to accept his drinking water and were at least able to get that point across. Not to be deterred, however, he emptied the contents of his bag into our parched radiator.

Then he refused our efforts to pay him for his kindness. So Dad disappeared into Fred's Hotel (our affectionate name for the trailer) reappearing shortly with a bottle of Tequila and two glasses.

The trucker's eyes brightened and soon a friendship blossomed as Dad and our benefactor each took turns toasting everything and anything, with the bottle's fast dropping liquid level moot testimony to the success of these frequent salutations.

Meanwhile a din of hooting, honking and yelling filled the mountain air behind the semi which was blocking a line of cars easily a quarter mile long.

Our pal's but casual concern over the obstruction he had created was obvious as he would smilingly accept another refill and deliver yet another toast.

- - - - - - - - - - - - -

All this had occurred in 1946. A full ten years later found me, now fluent in Spanish, with four years of living in Peru under my belt, having married a lovely Peruvian lass and residing in Hermosillo, Mexico which was clear across Mexico from where the trucker had helped our family with his drinking water.

I was driving on the long and lonely stretch between Guaymas and Ciudad Obregon in western Mexico when I noticed a couple standing forlornly beside their auto and its dry gas tank.

In my car trunk I always carried spare gas. So I stopped and emptied the contents of my container into their gas tank.

While all of this was in progress several other motorists, including one trucker, stopped to lend a hand.

The recipient of this assistance, a Mexican, then took out his wallet to pay me. I said, "Not on your life. You lovely Mexicans have always been more than kind to me and my family and it is rather we that still owe you a debt of gratitude."

Then I told this couple, and the others standing around, the story of the Mexican trucker who many years earlier had been so very kind to us way on the other side of Mexico.

The trucker who was listening raised his hand and said, "Yo fui ese camionero. (I was that trucker)." He even remembered the sign we had placed in our trailer window that said "Fred's Hotel."

Clearly this man was a living example of the "Good Samaritan." And those he had already stopped to help in his lifetime must have been legion.

* * *

Manna House, Mariposa's long-standing free-food ministry, did not "just happen." It has been the product of those who love their fellow man and then, through their actions, have demonstrated that love.

Born almost two decades ago, this cradle of caring for the needy, staffed completely by volunteers, stands like a modern day Ellis Island, assisting society's aliens because of economic misfortune and high-lighted by hunger pangs.

It has been thanks to all the local churches, to our great and generous public school students, to our supermarkets and their special discounts, to other many businesses, to the CYA men, to the Sheriff's Dept. and to the populace at large all marching together to the tune of "Love Thy Neighbor," that has made this outreach such an overwhelming success. People, lots of them, stepping out of their comfort zone to make it all happen.

So here we are, once again in the wonderful Christmas season, with Manna House bulging at the seams with activities on many fronts. Staff meetings to plan, organize and execute, all under the outstanding direction of its president, Barbara Kohles.

A typical day at the Manna House, just uphill from the Happy Burger, goes something like this:

A lad walks in, an earlier recipient of an unusual emergency loan, and hands to one of the MH staff full re-payment. His smile says it all, "Thanks for your help, but especially for your trust."

Lines of needy folk waiting for food for their barren larders, or to sign up for the upcoming Fairgrounds Christmas dinner hand-outs (to include a voucher for a frozen turkey), or a just-released jail inmate needing some urgent help while scrambling to get back on his feet, or $600 dollars (from an anonymous donor) which was enough to pay for the replacement of one of MH's ailing refrigerators, or Toys for Tots which were sent over to our exemplary Sheriff's Department that directs this caring program as well as coordinates emergency lodging, or Mariposa Photographic Studio 49 for their generous help, and surely there are many others who could be named or who otherwise wish to remain anonymous but whose great assistance has contributed immeasurably to the unquestionable success of this program.

Yes, a day, a precious day in the life of an MH staffer.

And why all this fuss? Because of simple obedience to the Divine Giver, to Him whose words, "Whatever you do to these, the least of My brethren, you do to Me," say it all.

*   *   *

BANDIT

This is a story about a dog, a black Labrador Retriever named Bandit. Isabel and I first met that gentle 12-month-old canine when our son, Peter, asked us to dog-sit Bandit for a little while. That little while stretched to fourteen years. Needless to say all in our household developed a very strong bond of friendship with Bandit.

Then one day we shed not a few tears as our dear companion, wracked with cancer, finally breathed his last on our Mariposa living room floor while we knelt in prayer beside him.

We are certain that Bandit knew he was loved which, we feel, may well have helped to account for his longevity, since we are told that Labs usually do not last beyond 12 years and not the 15 that Bandit lived to be.

A member of the family, he oftentimes accompanied us to the beach, during our earlier Ventura County residency, where he would delight in racing along the wet sand in mad pursuit of seagulls that would screech loudly while scrambling to become airborne barely ahead of their pursuer.

For hours on end Bandit would play fetch the ball with any and all willing throwers, faithfully depositing the slobbery fruit of his retrievals at the feet of soon to be arm-weary masters. Children adored playing with him, laying on him, tweaking his nose, pulling his ears while Bandit said nothing and did nothing, all the while enjoying being the center of attention.

I once learned something quite interesting relating to the intelligence and temperament of the Labrador Retriever. It occurred while I attended a several day, international seminar on solar cookers held at the University of the Pacific in Stockton.

A dear friend, Owen Schumacher, who was a fellow classmate during the missionary school my wife and I once attended, subsequently wrote me from his missionary base in Afghanistan. In that letter he asked if I would attend an upcoming seminar on solar cookers and then send him my gleanings from that conference's proceedings. The reason for his interest was because in Afghanistan wood for making fires oftentimes is hard to come by, while sun doesn't cost anything and is readily available.

So I obliged. It was a fascinating experience. People from every continent were present. One of the speakers was a blind lady who made her way up the stairs to the rostrum with not a police dog but a yellow lab at her side. Later I approached her and was soon made aware that the use of seeing-eye dogs is now gravitating toward Labs over the traditional police dogs because the Lab is considered by many to be smarter and with a more even temperament.

But back to Bandit.

During his declining months, Bandit did an unusual amount of sleeping. And when I would take him out to do his numbers, just plain walking was an effort for the poor dog. He would pant more than I, one of his octogenarian masters who erroneously thought he had a corner on the panting market.

When we knew the end was in sight because both his intake and outgo were nil, coupled with our conviction that he was in substantial pain, my son and I opted for having him put down.

However Isabel, remembering the Holy Scripture which reads, "The Lord giveth and the Lord taketh away, blessed by the name of the Lord," wanted God to exercise His right. Isabel finally, although with great reluctance, agreed that if Bandit did not go to dog heaven by 4 p.m. when the vet was due, then she would permit his being put to eternal sleep because of his sufferings.

Thirty minutes before our wonderful vet, Dr. Eileen Bissmeyer, arrived, Bandit breathed his last. We were all greatly relieved, if saddened, but Isabel's gratitude to Our Lord far outstripped ours.

Those final hours of Bandit's life taught me a very strong lesson, which was to trust more in God who is merciful and who is intensely interested, not only in our lives and in our prayers but particularly in our faith in Him.

Isabel's faith had been stronger than mine.

*　　*　　*

VALUABLE SLIP

While attending Georgetown University's School of Foreign Service I chose to major in international trade, one of three majors offered at that school, the other two being diplomatic corps and transportation. The course of study was basically the same for all three up to the last year when specialized subjects then distinguished each major from the other two.

A number of my classmates chose the diplomatic corps. One of these, and a good friend, was Frank Ortiz who went on to become ambassador to Argentina. Both of us were active participants in the Latin American set during our time at the university and oftentimes we double-dated. My particular goal in life, later to be realized, was to develop a career south of the border.

I recall once attending a huge masquerade ball thrown by Elena Ivanissevich, daughter of the Argentine ambassador. The embassy crowd turned out en masse to this gala affair, an event heavily covered by the press. Since I was living on a very strict budget at the time, I could not afford a fancy costume. So I decided to go as a tramp which wound up being in stark contrast to all the scintillating costumes that graced the embassy that evening. To my amazement, Look Magazine published a full page photo showing me, in rags, bent over a crooked cane while looking up at our hostess, Elena, dressed in stunning attire.

But, to the main thrust of this narrative. A fellow student, who was majoring in diplomatic corps, since he had chosen to be a career diplomat, was targeting the State Department for employment.

Now, to qualify for consideration by the State Department, it was necessary to get high scores on a series of very rigid entrance exams. The toughest of these and dreaded the most was the oral.

At the appointed hour my Georgetown colleague entered the oral exam room and began walking along the highly-polished and very slippery marble floor toward his panel of inquisitors, all high State Department officials.

As he approached the stern-faced board, his new, slick-soled shoes caused him to slide and then crash unceremoniously to the floor. With great aplomb he picked himself up as if nothing had happened and continued forward.

He stopped before the amazed examiners, smiled at them and awaited their instructions.

They looked at one another, hurriedly huddled, and spoke in hushed tones. Presently one of them, clearly reflecting the admiration of the others, face beaming, pronounced, "You have just passed your orals."

*   *   *

A Death in Hermosillo

At one time my lovely wife, together with our new-born twins and a Peruvian duenna lived in Hermosillo, capital of Sonora in northwestern Mexico.

Locally I was known as an entomologist for my stateside employer, Stauffer Chemical Company. But entomology was merely my assigned front. My primary, albeit secret assignment, was to ferret out the details of how our company's super-distributor, an American working in Mexico, was stealing from us.

We resided in Hermosillo for some three years and never had we experienced either before or since such intense heat. Indeed, there is a local saying that says: "When a Hermosillan dies and goes to Hell he asks for an overcoat." It was not uncommon for inside temperatures at midnight to hover at the century mark. Oftentimes our family of five would crowd into our only bedroom with refrigerated air where, at 85 degrees, we all felt greatly refreshed.

Our home was a small duplex on a dirt road. During our stay in Mexico we socialized with our Mexican neighbors and grew to know and love those very warm people.

It was a tightly-knit community with much visiting back and forth. Oftentimes we would be the recipients of a cake, or some other goodie prepared by a friend. And at other times Isabel would take one of the fruits of her culinary efforts over to a friend.

One day tragedy struck. A teenager, driving too fast, ran over the small child of one of our neighbors.

The open casket wake took place in the living room of the deceased where we, and many more, gathered to pay our respects, to eat and to console the bereaved.

It was moments like these of great intimacy, emotion and compassion which truly bond friends together.

When we returned to the states a part of us remained back with those lovely, hardworking, dedicated Mexicans who had generously shown us by their example the art of loving one's neighbor.

*　*　*

It is my privilege to be associated in the role of chaplain with Mariposa county's adult Detention Facility where I have been serving now for over 18 years, and a finer jail I would be hard-pressed to find anywhere.

Not only is this facility squeaky-clean, as opposed to many others where the fetid air is offensive to inmate and visitor alike, but of far greater importance, the model staff there treats its detainees with great decency and respect. This is not to say, in the interest of maintaining order, that when disciplining is necessary it is withheld.

During my many, many visits to this jail, never have I ever been treated with anything but sincere courtesy by its sharply groomed, kind and efficient deputies.

Most inmates do not hesitate to give these jailors high marks. But whenever a Mariposa inmate occasionally grouses to me about the poor conditions and lousy treatment, I quickly remind him that I am quite familiar with several other California lockups that would make this Mariposa one truly seem like a plush country club.

Prior to becoming a volunteer chaplain for Mariposa County attending to the spiritual needs of our jail's inmates, I was involved in bringing the message of eternal salvation to prisoners at the Los Angeles County Jail, California Men's Colony, Boy's Town of the West and Whispering Pines Correctional Center.

So it is that I salute our Mariposa Jail and all those responsible for making it a shining example of how, with caring, dedication and smarts, a prison can be something more than just a human warehouse.

Our Sheriff-Coroner, under whose purview falls this jail, demonstrated his feelings toward the work we chaplains do. He submitted our names to the White House for recognition. Today the writer and his fellow chaplains gratefully display our certificates signed by President George Bush.

In my case I have personally recorded 1,500 inmates of whom I am aware who asked Jesus Christ into their hearts. Due to the low rate of recidivism among such "saved" inmates (i.e., 15% versus 85% among unsaved inmates), this represents an annual saving to our penal system of over $50 million (with the big figure being a cost of $50,000 per annum per inmate).

* * *

This is a story about honesty, that elusive commodity, so unknown in today's world of hustle where anything goes and where morals and ethics too often take a back seat to rationalizing, to the philosophy of "finders keepers."

It was in the late Summer when Bob and I had decided to try our luck in the high Sierras. We loved trout fishing. But this particular day it was the legendary golden trout we were after.

So we drove to road's end, Saddlebag Lake, elevation 10,087 feet and there we loaded ourselves and gear into Saddlebag Lake Resort's ferry service that took us to the lake's far end.

Then it was hike, hike, hike.

At day's end, Bob had his Golden and I had tired feet. Yet because of the spectacular scenery, the exercise and pure mountain air that cleansed our lungs, we were both happy, if pleasantly tired.

But it wasn't till that evening as I was unpacking and stowing my gear that I learned to my dismay that my prize Swiss altimeter was gone. I just knew it had to have fallen from my fishing vest "somewhere" along the John Muir wilderness trails we had threaded our way earlier that day.

Needless to say, I gave the altimeter up for lost.

Some two months later, Bob and I found ourselves once again at Saddlebag Lake, anxious to limit out this time.

I said a quick prayer that somehow, miraculously to be sure, I might find my treasured instrument.

Then I walked up to Saddlebag Lake Resort's lunch counter and said to the waitress, "Miss, this may sound ridiculous, but I'll say it all the same. Two months ago I was up here and lost my altimeter. I hiked so much that day that it could literally be anywhere."

"Could you describe it," she said, so I did.

Sixty seconds later she returned smiling and handed me my treasure. She told me the owner, Don Steenerson, had found it.

For a minute I was speechless. When I finally found my voice, I thanked her profusely and asked to speak with the owner.

Soon I was in animated conversation with Don Steenerson. After acknowledging my gratitude, he pointed up to the rafters. There I saw hanging hats, fishing gear, radios, you name it – all waiting to be claimed by their rightful owners.

How refreshing, how marvelous to be a part of Don's on-going story, a story that says, "If it's found, I'll hold it till claimed."

My prayer was indeed answered that memorable day at Saddlebag Lake.

* * *

INSPIRATION

One summer morning I recall walking toward a building in Woodland Hills, California when a voice aimed at me.

"Can you please help me?" it softly said.

I turned around. There I saw a smiling lady in an electric wheelchair, so I approached her.

She had been using a key unsuccessfully to close the ramp door to her van.

It was little wonder that she was having difficulty because the only movement I could discern in her entire body was limited to her fingers and face.

Once the door problem was solved, we fell to talking. It was immediately evident that I was speaking to a most unusual person.

With eyes that sparkled and danced and lips which spoke with such love and vivacity, world-famous Joni Eareckson Tada soon had lifted my spirits to a new and exciting level.

I learned that she was on her third book, was deeply involved in her water-color painting (the brush she holds in her mouth) and was running a company, all at the same time.

And as if that wasn't enough, she also had a busy speaking schedule (with Billy Graham and others) besides the campus-witnessing for Christ she was heavily committed to.

As I walked away in the afterglow of that momentous encounter, I found myself mumbling, "Walker, don't you ever, ever complain again about your lot in life. You have just been in the presence of a REAL overcomer."

What an inspiration!

* * *

LOVE IN ACTION

Today I was in the waiting area of a Fresno restaurant when a man, carrying a bassinet in one hand and a young girl in his free arm, sat down beside me.

He and the little girl were clearly anglo saxon. The tiny baby was black.

After I complimented him on the two children he told me that they were both adopted.

"Their mothers," he said with eyes downcast, "are in jail."

"My wife recently died when she fell and hit her head, so I am carrying on as a single foster parent," he added.

The seating hostess then called his name. While rising he turned to me and with a smile gently said, "My wife and I have raised 29 children this way. I love children."

I watched him make his way over to a table and thought, "My what wonderful people there are in this world. And how I wished the media would devote more column-inches to stories like this, that uplift.

"The public is so hungry to learn about the noble in mankind, and indeed there is much noble to be recounted."

*   *   *

MANOLETE

My Dad in his mellower years became an art collector. Oftentimes he would don his oldest clothes and, with shoe soles flapping, wander through antique, art and curio shops hoping to pick up valuable paintings for a song because a proprietor hopefully would be unaware of their true worth, with father's hobo accoutrements designed to encourage rock bottom prices.

Over the years he acquired a number of fine works of art at bargain prices using this technique.

One evening he threw a party at his home. An invitee called him to say he would be delayed because some guests had unexpectedly dropped in. "Please have them come along with you," Dad offered, and they obliged.

So it was that Dad became acquainted with Mrs. Lock Milam whose father had founded the Lockheed Aircraft Company.

Mrs. Lock Milam was herself an art fancier and she spent much time examining Dad's collection. One work she liked especially. So Dad, normally a generous person, but doubly so after the few drinks he had already consumed, was flattered by her interest.

"Do you like it?" he purred.

"It is marvelous," she gushed.

"It is yours," said Dad as he removed it from the wall and handed it to her.

"Don't be silly, I can't possible accept such a gift," she responded with pained gratitude as she replaced it on its nail.

Manolete

"Oh, but I insist," retorted Dad as he once again took it from its mooring and placed it in her hands.

This sequence of "Please accept it; no I can't" continued into the wee hours.

When Mrs. Milam finally left, the painting was tucked under her arm.

Two weeks later Dad received a dinner invitation from Mrs. Milam. At the appointed hour he pulled into her Kentland driveway and parked alongside her Rolls Royce, the same car, dad was to learn, she would have flown, together with her chauffeur, to Europe whenever the travel urge would hit her.

Soon, with drink in hand, he was being given a tour of her marbled mansion. He nodded at the statuary and exclaimed over the tapestries.

Suddenly he was transfixed when he gazed at a bullfighter's suite-of-lights hanging on the wall. Below it appeared the caption "Manolete's Suit-of-Lights.

Dad was a taurine lover and over the years had acquired a number of paintings of bullfight scenes. So he knew very well that Manolete was to bullfighting what Da Vinci was to painting. Mrs. Milam could see he was ecstatic, so she whispered, "Do you like it?"

"Like it!" he sighed, "It is truly magnificent!"

So she reached up, took it from the wall and presented it to him.

Dumbfounded, Dad stammered, "But, but I simply can't," as he reluctantly yet tenderly put it back in its place of honor.

"Oh, but you must have it," she insisted as she replayed the familiar scene she had been a party to just two weeks earlier at Dad's home.

When the "But you must, no I can't" scenario was finally played out, Dad bade his generous hostess goodnight and reverently deposited Manolete's suit of lights on the back seat of his car. *(See photo.)*

*   *   *

MARTHA

This is a story about a lady who cares about others and about a loyal employer who appreciated her. Martha's winsome smile and kind words to everyone who pushed their shopping cart up to her check-out station had become a legend.

Then she fell deathly ill and was rushed to Modesto's Memorial Hospital. She was six-hours under the knife. For the longest time following her surgery the prognosis remained grim. Pale, weak and frail, Martha began her long road to recovery which included protracted and debilitating chemotherapy sessions.

During that great trial, her employer, Pioneer Market, her co-workers and her many friends, all showered dear Martha with flowers, visits and get-well notes of encouragement.

Today, one year later, Martha is finally well. And Pioneer Market management, in a truly heart-warming expression of loyalty and compassion, has welcomed her back.

Now at the market we Mariposans will once again be treated to Martha's warm smile and sweet words.

*   *   *

A Refreshing Encounter

Andrew Wilson is black, middle-aged and a trucker. He was delivering shoring posts for an apartment house complex I was building in Canoga Park, California, when I met him.

From the start I liked the man. Peaceful and smiling, he had an aura that attracted.

Soon I learned he was the father of seven children and had been married 28 years.

He talked with understandable pride about his son, Freddie, who, at six feet, was the shortest player on the University of Nevada at Las Vegas' championship basketball team.

The reason why Andrew chose to be a local trucker was so that he could be home every night with his family. He said he decided many years ago that he did not want to make the same mistake his father, a Baptist preacher, had made by spending so much time away from home that he never really knew his family.

So I told him that America needs more families like his and that I wished I had not waited so long before I changed professions, precisely so that I, too, could get to know my family better.

Soon his truck was unloaded. Andrew smiled and waved as he pulled away from the curb.

There went a man happy over his choice of priorities. What a refreshing encounter.

*   *   *

This is a story about a speeding ticket and why I wish to commend the CHP officer who gave it to me.

Not too long ago I dropped my wife off at Mariposa's John C. Fremont Hospital so that she could visit a patient there. Her parting words to me were "Please be sure to pick me up no later than one hour from now as I have important things to do."

"Don't worry, honey, I'll be back in time," I reassured her.

Soon I was near Catheys Valley, stopped by the road, taking photographs I hoped to enter in the upcoming County contest.

Suddenly I glanced at my watch. Yipes! I was good and late. So I swung into the driver's seat and took off in a cloud of burning rubber. I knew I was speeding but since I didn't see any airplane spotter the road sign announced, I figured, "Hey, no problem."

Then a Christmas tree lit up in my rear view mirror and I knew it wasn't December. So I pulled over, hauled out my driver's license and waited for the officer to give me the grim news.

Presently I was greeted by Officer Coronado, one of the nicest, most polite persons I could ever hope to meet.

My opening words were, "Officer, I was clearly in the wrong and you are totally in the right by ticketing me." I thought I saw him do a double take as he took my license and walked back to do his paper work.

Presently he returned and, with a slightly pained expression, handed me my "Notice to Appear."

We exchanged parting pleasantries and as he turned to head back to his patrol car I noticed that his eyes were moist.

How refreshing! Here was a patrolman, clearly doing his duty, yet showing the milk of human kindness by letting his eyes express the compassion that he felt.

Hats off to the California Highway Patrol!

P.S. One of the photos I took that fateful day I am entering in the contest. I call it my $162 picture (fine plus traffic school.)

*   *   *

Back in the sixties I had just flown into San Francisco's international airport from Brazil where I was living.

My Dad was at the airport to greet me. After we hugged and exchanged our father-and-son words of endearment, he said, "There is someone I would like you to meet. He's in the bar."

So we repaired to the watering hole, also known as the place of "attitude adjustment." He walked up to a very black distinguished master sergeant, put his arm around the serviceman's shoulder and pronounced with fatherly pride, "Sergeant, I want you to meet my son."

Now in order to appreciate the import of what then followed it is necessary to say that this period in our nation's history was seeing the problem of Negro suppression reaching new heights. Men like governor Orville Faubus were flaunting their bigotry and too many people were allowing such anti-American behavior to go unanswered. But not Dad.

He turned to face all in the crowded airport tavern and, with his arm still encircling the black master Sergeant's neck, shouted for everyone to hear, "Ladies and gentlemen, this is my answer to Orville Faubus."

That was my father and I am proud of him. Always will be.

* * *

JOE FEENEY

There are not too many singing talents that really captivate me, but Joe Feeney is one such standout.

It was back in the seventies when I had the privilege of being present in the audience during the taping of a Lawrence Welk television show.

That memorable afternoon this gifted tenor cranked up and let fire with the most beautiful rendition of "Danny Boy" that I had ever heard.

So moved was I, that tears of joy and appreciation welled in my eyes as I sat, awed at such a God-given talent.

Years later I listened to a re-broadcast of that particular program, but I must confess that this electronic age we live in, as advanced as it is, still cannot capture the same voice quality that a live audience hears.

I cherish the memory of that brief moment in the presence of one of the great voices of our time.

-----

* See photo

Nestled in a small, remote subtropical valley in Brazil's coastal mountain range, known as A Serra da Bocaina, is an inviting retreat. Comprising many acres of stately pine trees and trout-filled streams, it belonged to my close friend, William Marinho Lutz. During my Brazilian residency Lutz managed the power and light company for South America's largest city, São Paulo, where our family resided.

He once told me that the materials used to build his comfortable high-country escape were brought in on the backs of many mules, since mountain trails provide its only access to distant roads. And indeed, I had saddle sores after the five-hour ride to his place from where I had left my jeep, mute testimony that no vehicular traffic had ever tarnished this delightful Shangri-La that was sandwiched, amazing as it may seem, close in-between Brazil's two greatest cities, Rio de Janeiro and São Paulo.

Being a fly fishing addict, I always treasured the occasions when Lutz would invite me to his alpine hide-away.

On one of my piscatorial visits, in the company of other fishing guests, I found myself elected to tie a supply of flies to "match the hatch."

Since it was grasshopper season, I homed in on "Joe's Hopper," a reasonable facsimile of the real thing. However, there was a slight hitch. Our refreshment center featured cachaça, a powerful local rum to whose snares I had unwittingly fallen prey.

But it wasn't my resultant unsteady gait that bothered me so much as it was the multiple vision this drink had produced. (Of course, if I tried that same drinking stunt today, forty years later, I'd wind up pre-embalmed, much to the disappointment of the funeral parlor whose fee would have to be correspondingly reduced.)

So while the guys continued to deplete the cachaça supply, fly-tyer Walker sat in front of his vise, inserted a hook which initiated the procedure that was to be repeated long into the night.

Well, I don't have to tell you the problems that double, maybe even triple vision can cause in general and much more to fly tying, a hobby which can be likened to micro surgery in its demands for precision.

Threads that shouldn't have been cut, were. Feathers whose whole purpose was to simulate insect wings looked like they'd been pasted on by a preschooler and hackles and tails were all askew.

I had created unique, wretched messes that no more resembled a grasshopper than I did.

At dawn I parceled out to each of my companions his allotment of my previous night's disastrous encounter with hook and feather while, to a man, all stared incredulously, gulped and then glumly fanned out to try their luck.

That evening as our group of budding Isaac Waltons sat around a crackling fire, the air was electric with excitement. All had made a killing. Incredibly, everyone had limited out on my wretched messes. I was astounded more than I was proud.

Abercrombie and Fitch, at one time one of America's premier sources of quality fishing tackle, would sell flies at fancy prices that were true works of art. So realistic were they that live male flies (rumor has it) would stand in line waiting their turn to mate with the A and F decoy.

That experience drove home to me a very salient point. Trout could care less about how meticulously flies are tied.

So to you, purveyors of fly tying equipment, may I present a thought? Try including in each kit a couple of bottles of cachaça. It's a sure way of guaranteeing a wretched mess every time… and will the trout, and their Homo Sapiens stalkers ever *love* you for it.

*　*　*

BIRDS ARE FOR THE FLIES

Knowing of my love for fly fishing, one Christmas my wife surprised me with a fly-tying kit which I soon put to use, thanks to the fine instructional skills of my fishing buddy, Datus Proper, an expert fly fisherman AND fly-tyer.

Soon it became apparent that a wider variety of feathers would be needed for the more exotic fly patterns than what my then limited inventory provided.

We were living in São Paulo, Brazil at the time. So I approached São Paulo's zoo keeper. "What do you do with the bird carcasses after your birds die?" I asked.

"Oh, we feed them to the fish," he responded matter-of-factly. But he warned that his birds were usually long-lived and only very occasionally was he faced with having to replace a dead bird.

"Can we work a deal?" I quickly voiced. "I'll give you 50 cruzeiros per carcass. All you have to do is call me when a bird dies and I'll come right over."

With a smile he intoned, "You're on."

A few days later I got his first in a number of surprisingly frequent phone calls. "Got a couple of dead ones for you," he would proudly announce with cruzeiro signs dripping from his voice.

The next week several more calls and so it went until my supply of rare bird plumage could have put me into a feather business of my own.

It finally got to the point where I had to tell him that I could not buy any more for awhile. Presumable his diminishing bird population stabilized shortly thereafter.

I can just imagine how it must have been at the zoo's aviary section before I entered the scene. A father, with young son in tow, pointing an instructive finger at one of the many unusual birds, "That, my son, is a One-Wattled Cassowary."

After Walker's deal with the zoo keeper and the resulting nose dive in the zoo's rare bird numbers, I could just visualize the same father walking up to one of the few remaining birds and pronouncing, "Son, that cute chicken over there is a Rhode Island Red."

*   *   *

THE PIRACEMA

This particular narrative has as its setting South America's two largest countries, Brazil and Argentina, and is about the Dorado, a fresh water game fish of legendary fascination.

Sport fishing enthusiasts from around the globe often converge on Brazil and Argentina to do battle with this gold-sided, hence its name "Dorado," powerful tropical cousin of the salmon.

Ranging up to 20 pounds or more, the Dorado (spelled Dourado in Portuguese-speaking Brazil) inhabits fast, turbulent and warmer waters rich in oxygen.

The Dourado angler early on succumbed to the necessity of employing steel leaders to which his lures were attached. Regular nylon terminal gear the Dourado invariable would soon snap in two with its razor sharp teeth during its pirouetting, tail-walking, gill-shaking struggle for freedom.

Fishing enthusiasts Henry Ford II and President Dwight Eisenhower, among many other world figures, on more than one occasion came to stalk this noble if belligerent denizen of South America's sub-tropical rivers.

120

A favorite spot frequented by the Dourado was just below the massive waterfall known as Iguaçu situated at the confluence of the Brazilian, Argentinean and Paraguayan borders.

So huge is this cataract that former first lady, Eleanor Roosevelt, once wrote in the guest register of a nearby hotel, "Poor Niagara!" On many occasions I have flown over Iguaçu en route from São Paulo to Buenos Aires and at 40,000 feet these falls were still clearly visible.

All of which now brings me to the title of this account, The Piracema, which is Portuguese for "the spawning trek."

From our Brazil home I once took my young sons to where a Dourado "piracema" was in progress. As we looked down from a bridge vantage point, we could see a nearby waterfall emptying into a pool just below us.

There we gazed in delight at a sizable circle of Dourado, their dorsal fins slicing the water's surface, as they slowly spun en masse like a huge revolving wheel.

Then methodically, as if by pre-arranged signal, one Dourado after another would peel away from that densely packed wheel of fish and, with tail fin wagging at blurring speed, race toward its cascading target.

With a mighty burst of raw power we witnessed each fish become air-borne and then, like a bar of sparkling gold sinking into fresh snow, slip into the foam en route to its upstream rendezvous to perpetuate its species.

When we finally turned to leave, I could not help but reflect with deep admiration on the majestic Dourado's richly earned reputation among international fishing connoisseurs for its beauty, exhilarating power and combativeness.

* * *

PERU'S DESERTS

I lived and worked in Peru for a number of years, traveling quite extensively in that country, mainly up and down its long and parched coastline, while working with an international commercial fishing consortium.

Then years later I found myself engrossed in an entirely different field, namely farm chemicals. From my Brazilian base of operations, I would periodically return to Peru to resume my relationship with that enchanting part of South America.

That land-of-the-Incas' agriculture is largely dependent upon water from those relatively few rivers flowing westward from the Andes that are large enough to survive their moisture-sapping trek through Peru's bone-dry western coastal desert where most of that country's crops are grown.

At one time a Peruvian friend, Guillermo Ganoza, a Trujillo industrialist, and I planned to go into business together. Our idea was to use Pacific Ocean wave power to run a network of reverse osmosis plants up and down the coast. By producing great quantities of fresh water from sea water we could cause Peru's deserts to blossom like a rose. For a variety of reasons, however, that dream never materialized although I remain steadfast in my conviction that the idea remains basically sound. Interestingly, the Peruvian government does have intentions of alleviating its severe water shortage problem by looking to the lofty Andes mountains for a solution. Involved here is selecting a number of large mountain lakes and creating outlets in each by drilling through the Andes to allow water to drain to the west. It is there where Peru's demography and croplands predominate. Conversely, east of Peru's Andes lie the Amazonian rain forest lowlands where both populations and farming are sparse.

Oddly, there is a plus side to that nation's water deficit. I was made sharply aware of this following a lecture on the use of crop pesticides I once gave to farmers and agricultural technicians at La Molina which is Peru's large, federally-funded agricultural college. My subject was the use of chlorinated hydrocarbons, organo-phosphates and other synthesized insecticides of that era which at the time were employed widely in many parts of Latin America to control farm insect pests.

After my lecture, slide presentation and questions from the floor all had ended, the government's leading entomologist came forward and politely told me, "What you have said may be all well and good, but we will not allow your company, nor any other pesticide firm, to sell chemicals that upset the natural biological control system which we have worked hard and successfully to establish. The chemicals you speak of literally decimate our beneficial insect populations thereby causing crop-damaging insect numbers to explode and crops to suffer correspondingly. Currently," he went on to say, "our government is committed to a system of biological control. We are constantly raising billions of beneficial insects which we are making available to farmers, at very low prices, all up and down our desert coast.

"These good insects stay where put and perform very effectively in curbing bad bug activity. The reason they do not migrate elsewhere before having the chance to do their job is because the surrounding deserts block all escape."

Fortunately for my employer, an important manufacturer of insecticides, biological control in most of the remaining countries of South America, where lush growth is common, was not (and still is not), a viable alternative.

122

Lack of aridity in the more tropical countries of South America simply makes it impossible to contain the beneficial insects until they can do their job. Clearly, however, unless damaging insects can be kept in check, crops obviously will suffer.

Hence I was still able to put food on my family's table in spite of our setback in Peru and Rachel Carson's book, The Silent Spring, with the furor the latter ignited over the evils of pesticides.

*   *   *

ARE YOU STILL MAD?

Back in the early fifties I was working in Peru for a large, San Francisco-based fishing company. An assignment I once was given involved handling all the towing and dry-docking arrangements for one of my employer's refrigerated barges.

In the process I sought bids from several ocean-going tug companies since our barge had to be brought from near the Ecuadorian border for some 500 miles south to a dry-dock at the port of Callao.

The best price was provided by a firm run by an Italian. But when the time came to sign the contract he went back on his word and upped his price.

So I snapped at him, "Because you reneged on your promise, even if your new price was still the lowest, our company would not do business with you just on principle." Then I marched off in self-righteous indignation. I told my boss the story. He then asked me, "Frank, who had the best price?" Gulping, I responded, "The Italian" (since, even after his unfortunate upward price revision, his quote was still the lowest).

"Let's sign him up," ordered my superior.

Red-faced, I went back to the Italian. When I arrived he was out but expected back momentarily. I noted photographs on the wall showing him beside his private airplane and I planned my conciliatory comments accordingly.

Presently he strode through the waiting room, saw me, and sneered, "Well, Mr. Walker, have you gotten over your pique yet?" He, of course, surmised why I was there before I even opened my mouth.

"You must have been quite a pilot," said I appeasingly while wolfing down generous portions of crow. Through half-drawn eyelids he peered condescendingly at me and then flung offhandedly over his shoulder, "Oh, that was many years ago," as he disappeared into his corner office.

I sweated for 45 minutes and was finally led to his inner sanctum. Crossing the threshold I saw him, feet on the desk, wave me to a chair with one hand. His other hand was being held by his secretary who, with great flourish, removed his two-carat diamond ring. She then placed it in a bowl of soapy water and meticulously cleaned it right before my bugged-out eyes. After she had dried and polished it she, with utmost reverence, slipped it back on his finger.

All the while the Italian's smile told me that he was relishing this moment with uncommon delight.

All conversation was frozen while this ritual was in progress.

The contract was signed at the new price and as I walked out I could not help but wonder how many other victims there had been before me or, for that matter, how many more lay ahead who would be subjected to the same ring-cleansing ceremony.

*   *   *

MAE JEANNE CHANG

In Brazil good secretaries were hard to find, especially ones who were at least bilingual but ideally trilingual, since the territory assigned me by my stateside employer was all of South America; hence my constant need for English to communicate with my home office plus Spanish and Portuguese.

So from my office in São Paulo I found myself occasionally faced with having to advertise for a secretary.

One day I received a phone call. The voice was that of a mature and refined lady whose accent appeared to be Oriental. She was answering my ad for a steno on behalf of her daughter who was soon to graduate from the University of California at Berkeley and would be seeking employment in São Paulo.

I encouraged her to have her daughter, Mae Jeanne Chang, see me as soon as she arrived.

However, even before Mae Jeanne's appearance, her Chinese parents called at my office. They were a distinguished couple who clearly wanted to size me up in advance of their daughter's scheduled interview.

During our conversation I learned that both Mr. Chang and his wife had served under president Chiang Kai-shek. He was China's soybean tsar while Mrs. Chang, herself an Oxford graduate, was pre-Communist China's minister of economy.

124

Soon after, a tall, young and well-dressed Chinese lady stood at the door.

This was my first meeting with Mae Jeanne Chang, nor was it to be the last.

I showed her into the office. Guilty of pre-judging her, I must admit that I was a bit skeptical about her claims of Spanish fluency. However that fear was allayed as soon as I switched to Spanish.

"Would you kindly sit down at the typewriter," I then asked, "and tell me about yourself."

A short time later I was handed a neat, well-organized and informative resume.

"Miss Chang," I remarked, "You will notice my two filing cabinets. Would you mind quickly leafing through the folders in those eight drawers to familiarize yourself with the general content, and then start filing these papers."

I watched her out of the corner of my eye as she began her filing assignment. Shortly I saw her pick up a letter. Without even opening the filing cabinet she approached me saying that I had no file for that subject. "Shall I open one?" she inquired.

"My heavens," I thought, "this girl has total recall!"

She was hired and in no time added Portuguese to her impressive list of languages.

She served me long and with great efficiency and loyalty.

Then one day she left to join UNICEF in Europe where she felt she could better use her six languages……. And I lost the best secretary I ever had.

*　*　*

ANACONDA TIRES

A fellow laborer of mine in the pesticide business in Brazil was also an American. We were friendly rivals and our families socialized. I represented Stauffer Chemical Co. in Brazil while his employer was Rohm and Haas.

Since he was in Brazil for the long haul, he had made investments there to include a piece of wooded land along a river in the wilds of Mato Grosso. After this purchase he struck a share-cropper deal with a Polish immigrant who cleared the land and then planted rice. Profits were split down the middle.

One time he journeyed with his wife to visit their new farm. The trip, just one-way, entailed several days of tough going.

First they took a DC-3 because that craft was sturdy and had a low stalling speed and thus was able to negotiate the short, pot-holed landing strips prevalent in that backward part of Brazil's western hinterland. Then it was into a four-wheel drive Jeep for many grueling hours over paths optimistically labeled as roads.

When that teeth-rattling leg of their trek finally deposited them on the banks of the large Mato Grosso river their property was on, they embarked on the final leg of their odyssey. Gingerly stepping into an unstable dugout canoe, they then fired up the outboard and sped off.

Presently my friend's wife pointed while exclaiming, "Look, honey, a stack of truck tires right over there on the bank."

Suddenly that pile came to life, so he queried, "Dear, are you still willing to call that massive anaconda a product of Akron, Ohio?"

Mato Grosso happens to be noted for its huge pythons. Indeed, Teddy Roosevelt on one of his hunting safaris to this part of Brazil wrote about the boa constrictors he found there, and brought back photographic proof of their great size. Col. Percy Fawcett, author, British surveyor and South American adventurer, spanning a number of years, mapped much of the common border between Peru and Bolivia located in the upper reaches of the Amazon. His assignment was to establish once and for all the definitive border between those two countries. Until then, whenever a river common to each country would change course, out would come the rifles and shooting would start.

Fawcett is on record as saying that some of the mighty anacondas he has seen reached 70 feet in length. And statements, from local Indians he trusts, emphatically declared that these snakes have reached an astounding 90 feet.

The longest one I ever saw, however, measured 30 feet. It was a skin hanging at the world-renowned snake institute known as O Instituto Butantan in São Paulo.

Back in 1990 my wife and I spent an exciting two months in jungle-covered Malaysia. While there we met an architect named Allen. One evening over dinner he told us of his excursion experiences into Malaysia's jungles.

Because the tropical growth was so dense and paths so badly overgrown, he always carried a machete to hack his way through. But his trusty machete also served another very useful purpose. Pythons oftentimes could be found purposely dangling from trees hoping they would be mistaken for vines until it was too late. So he would always thread his way along jungle trails with his machete handle held low, blade tip high, cutting edge facing forward. That way, should he ever be encircled by a boa constrictor, the snake, in theory at least, would cut itself in two before it had time to kill him.

* * *

THE AMAZON ICE CAVE

Our family was living in South America's largest city, São Paulo, Brazil when an American neighbor and friend phoned, "Say, Frank," she said, "would you and Isabel like to come over this evening? I have a visitor who is an explorer. He just returned from a two-year odyssey along the Amazon River and is putting on a slide show."

It was indeed a fascinating evening full of eye-opening photos and accounts. This man was a Polish explorer-adventurer who had just returned after tracing the mighty Amazon from its inception in the Andes Mountains far to the west to its 200-mile-wide mouth 4,000 mile to the east.

To put into perspective some of the amazing highlights when we mention the Amazon this man traveled through, we should include the following:

1. This river carries 20% of the entire world's river water.
2. The area it drains, known generally as the Amazon rain forest, is two-thirds the size of the United States.
3. The U.S.'s largest river, the mighty Mississippi, discharges one-tenth the water the Amazon does.
4. I have flown over the Amazon many times and can attest that this river's chocolaty water (so colored because of all the top soil its tropical rains strip and carry with it) is visible over 60 miles into the Atlantic Ocean from its mouth. So great is the volume of water it discharges that it literally plows through the salt water that far out to sea.
5. The Amazon has over one-thousand tributaries of which 17 are major rivers with each of these measuring over 1,000 miles in length.
6. This river drains water from nine countries.
7. Over two thousand species of fish make their home in the Amazon, far more than in any other river system.
8. Its bird species exceed 3,500 or approximately one-half of all this planet's known kinds. It is literally an ornithologist's paradise.

9. More than 8,000 species of insects inhabit this rain forest, making it also an entomologist's dream. Needless to say, the area likewise teems with many other forms of animal life; the jaguar, the tapir and the anaconda to mention but a few.

10. The Amazon basin has been called the "lung of the world" because its vast forests produce so much oxygen. But today ecologists from many countries are deeply concerned that Brazil's colonizing policy that allows slash and burn and soon could cause a major disruption to weather systems round the world as well as affecting the availability of oxygen which felled trees can no longer produce.

11. Large ocean-going freighters can, and oftentimes do, sail up the Amazon clear through Brazil to the Peruvian port of Iquitos, some 1,800 miles from the Atlantic Ocean. Smaller ships go even further upstream.

12. Much of Manaus, the Amazon's largest river city, is built on pontoons since the river during the rainy season has been known to rise over fifty feet. Fortunately its large and very ornate opera house is on ground high enough to escape those flood waters. That opera house, by the way, although seemingly incongruous, given the jungle setting around it, was erected during the great heyday of the rubber barons when money was no object. Among many notables who once sang there was the legendary tenor, Enrico Caruso.

These are but a few of this huge river's superlatives, but they help to explain the enthusiasm that fired our European explorer during his two years of exploration through that "green hell," as this area is oftentimes called.

As mentioned earlier, he first located the very beginnings of the Amazon River which were drops falling from an icicle in a Peruvian ice cave in the lofty, oxygen-starved Andes not far from the Pacific Ocean.

That cave was his starting point. From there it was all downhill. For a relatively short distance he traveled by mule and then, when the river grew large enough, by raft.

Two native guides accompanied him.

His baggage consisted of one trunk filled with medical supplies. A second contained all his photographic equipment and the final one was for everything else. The camera he used was a heavy, professional movie studio 35 mm and the slides we were shown were excerpted from that film.

At one point during his trekkings he was the uneasy guest of the head-shrinking Jívaro Indians. It seems that a small Jívaro girl in one village that was hosting him, greatly weakened by high fever, was not expected to live. After he treated her she recovered. Henceforth the Pole could do no wrong.

Quickly Jívaro drums spread the news down river of this white witch doctor's medical magic to where his journey was met with lavish hospitality wherever he stopped in Jívaro country.

He spoke of the terrible mosquito infestations that frequently made sleep impossible. Soon he learned to seek out a rubber tree, slash it and smear the milky latex exudate all over his body. This make-shift wet suit did the trick and stymied the puncture intentions of his anopheles antagonists.

Our hostess during that slide show later told us that she helped him establish contacts in Hollywood. Whether or not his adventures were made into a movie I cannot say, since we ultimately lost contact with that neighbor when we moved back to the United States.

Years later I had occasion in Manaus to meet the "king of the Amazon," as this diminutive, wizened Portuguese immigrant was known by throughout that part of Brazil. My meeting as a visiting Gulf Oil representative, was to open hydrocarbon negotiations with this man who had the only refinery on the Amazon.

But that was only a small part of his commercial empire. He controlled most of the hardwood exports, had the Amazon's only plywood factory, monopolized the animal skin market and the list of all that he dominated went on and on.

I recall landing at Rio following a tiring, non-stop flight from New York and rushing to catch a smaller domestic plane north to Manaus for that meeting with the "king." But somehow my plane had been overbooked and the airline agent told me I was out-of-luck.

My tight schedule, however, was such that I absolutely had to make that flight. So I slipped the agent enough cruzeiros to widen his eyes. "I'll see what I can do," he quickly said with a smile….. and I was soon on that flight.

As my plane neared Manaus, I was saddened to see the vast scarrings to this majestic forest which chainsaws, controlled burning and bulldozers had inflicted on this, nature's huge but shrinking crown jewel.

*　*　*

I was ready to walk out of a floral shop in downtown Lima, Peru with a bouquet I had just purchased for my lovely Peruvian fiancée when I noticed an American customer struggling to make himself understood in English to a saleswoman who only knew Spanish.

"May I be of help to you?" I asked in my California English.

"Shay, pal, can you ever," as he blew at me an alcoholic gust that almost wilted my flowers.

It seems this man had only been in Peru for a few weeks and was late sending wedding anniversary flowers back stateside to his wife. So I helped him wire what he figured would extract him from the dog house.

With mission accomplished, he insisted on buying me a drink. So we walked across the street to the Bolivar Hotel's bar that fronted on the Plaza San Martin.

By our second beer, I had learned why it was that he had felt no pain back in the flower shop. Earlier that same day the poor fellow had been drowning his professional worries at a nearby bar.

He was a pilot who had just been hired by Faucet Airlines. Elmer Faucet had been a member of Claire Chennault's famous WW II Flying Tigers who later established what soon became Peru's leading airline. Using a fleet of WW II surplus C-47s, also known not only as the DC-3 but, during the war, as "The Workhorse of the Pacific," Faucet planes pretty well serviced all of Peru.

"Frank," he said, "before they can put me in the pilot's seat, I have to log some hours as a co-pilot while getting used to the routes. And I'm telling you, some of this flying is downright scary. Why just yesterday we took off and headed for a town way up in the soaring Andes. Faucet's DC-3s are not equipped with radar, yet we were threading our way through mountain passes which oftentimes were enveloped in clouds.

"When I would ask the pilot how in heck he avoided becoming one with the mountainside while flying on instruments, his casual, yawn-punctuated answer would come back, 'We cruise along for a few minutes on this heading and then hang, oh, around a 30 degree right for another minute, give or take.'

"I tell ya, Frank, I don't think any life insurance company in its right mind would touch these pilots!"

Our budding friendship ended up being short-lived. My friend, not surprisingly, wound up declining his piloting assignment and returned to the U.S. and to the object of his tardy floral attentions.

<u>Author's Note</u>: Today, some 50 years later, Peru's national airline is modern and competes with the best.

*   *   *

A BONE JARRING RIDE

Back in the 50s while still living in Hermosillo, Mexico, I once received a long distance phone call from a high executive with the San Francisco-based company I worked for.

"Frank," he said, "a close friend of mine, who plans on retiring, wants to buy a piece of property down your way, build a home on it and move there. Do you think you could give him a hand with some of the particulars?"

That was how I got to know and develop a lasting friendship with Guy Daniel, a man of legendary charm who ran one of William Randolph Hearst's biggest money-makers, the advertising department of the San Francisco Examiner.

His choice of a retirement place led him to the village of Mulege situated on the east coast of Baja California and just across the Sea of Cortez (also called the Gulf of California) from Guaymas. Apparently Daniel, before I ever got into the picture, had located just the piece of land he wanted. Proudly he showed me a maquette of his intended Baja retirement villa.

My mission was to help Guy close the land deal with its owner, a wealthy farmer and businessman named Pierre Mayieux, who conveniently happened to be a fellow Hermosillo dweller.

At one point in the negotiations it became necessary for me to visit Mulege and…. was that trip ever an experience!

My work demands frequently took me to Baja anyway. Customarily I would drive to Guaymas, leave my car at the airport and hop a milk-run DC-3 for La Paz with intermediate stops at Santa Rosalia and Loreto.

While flying across the Sea of Cortez, I would not infrequently see the huge Manta Ray basking close to the waters' surface. As the shadow of my plane raced by those wing-appearing fish, I recall calculating their span, using as a reference the known dimensions of the aircraft I was on. I concluded those monsters reached an astounding 20 feet in width.

My memory would then flood back to the days when I worked for the Peruvian subsidiary of a large stateside commercial fishing company. Among the types of fish we were after was the shark because of the desirable oil contained in its liver. Occasionally our small shark fishing boats would accidentally hook a huge manta ray which not infrequently would soar out of the water while trying to throw the hook. The very real danger was that the massive ray during its aerial pirouettings would, as it sometimes did, come crashing down on top of the small fishing boat and demolish it.

On one of my many visits to La Paz, I recall being the week-end guest of the Territory of Baja California's governor, General Miguel Olachea, who later was to head up Mexico's only political party, the Partido Revolucionario Institucional or PRI for short. The purpose of that visit was to conduct a lecture and slide presentation, at the governor's request, for the farmers of that area. My theme was *how to control cotton insect pests*, since at the time that was one of my areas of expertise.

After my lecture, the governor threw a luncheon that had umpteen courses and lasted for over two hours. All of us rose from the table bloated. Then smiling, Olachea said, "Gentlemen, I think I might be able to ease your stuffed feeling. Come with me," whereupon he led us to a small nearby out-building.

It was a well house. He then proceeded to fill glasses with an odd smelling liquid which he handed to each of us.

I was astounded, as were the governor's other guests, because within thirty minutes not only was the discomfort of our over-eating erased, but some of us were actually ready to resume with knife and fork. Whatever it was we had drunk had remarkably sped up the digestive process.

But to return to the account of my involvement in Guy Daniel's land deal. With my farm chemical work concluded during one of my business visits to La Paz, I sought out transportation that would deliver me to Mulege where I had loose ends to wrap up for my friend. A plane was out of the question. Mulege back then had no landing strip.

This was in the years when the modern highway down the long Baja California peninsula had not yet been built, which fact was to become painfully apparent to me practically from the outset of my bone-jarring, nerve-jangling overland odyssey from La Paz to Mulege.

I had hitched a ride on a stake bed truck. My seat was atop a 55 gallon gasoline drum with the wind whistling past my hirsute shy scalp. That adventure lasted 23 hours to traverse a scant 250 miles, mute testimony to the primitive condition of the road or path or trail or whatever it was called.

The driver wore several hats. One was that of mailman, so that frequently he would slow down upon approaching clusters of adobe huts and toss out a mail sack. Once, however he pulled up to a building and with great care gingerly eased a sack into eagerly awaiting arms. Later I learned it contained not only mail, but bottles of booze as well. I guess as an underpaid postal employee he had to supplement his earnings.

Finally, FINALLY my mirage-like destination lay shimmering in the distance. It was the small desert oasis of Mulege, a sleepy little pierless port village, beside which babbled a clear stream that immediately emptied into the fish-ladened Sea of Cortez. Nestled among palm trees, this delightful miniature mecca was a sight for sore eyes (and sore backs). No wonder my friend had chosen Mulege to live out his last years.

Once I had concluded my Guy Daniel business, I then spent a while touring Mulege. Soon I learned that cotton yields were fabulously high, about twice the famously high yields obtained in the San Joaquin Valley!

My cerebral wheels began to spin over the prospects of going into a lucrative farming venture in Mulege, but, like the best laid plans of mice and men, these were soon to be dashed once I reflected on the impossibly high transportation costs.

Oh well, there was always tomorrow.

*　*　*

BRAZIL'S KILLER BEES

Brazil's Biological Institute, known as O Instituto Biologico, is located in the megalopolis of São Paulo, a city where my family and I lived for eight years. That federal institute once became heavily involved in creating what has now become a Frankenstein monster affecting the entire Western Hemisphere, for they unwittingly loosed the infamous killer bees.

Because my responsibilities included getting my stateside employer's farm pesticides tested and registered for use in Brazil, it was necessary for me to maintain close contact with that same Biological Institute, for without their nod we could not sell our chemicals in that country.

During my residence in Brazil technicians at the Biological Institute had imported certain strains of aggressive but highly productive African bees which they planned to cross with those Brazilian bees noted for their docility. This was a project locally publicized and well-known to many. The Institute's intent was to produce a super bee, one which excelled in pollinating performance and honey output, but which was relatively inoffensive.

Somewhere along the line, however, a researcher's assistant goofed big time by mistakenly releasing all of the highly dangerous African bees before they could be bred with their meek Brazilian cousins.

Our family can attest personally to that killer bee's hostility. One Saturday I had driven my wife and our five children not far from São Paulo to a beach near Santos for a day's outing. We were enjoying ourselves, minding our own business, when from out of a nearby thicket a massive swarm of bees raced unprovoked toward us. Their hum was deafening and their purpose clearly anything but friendly.

We all sought cover under water, emerging only long enough to gulp in air and flail at the angry, buzzing cloud.

Our assailants finally left.

Subsequently we learned that those same hymenopterous aggressors did indeed have their origin at the Biological Institute.

It then took several years for those bees to travel, breeding along the way, northward out of South America, through Central America and Mexico to where, today, they can be found in the United States.

Frightening experiences similar to ours, as well as far worse to include death, now abound.

*　*　*

BRAZIL'S SUICIDE BIRD

My family and I lived in Brazil for a number of years and we were privy to many fascinating accounts of national happenings that unfolded during our residency.

São Paulo's leading daily, the O Estado de São Paulo, once ran a series of stories about an airline tragedy.

134

It seems that a C-47 had developed engine trouble en route to Manaus and made a forced landing onto tree tops deep in Brazil's Amazonian jungle.

The plane's weight caused the aircraft to sink into the dense foliage canopy which quickly closed behind it thereby erasing all traces of its presence. For that reason it was almost a month before rescue teams were finally able to locate the airplane.

There were no survivors, however one of the dead had initially been injured badly enough to where he could not leave the crash site. But, still mentally alert, he kept a diary until, that is, exposure and lack of food caused his death.

It was that diary that enabled the O Estado de São Paulo to run its series of eye witness accounts of what had transpired until the last of the victims perished.

Immediately following that accident, those surviving passengers and crewmembers who were still ambulatory fanned out in their quest for help. Many never returned. Those that did brought food back to the maimed and then struck out repeatedly for assistance.

But ultimately none returned to the plane and the injured narrator subsequently died.

It was the opinion of experts, guides who were skilled in jungle survival, that the "suicide bird" (also called the bell bird) was probably responsible in large measure for the lack of survivors.

This bird's call sounds very much like the tolling of a bell. It was surmised that the plane's occupants were not wise to the ways of the jungle and probably mistook the cry of the suicide or bellbird for the tollings in a church belfry and would strike out in that direction. The bird would then fly off in another heading and sound its call once again.

Confused, the survivor would change his course to the new bell location and before long he would be hopelessly lost.

Without jungle survival smarts, one can easily perish in the Amazon. Exhaustion, lack of food, poisonous snakes like the dread and aggressive bushmaster, the anaconda, jaguar and flesh-eating ants (known as the marabunta) that travel in armies numbering in the millions, to say nothing of the deceptive suicide bird, all help to explain why that jungle is aptly dubbed the "green hell."

*   *   *

Pete had an odd sense of humor but perhaps that was acceptable to many, given the fact he was a multi millionaire. I didn't know about his penchant for the practical joke until after I had set him up as one of our farm chemical distributors in Western Mexico.

One day I bumped into him in downtown Hermosillo, Mexico, a town where we both lived.

"Frank," he said, "I'm having a few friends over tonight for a showing of the movie I took during my last African hunting safari. Can you and your wife make it?"

I told we'd be glad to come.

So that evening Isabel and I arrived. We were one of six or seven couples.

His living room walls were covered with big game trophies from all over the world.

Soon the lights were dimmed and the flicker began. All of us had anticipated something quite different from what Pete had in store. We weren't more than a few minutes into the movie before we became unwitting (and uneasy) spectators to a pygmy circumcision rite.

And as the details unfolded before us, I observed Pete off in the corner chuckling to himself almost obscenely, fully aware of the crimson faces his escapade was producing, especially among his distaff guests.

Later I told a mutual friend about that home movie experience. He was my dentist and knew Pete extremely well. He responded, "That's Pete alright."

"Let me tell you a few stories about that man," he said.

"It was Pete's wedding day. He had just married this French lass, his third wife, and had retired to a beachside cottage in Guaymas for the honeymoon.

"After carrying her across the threshold, he said, 'Wait here, honey, I have to go out for a few minutes.' When he returned, his new mate was standing on a table, clutching her skirts and screeching.

"Slowly circling the table legs was a large python.

"That marriage, by the way, did not last," he added.

With the scene now set as to this man's weird sense of humor, an interesting turn of events took place.

My dentist friend continued, "Here's another gem. I happen to be one of Pete's hunting buddies and sometimes brunt of his off-the-wall practical jokes.

"It seems that Pete liked to go off into the highlands of Sierra de la Giganta on Baja California in quest of the elusive mountain sheep. On one particular expedition he bagged a sizeable specimen, had the head mounted and hung it on his wall.

"During a visit to Pete's home, I remarked, 'Say, Pete, how come you have that sheep trophy hanging there collecting moths and dust?'

"To which Pete responded, 'What's the matter, would you like to have it? It's yours if you want it.'

" 'Don't mind if I do,' " I said and carried off my newly-acquired prize.

"Realizing that this trophy was indeed a potential award winner, I submitted it as a candidate to the appropriate judges. Soon I was honored with a plaque plus a very expensive Weatherby rifle, complete with gold-plated trigger, because that set of horns wound up being the second largest on record.

"Triumphantly I drove over to Pete's home, walked up to the front door with weapon in hand and gleefully punched the bell. My planned words of retribution for all he had inflicted on me over the years were already well-rehearsed.

"Pete came to the door and I greeted him, 'Hi, Pete, I got an interesting story to tell you,' while flaunting my ballistic treasure."

Ah, sweet revenge, but what a shame Pet's "python" bride plus myself and all the other victims of Mayieux's odd sense of humor, could not have been present as a body to rub our hands in absolute glee over this touché, Weatherby encounter.

Then there was another time that sweet retribution visited our protagonist. One of Pete's flourishing enterprises in Hermosillo was a farm implement and supply distributorship. He had just acquired the representation of the Shepherd tractor. So with great pride he ran full page ads in the local paper as well as on the air waves of Hermosillo's radio station announcing a great barbecue and tractor demonstration.

With free eats, people naturally arrived in droves. After his introductory speech, Pete proudly mounted his newly acquired tractor and with an ear-to-ear grin, turned the ignition key. Errrr, errrr, errr whined the starter. His little gem simply would not oblige.

Snickers raced through the crowd, mostly from those who had already been victimized by dear Pete's crass sense of humor, myself included. Presumably one of them had to have been the jokester who had made sure the thing would not start.

By chance I later happened to be in Pete's office while he, red-faced and with swollen neck veins, was chewing out Shepherd's factory representative.

*　　*　　*

Back in the 60's I lived in São Paulo, Brazil and from that base covered South America for my U.S. employer. While there I once surreptitiously engaged (to my lingering regret) in an act of smuggling. Here is the story.

One of my close friends was Mauricio, a Brazilian attorney who had a ranch half-way between São Paulo and Rio.

Located in the coastal mountain range known as Serra da Bocaina, Mauricio's spread was a delightful, if rustic, place to unwind for a few days. There we would ride, fish for trout, hike and observe the natural wonders of this inviting part of Brazil's sub-tropics.

So it was that my swelling indebtedness to Mauricio caused me to seek ways of repaying his many favors.

An opportunity came soon after I told Mauricio that our family would be vacationing in Europe.

He asked, "Frank, will you be going to Belgium?" I told him yes.

Then he said, "There is a special Belgian-made shotgun I would love to have. I'll give you the money if you would be willing to buy it and bring it back."

"Why of course, Mauricio, consider it done," I replied with a magnanimous wave not realizing what was to lie ahead.

Before our departure for the old world, Mauricio and I met again. It was then that I received his disquieting instructions.

"Frank," he said, "the easiest way to handle getting the gun through Brazilian customs is for you to hide it in one of your trunks by building a false bottom and stashing it in the void between the two bottoms."

Gulping, I then asked, "But how can I be sure they won't find it?"

"Not to worry, Frank," he answered with a smile, "I know the head of customs."

I gulped again, perspiration beading on my forehead.

The shotgun was acquired in Liege, Belgium, and we returned to our vacation base in Paris where my brother-in-law, Pierre, lived.

"Pierre, I need your help," whereupon I explained my plan.

Excited over the intrigue of it all, Pierre pitched right in and between us we carefully removed the cloth that lined the trunk's floor. Next we disassembled the shotgun, wrapped it well, placed it at the bottom and affixed a plywood sheet on top of the weapon.

Right after we had glued back the cloth to cover the new false bottom, we stood back to admire our masterpiece of deception.

When our ship reached its Brazilian destination, we saw Mauricio looking up from the dock below. He gave me the 'everything's-taken-care-of high-sign'.

Soon we were in a long customs line awaiting our turn to have our baggage examined. I watched with intense concern as the inspector with a very fine toothcomb went through the luggage of passenger after passenger ahead of me. He was gruff, uncompromising and many items were being confiscated.

Clearly shaken, I was convinced that Mauricio was dead wrong when he had insisted our escapade's success was pre-wired. Instead, I was certain Brazil would soon have me earmarked for residency in one of its more obscure jails. With my adrenaline pumping as fast as a sprint cyclist, I muttered under my breath, "My Heavens, this inspector not only has x-ray vision but he can mind-read better than any polygraph."

Then the moment of truth came. The inspector looked at me with his penetrating stare and demanded, "What have you in this trunk?"

I leaned toward his ear and, to further insure confidentiality, replied in a muffled tone out of the corner of my mouth, "This trunk has a false bottom which conceals a shotgun that I am bringing for a friend."

Dumbfounded, I heard him say with a wink, "No problem." Then he patted the trunk without opening it and waved me on through as he yelled "next" to the person behind me.

*　*　*

A BRAZILIAN DRAGON

This unusual picture of a poisonous snake venom milking operation I took at São Paulo, Brazil's world famous snake institute, O Instituto Butantan.

Because of the strange tongues of flame appearing to emit from the nostrils of this venomous snake, I submitted this photo to Butantan's board of directors for analysis and interpretation.

However I was unprepared for their astounding response. They concluded that this snake, a Bothrops Jararaca, had coincidentally snorted at the very instant I snapped this picture.

Brazilian Dragon

The moisture in that snake's expelled breath was picked up by the sun's rays producing a rainbow effect in the form of tongues of flame.

To duplicate such a picture would defy million-to-one odds they said. *(See photo.)*

*   *   *

BRAZIL'S DEADLY TRAFFIC

I lived in Brazil for eight years and although I fell in love with the country and its people, I must admit that the wild traffic there remained an eye-opener right up to the day our family moved back to the United States.

One day while driving in downtown São Paulo, population then seven million strong, I saw a pedestrian frantically trying to cross the street. Several times he stepped from the curb only to make a diving return, much like the overly-optimistic base runner taking too long a lead off and then having to scramble back to avoid being tagged out.

Overcome by a sudden wave of brotherly love, I stopped and motioned for the desperate fellow to cross, an act virtually unheard of in this land that placed a bounty on pedestrians.

Clearly stunned he glanced suspiciously at me, then at the street ahead of him and then back at me.

It soon became evident he had made up his mind. Up went his index finger which he slowly waved back and forth at me, the Brazilian equivalent to our "no siree" headshake.

He knew the pedestrian was about as expendable as a cockroach and figured I merely wanted to lure him into the middle of the street where I would have a clear shot at him.

*   *   *

MY SPANISH AND PORTUGUESE LECTURING DAYS

While in my early 20s during my WW II U.S. Navy days in the Philippines, I got my first taste of Spanish. A local family with whom I had developed a close friendship, spoke both their native Tagalog as well as Spanish at home, besides, of course, English for which I was relieved since at the time I only knew English.

However over the intervening years I acquired both Spanish as well as Portuguese as necessary tools of my trade because I was to end up living and working among the people of most of Latin America for 21 years. The acquisition of these languages, however, was not without certain heartaches along the way.

The early seed of desire to learn Spanish must have been planted during my Philippine residence, for in my subsequent college years, I found myself watering the latent yen with two years of formal Spanish. My professor was a Madrileño and so we students were expected to pronounce certain words with a definite lisp, a practice I was later to suppress in deference to the Latin Americans with whom I was later to become closely associated and who had broken years before with that old world tradition of the lisp.

I remember during my final college oral board one of the native Latin examiners asking my, "Y que tomó Ud. esta mañana por desayuno?" (What did you have this morning for breakfast?"

So I reeled off a list of appropriate food items. But, feeling I should impress my inquisitor by adding one more vocabulary tidbit for good measure, I then said, "y ensalada también." (and salad also), as I leaned back, smugly happy with my performance.

"Ensalada por desayuno?" I next heard him gasp incredulously while staring at me through saucer-wide eyes.

Despite my "salad" punctuated breakfast, I managed to pass the course.

My first job out of college was aboard a mother ship, a freezer. It was the nucleus of a large broadbill swordfish fishing operation off the northern coast of Peru, with me the only English speaker aboard.

Needless to say, that total immersion experience into the real world of Spanish put my university studies to the acid test, which got me off to a sputtering if humbling start.

Quite frankly, for the first month I didn't know which end was up. I felt totally lost as machinegun fast sentences zipped by me and I would hastily thumb through my soon to be dog-eared Spanish-English dictionary to salvage at least some meaning from what was being said.

Once in the galley I recall the chef asking me, "Como quieres tu pollo?" (How shall I fix your chicken?).

Since he was not the world's best cook (a euphemism at best), I figured that I couldn't go too wrong if I had him simply boil it. So I replied, "Enganchado por favor." Translation: "Meshed, please." (That's meshed as in when gears mesh together). Well the guy practically expired laughing and it wasn't long before the entire crew was guffawing over my order for "meshed" chicken.

You see, what I had meant to say was the similar-sounding "sancochado," the Spanish word for boiled.

And I was to make many more similar gaffes along my journey of hard-knock Spanish, some a lot more embarrassing, like the time I was lecturing in Guatemala City years later to a group of farmers and agronomists. At the conclusion of my talk, I threw the session open to Q and A as was my custom.

But a joker, a wise guy, was present in the audience who wanted to have a little fun. So he reworded one of my earlier statements by inserting a few double-meanings I was unfamiliar with which changed my innocent enough assertion to one having strong sexual overtones. Then he asked, "Is that what you meant?"

"Absolutely," I replied and the room erupted in laughter, all except for one of the few ladies present whose face promptly turned bright crimson.

142

Later my local distributor, Juan Maegli, came up to me and told me that they were not laughing at me but at the perpetrator's sense of humor. That was one more phrase I never forgot.

When my family and I moved to Brazil where we lived for eight years, I was bound and determined not to mix my Spanish, which by then I already knew well, with my newly-acquired Portuguese, a Latin based language and quite similar to its Spanish cousin. I say this because I was soon to realize that many Italian and Spanish immigrants spoke a cocktail which made me cringe. It was either a blend of Italian (also Latin based) and Portuguese or else Spanish flavored with Portuguese.

My technique for avoiding that pitfall was to pay attention to the way my mouth felt, especially my tongue and lips, whenever I switched from Portuguese to Spanish during my trips from my home base in São Paulo, Brazil to Buenos Aires, Argentina, or other Spanish speaking countries of South America.

And the reverse was also true when I landed at Viracopos Airport in Brazil from a visit to a Spanish-speaking country. If I sensed that Portuguese feel to my mouth and nose upon shifting to Brazil's often nasalized language, then I knew I'd succeeded in leaving my Spanish behind.

If I were to pass on to anyone wishing to learn a new language, the best advice I could think of based on my own experience, it would be this. Never attempt to translate literally from your own native tongue to the new one you're in the process of learning. Instead, memorize the phrases that convey the meaning you want to get across. And if those phrases have the words jumbled about and not in what you feel to be logical order, don't sweat it. Merely accept the strange sequence, master it that way and live with it. Soon you will shed the strange feeling and all will quickly seem quite natural.

It is not all that hard, once one develops working usage of a language, to detect without much difficulty an accent in the voices of others. And I am sure that, despite my fluency in Spanish and Portuguese, others can detect my accent. Although, once I am into the swing of either of those two languages then I am told my accent is scarcely detectable.

However, my wife has an unusual talent. She speaks four languages, three of which (French, Spanish and English) she grew up with and there is absolutely no trace of an accent whatsoever in any of those three. The other day here in Mariposa, California, where we presently live, a French tourist asked her for directions. Later he told me that he thought my wife was a Parisian!

Isabel's Portuguese learned later in life during our Brazilian residency does have evidence that gives away her non-native origin.

Our Spanish speaking friends would often, with tongue in cheek, remark that Portuguese was actually poorly spoken Spanish. But when we moved to Brazil, our local friends there declared that the Spanish linguists actually had that assessment completely backwards.

*　*　*

TRULY EMBARRASSED

Chet, an American, and I worked for the same U.S. based fishing company in Peru. It was during Peru's heyday as the world's largest exporter of fish products.

Spanish was not one of Chet's fortes, but he tried hard. Once he confided that the formula he often employed to get him out of a language scrape was to insert an English word whenever he could not remember the Spanish one, tack an "a" or an "o" at random onto the end of it and give it a Spanish accent. Then he would cross his fingers and hope for the best.

One afternoon he was attending a garden party. It was a very ritzy social gathering and Chet was speaking to a group of blue-blooded high society ladies in his fractured Spanglish.

When he got to the punch line which was, "Boy, was I embarrassed," he could not for the life of him remember the Spanish word for "embarrassed."

So… trusty formula to the rescue.

And out came "Estuve muy embarasado." Translation: "Was I ever pregnant." His formula had just laid an ostrich egg.

The ladies did their utmost to hide their smiles behind lace hankies.

Later when Chet learned of his gaffe he said to himself, "Oh my gosh! Well, that's one more word I'll never forget!"

*　*　*

A FEW PERUVIAN RAMBLINGS

During my high school days in San Francisco the talk I kept hearing at home and elsewhere concerned the rapidly climbing divorce rate. Back then (late 30s and

144

early 40s) it had reached 25%, considered staggeringly high at the time when compared with but a few decades earlier (yet little could one imagine that by the end of the century this 25% figure would more than double!).

Subconsciously I must have feared that the odds were stacked against a marriage being successful in my home country, because I found myself directing my course of university studies toward what might later qualify me for work in Latin America.

That area to the south attracted me for many reasons, not the least of which was the Latin set of solid family values that can rightfully boast a lower rate of broken marriages than in many of the so-called more advanced countries.

As it later was to turn out, I did marry a lovely Peruvian lass. That was 58 years ago and we're still going strong. We became the parents of five fine children and now have six grandchildren…. But I am getting ahead of myself.

- - - - - - - - - - - -

So it was that in 1949 my first job out of college found me in Peru working for a San Francisco based, international fishing company.

Peru in that era of the 40s and 50s had become the largest exporter of fish products in the world, surpassing such traditional leaders as Norway and Japan. The cool Humboldt ocean current, originating in the Antarctic and traveling north through warmer waters close to Peru's coastline, created conditions ideal for the growth of vast amounts of plankton. That gave rise to a prolific and highly marketable food chain which included the small anchovy, several members of the mackerel family such as the bonito, skipjack, albacore and its larger cousin, the yellowfin tuna; and the great broadbill swordfish.

My first assignment was offshore near the dinky but key fishing port of Mancora in northern Peru close to the Ecuadorian border. I lived aboard a freezer ship working the commercial aspects of a broadbill sword fishing operation. This ship had formerly been a U.S. navy landing craft. We called her the "Ayacucho."

Our fleet comprised this freezer-mother ship plus some 30 wood-hulled fishing boats dedicated primarily to the harpooning of the broadbill. Daily their catch would be winched onboard the "Ayacucho" for processing. These broadbills averaged over 300 lbs each and our company set the world record for the most harpooned in one month, 929!

As soon as the "Ayacucho's" hold was filled with fish, which was often, we would weigh anchor and head for the nearby, larger port of Talara, to offload our frozen cargo onto a W.R. Grace ship which was a combination passenger liner and cargo vessel, bound for the U.S. I relished those moments aboard Grace's ships for I would dine to the manner born, since the "Ayacucho's" greasy spoon was just that.

In fact, lack of sanitation in the "Ayacucho's" galley and elsewhere aboard the craft ultimately gave me acute hepatitis which, my hospital doctors later confessed, came dangerously close to killing me.

- - - - - - - - - - - -

Not all was routine in our fishing operation. I recall that one afternoon a small "picudo," as we called some of our fishing boats, failed to return from its day of harpooning broadbill swordfish. Two search boats were then dispatched. They found the crew floating in the water but their craft was nowhere to be seen. A marlin they had harpooned earlier in the day, instead of sounding when struck by a harpoon the way the broadbill does, turned on them and with its bill rammed their boat, sinking it almost immediately.

- - - - - - - - - - - -

Interestingly, much of the film version of Hemingway's Nobel-Prize-winning-book, "The Old Man and the Sea," took place off Cabo Blanco just a short distance south of Mancora. Cabo Blanco is noted for its unusually large marlin.

Our customary anchorage was in a cove some 400 yards off-shore from Mancora. This locale was literally seething with activity. Large numbers of fishing craft, refrigerated barges and refrigerated mother ships filled that cove.

- - - - - - - - - - - -

Mancora itself was but a wide spot on the narrow Pan American Highway, largely dirt, which threaded the length of Peru's arid coastline. Mud huts were the rule rather than the exception in Mancora. It was a port with no pier. There was no beach (unless you want to call fist-sized stones a beach) and no restaurant (again, unless one considers a bill-of-fare that features fish-flavored eggs and fish-flavored bacon as adequate credentials to qualify as a restaurant). You see, the town's chicken and pig population would forage along the beach, feeding on all the fish heads, fins and offal that washed to the bay's edge.

Whenever we went ashore to Mancora we did so in a rowboat and, at certain risk, had to ride the breakers onto the rocky beach. I recall that a wave once flipped an oar-powered skiff over and crushed to death one of its passengers.

One particular Sunday, our only rest day, the "Ayacucho's" crew was relaxing on deck, either fishing, sunning themselves or snoozing. Two drop-line fishermen were on a nearby balsa raft testing their luck. Suddenly all eyes were riveted on one of those two fishermen who clearly had something very big at the end of his line. He struggled for over two hours before he was able to muscle his prize to the surface. It was a massive Jewfish, locally known as a Mero.

Much too large for these two rafters to do anything with, this monster we purchased since its meat was considered a delicacy and, as such, was quite saleable. After winching it aboard the "Ayacucho," we saw that it tipped the scales at 620 pounds. Several of our workers who played the guitar removed scales from this fish because these were both large and stiff enough to make ideal guitar picks.

- - - - - - - - - - - -

The temptation of making big money was so great during this fishing heyday that other nations sent fishing fleets to poach within Peruvian waters claiming non-recognition of Peru's declared sovereignty 200 miles out to sea. In the process these pirates found themselves trying to dodge shells from angry Peruvian warships and some of these interlopers were even escorted as captives to a Peruvian port and the awaiting and fuming authorities. The international press, naturally, had a field day writing about these incidents.

- - - - - - - - - - - -

During this fishing boom, ladies of the evening did a brisk business. I recall that our skipper, an old raunchy sea dog who liked his flings, came up to me one Monday morning. He was doubled over in laughter, guffawing raucously and slapping his knee insistently over whatever it was that tickled him so, to where I thought he would never get it out. Finally he roared, while tears of merriment poured down his cheeks. "Pancho," (my nickname) "Last night I took this gal to a hotel. They asked me to sign the guest register, so I put your name down." More belly laughs that could be heard all the way to shore. "Very, very funny," I wryly said to myself.

A sizeable cross-section of legitimate and illegitimate businesses headquartered on these boats and ashore.

International adventurers and out-and-out crooks abounded. And many an honest but unsuspecting fisherman was taken to the cleaners.

One such devious soldier of fortune I knew. His name was Cleo. He lived in a three-room tent on Mancora's beach. When I first met Cleo I thought to myself, "My, what a pleasant fellow. He sure talks with a nice, slow, southern drawl. He probably isn't too smart. Just what is he doing here anyway?" I was to learn subsequently that this apparent hayseed was in reality a big-time international swindler, on the lam after having cheated no less than magnate Henry J. Kaiser of steel mill, auto manufacturing, ship building and hospital chain fame.

Peruvians from all walks of life left their professions and, much like our gold rush frenzy of the 1800s, flocked to key fishing areas all along that country's coast.

I once knew, for example, a medical doctor from Lima named Figallo who closed down his practice and went to Mancora. He was convinced that his secret theory, if viable, would make him wealthy over night. Taking a long pole, he attached a stethoscope to one end. Then from his launch, which he maneuvered close in to the rocky shoreline, he would listen through the stethoscope while the pole's other end probed submerged rocks. His theory? To detect the sound of lobsters walking across rocks and then send divers down to grab these plentiful crustaceans.

Regrettably this doctor's hypothesis was heavily flawed and soon he returned to Lima and his medical practice. Stories like this one proliferated over beers at many a local pub.

- - - - - - - - - - - - -

On a typical late afternoon most of the fishermen would be back after their long work day. Tons of discarded fish parts would soon be floating all over the cove following the large cleaning operation. The air would be a din of seagull screeches. The huge and graceful winged Men-o'-War (also called the frigate bird) could be seen frequently out-maneuvering the Gulls in aerial dogfights and then snatching fish from their hapless beaks.

The Pelican was everywhere and its beak can indeed hold more than its belly can. Frequently it would be seen skimming but a foot or two above the water in prolonged glides until finding schools of small fish near the surface. At that point it would pull its joy stick back to gain altitude and then dive with uncanny accuracy. Almost always it caught what it was after.

The mighty Andean Condors not infrequently would be visible from their perches on the cliffs behind Mancora. Once I chased several that had lit on the beach to feed on dead fish. The massive thrust required for this eight-foot-wing-spanned monarch of the skies to become air-borne left six-inch deep prints in the wet sand.

A buddy of mine brought his shotgun to the beach one day and downed a Condor. If this had happened back in America where such endangered species are highly protected, he would subsequently have had ample time to memorize the names of all of his fellow inmates.

- - - - - - - - - - - -

During my Peruvian residency the government was on the horns of a real dilemma where the important guano industry was concerned.

For many years Peru's foreign exchange had been greatly enriched through its exports of guano. Guano, once an important fertilizer, comes from bird droppings, droppings which once were anchovies. But with the advent of fertilizer synthetics made from petroleum, the hand-writing was on the wall and the guano industry's demise but a matter of time.

Vested interests wanted to protect the ailing guano industry and discourage the seining for anchovy. They claimed that such activity would deprive the guano bird of its essential food supply.

Those that opposed insisted the Peru could make more money on export duties from fishmeal derived from the processing of anchovies. Fishmeal, high in protein, was (and still remains) a major food source for the stateside, high protein-demanding poultry industry.

The Guano interests ultimately lost the battle but not before expending valiant efforts to stay alive. At one point they brought in all sorts of new fish-loving birds hoping that they would leave their droppings in-between those of the guano bird in order to make harvesting more efficient. Unfortunately these feathered imports were a bit squeamish over where they relieved themselves, so the experiment flopped and the fishmeal industry continued to flourish at the expense of the guano die-hards.

- - - - - - - - - - - -

Following my Mancora stint I was then to become heavily involved in the importation and sale of fishmeal plants for use all up and down the Peruvian coast.

Odors were very distinctive in and about my workplace. Yellowfin tuna had one kind of smell, the swordfish another and rotting fish yet another. Ashore, in the absence of bathroom plumbing, erosion of adobe wall exteriors became a problem, but less so than the aroma such practices encouraged.

- - - - - - - - - - - -

It has been said that the vocabulary of stevedores and those in the building trade can keep the air about them quite blue, but my observations showed that the Mancora fishermen had 'em all beat.

And so there I was hanging on every word as I strove to expand my inventory of Spanish words in an on-going effort at bettering my communication skills. A noble, constructive undertaking I thought until, that is, my first R and R in the big and cosmopolitan city of Lima. Early on I realized that something was greatly amiss when, during what I thought was acceptable, polite tea-time conversation, eyebrows occasionally soared.

Thereafter, a major project for me, and which over my many years in Latin America proved successful, was the meticulous distinguishing between the "yes-yes" words and the "no-nos."

- - - - - - - - - - - -

Much more could be said about Mancora, but I hope I have left something of the flavor of what was for me a dramatic period, my first job out of college.

But more importantly, it introduced me to a country that later was to graciously allow me to take as a wife one of its loveliest and most precious own.

* * *

THE MAMBUCABA

When I learned my U.S. employer was about to transfer me to Brazil to assume new and exciting duties of chemical market development on the South American continent, I began to spruce up my fly fishing gear in anticipation of vacation forays in quest of rainbows, browns and brookies.

The legendary trout waters of southern Argentina were beckoning and were high on my list of desirable fishing meccas, along with the equally productive streams of neighboring Chile.

Brazil, however, being largely a low-lying, tropical country, was an unlikely candidate, erroneously I was to learn, for the line-tightening salmonids, those popular fresh water game fish historically associated with mid latitude climates of both hemispheres.

150

And so it was that early in my Brazilian residency during a routine business visit to São Paulo's noted Biological Institute, I was to have my jaw sag in complete disbelief. For there on a shelf, pickled in formaldehyde, I spied a 15" rainbow.

"Where in the world did that come from?" I gasped in amazement, convinced up until then that Brazil's predominantly tropical and sub tropical climates necessarily precluded trout from its warm waters.

Matter-of-factly the white-smocked researcher responded, "In the nearby coastal mountain range known as Serra da Bocaina."

Then he went on to elaborate. It seems that, following WWII, a couple of enterprising, former U.S. Air Force pilots, budding Isaac Waltons in their own right, aerially seeded trout, steelhead and salmon eggs in many of those fresh, cooler and well-aerated waters, those waters, that is, capable of supporting such aquatic life not only in Brazil but especially in southern Argentina and Chile.

Indeed it was thanks to those same seeding efforts in Argentina that I subsequently was able to experience many an exciting battle while stalking the powerful, if belligerent, land-locked Sebago salmon and its cousins, the steelhead and the rainbow.

But this particular story is meant to focus on Brazil rather than Argentina or Chile.

Naturally, my immediate goal was to ferret out those ranchers, "fazendeiros" as they were called, in the Serra da Bocaina region, a mountainous area that lay between Brazil's two largest cities, São Paulo (where I lived) and nearby Rio de Janeiro to the east.

My sleuthings were productive and soon I had ignited acquaintanceships that were to blossom into close and lasting friendships with two delightful São Paulo residents whose Serra de Bocaina holdings were precisely in the trout areas I had targeted.

Mauricio Neves de Oliveira, an attorney, was one of those two men, and the tale I am about to unfold relates one of numerous memorable fishing expeditions we took together. Our destination on this particular trip was a remote and fabled semi-jungle-shrouded valley whose name, the Mambucaba, was derived from the Mambucaba River that flowed through it.

Loaded to the axles, our two-car, trout-bound caravan bounced along, mostly in low gear with four wheel drives engaged, over roads better labeled as trails.

On one occasion we abruptly skidded to a stop just before what was once a passable wooden bridge. In a state of utter disrepair, its flooring was totally missing.

Our only hope of negotiating this risky crossing was to inch our way along two rounded and slippery logs that served as the only surviving remains of that structure.

With fingers crossed and perspiring nervously while trying not to peer at the crevasse beneath us, we were finally able to exhale our "whews" when we left that hazard behind us.

A half a day later we pulled up to Pedra Azul (translated "Blue Rock") which was Mauricio's mountain fazenda (ranch).

There we refreshed ourselves and early the following day, we loaded up our pack animals, hopped on our mules and, with topo maps in hand, off we headed toward our coveted goal, the elusive Mambucaba.

Even though our animals were the sure-footed mule, we were to meet with a near mishap. Along one of the trails we were threading, carved into a steeply-sloping mountainside, the ground gave way under the very beast carrying most of our provisions.

Down the animal tumbled head over hoof with the contents of its heavily ladened baskets spilling and cascading ahead of the startled, cart-wheeling critter.

Mauricio and I had visions of having to put our four legged friend out of its misery, but by the time we had slid, fallen and rolled numerous times en route to the animal's motionless body far below, we happily found that he was just badly shaken but had no broken bones.

With baskets finally mended, loaded and once again positioned on the jittery critter's back, our safari was then able to resume.

Apparently the region we were traversing had been, back in colonial times centuries earlier, an overland trade route, since we passed by occasional patches of stone paving, outcroppings amidst the lush tropical growth, which stonework surprisingly had survived the ravages of long abandonment.

Two days after our trek had begun we rounded a corner. There in the distance ahead lay our Holy Grail, the Mambucaba valley. We stood transfixed, eyes agog while smiling from ear to ear. It was as if we were passing into an Oz, a Shangri La. Wild flowers were uniquely brilliant, hues vibrant and fairly glowing.

Delicate orchids clung to hardwood trees that flanked our trail. Surely we were being treated to a most unique microclimate. I recall leaning from my saddle to pluck a multi-colored flower only to see it explode just before my fingers could touch it and then my laughing in astonishment as I witnessed its petals fly off. That flower had not been a flower at all but rather a cluster of exotic butterflies huddled together, deep in conversation no doubt, before I had unwittingly interrupted them.

Penetrating into the heart of this exotic paradise, we saw many more morphos of all shapes, sizes, colors and flying styles, bobbing across our paths like carefree yo-yos.

We could not help but smile at them while our eyes constantly swept about us in awe over nature's generosity – lush ferns, blossoming hardwoods and the panoply of wild flowers, the varied colors of which I had rarely been treated to. Then suddenly there it was, wending and babbling its way eastward, the object of our long piscatorial excursion, the scintillating Mambucaba River.

Clear, cool and busy in many places, this sight for sore eyes seemed to be calling for our artificial flies to entice its finned denizens.

So fish we did and with rewarding results.

Our lines were frequently to sizzle through deep pools or across riffles as many a fat rainbow, fighting for its freedom, lost the battle and wound up in our creels. But this entire Garden-of-Eden setting so delighted us that frankly we spent more time soaking in its beauty and exploring its many botanical treasures than we did fishing.

Way off in the distance we heard a muffled roar, its source hidden from view by tropical growth.

Making our way upstream past ferns and other mist-loving plant life, we finally gasped in wonderment at storied Mambucaba Falls.

Fishing was our initial justification for undertaking that trip, but the soul-restoring experience of communing with this very special blessing of nature was the real reason… and restore us it certainly did.

Indelibly etched in my souvenirs of Brazil will always be the unique enchantment of the Mambucaba.

*   *   *

A DOCTOR WHO LOVED

In a world where the almighty dollar or, in this case, the Peruvian sol, seems all too frequently to reign supreme, it is so refreshing to learn of those who reject that creed.

This is an account of one such person. His name was Dr. Victor Alzamora Castro. He was a Peruvian physician widely acclaimed for his manifold acts of charity.

Peru's largest city, which at one time happened to be my home, is Lima. It is also that country's capital. But more importantly, Lima is where the revered Dr. Alzamora lived and practiced medicine.

Although he had a sizeable paying clientele, he had a still larger number for whom he charged nothing, for these were the closest to his heart. They were the destitute and most of them lived in the barriadas, the vast slums that surround Lima… and it was there that Dr. Victor, as he was affectionately known by, felt most at home, donating his health-giving services to the impoverished.

Then one afternoon this young physician called for his wife who entered the room to find him lying on his bed. "Honey, could you please bring me a comb?" he asked. "I'm dying and I don't want to meet My Lord this way."

Throngs attended Dr. Victor's funeral. Many were those same impoverished patients he had lavished his love on. They marched en masse from Lima's barriadas carrying banners whose words spoke volumes of one who placed unselfishness far above the sol.

This love story was told me by one who knew and greatly esteemed Dr. Victor. Her name is Isabel, Dr. Victor's cousin. Isabel is my wife.

*　*　*

FLIGHT EXPERIENCE VIGNETTES

For 21 years Latin America was my beat and much of my travel was by air. What follow are vignettes of some of my flight experiences.

The most luxurious trip I can ever recall taking was before the jet age on a piston driven, triple tail, Pan Am Lockheed Constellation.

Our flight was a fairly long one. We took off from Caracas, Venezuela's Maiquetia airport and droned for hours over the Amazonian rainforest and on south, ultimately landing at Rio's Galeao airdrome.

My seat, because of its marvelous design, invited slumber. And I could have been seven feet tall and still would have had ample leg-stretching room.

The stewardesses smothered us passengers with pampered kindnesses, catering to our every whim – a preheated blanket, a glass of champagne, you named it, they obliged.

I felt as if the plentiful four star Michelin bill of fare could, with little effort, have done serious harm to my waistline. But how easy is it to refuse lobster thermador with a side order of medium rare prime rib? A choice of vintage wines? Most certainly!

That trip ended too soon for me and, as I stepped onto the tarmac, I turned and, with a wistful smile, looked back at Pan Am's airborne Waldorf Astoria.

- - - - - - - - - - - -

On one occasion in Argentina I took a business flight from Bahia Blanca, in an area known as the Pampas, to Neuquen way to the south on the shores of the Rio Negro River in the wind-swept Patagonian steppes of southern Argentina.

The plane was an old tail wheel, twin engine, twelve passenger Beechcraft.

There was a gentleman standing beside the aircraft's entry door taking our boarding passes. The same man, once we were all safely inside, climbed in, closing the door behind him.

After verifying that each of us had fastened his seatbelt, he passed out gum.

Then with a smile he made his way to the forward cabin, eased himself into the pilot's chair, put on his earphones……..and we took off.

The rest of us exchanged shrugs and smiles over this unusual one-man show.

- - - - - - - - - - - -

Holland's KLM flight had just lifted from Santiago, Chile's international airport and soon was banking to the east bound for Buenos Aires, Argentina.

We had to overfly the nearby towering Andes, so the pilot engaged in a maneuver that found us climbing in a tight spiral to gain the required altitude to avoid becoming one with lofty Aconcagua, the Western Hemisphere's highest mountain.

Finally the craft leveled out and I settled back in my seat, suddenly to lean forward as I noticed our pilot oddly had resumed once again his upward corkscrew path.

Later the captain turned over the controls to his co-pilot and made his way to the rear, exchanging pleasantries with passengers along the way. So I figured I'd satisfy my curiosity.

"Say, captain," I aimed my voice at him, "I wonder if you could tell me why it was that you engaged in a second series of spirals?"

His lips tightened. "I thought we were high enough to clear the mountains after the initial spiral series, but I was wrong."

"Ulp," I thought, "good thing he reconsidered. I had sorta counted on reaching B.A. in one piece."

- - - - - - - - - - - -

Vapam, a temporary soil sterilant, I had scheduled testing for my stateside employer on a coffee plantation in a relatively cool valley high in the Andes of largely tropical Colombia.

I had chartered a small Cessna. The man at the helm was a Colombian air force pilot moonlighting for a bit of pocket change.

His foot was resting on the dashboard, he was picking his nose and the gas gauge was flirting with "empty."

"Ahem," I gulped, "you sure we got enough gas in this buggy? Those mountains below us have zero places to land."

"No se preocupe (don't worry), señor, we have plenty of fuel left," to which I worriedly mused, "Then either his gas gauge is busted or he has reckless confidence in his ability to set his plane down on a 45 degree slope."

As it was, we wound up landing on a terribly short, makeshift, mountaintop, dangerously sloping strip.

He touched down at the low end of the field and used gravity plus wheel brakes to slow us as we decelerated going uphill, stopping barely short of the runway's end, with the drop off that followed an absolute delight as a take off point for any hang glider enthusiast.

* * *

THE ISLAND

My friend, Frank Novitski, and I worked for the same U.S.-based fishing company in Peru. Then each of us went his separate way.

I wound up in São Paulo, Brazil. A number of years later Frank moved to Brazil and our friendship resumed.

So we would vacation together, trout fish together and our families would socialize together.

It so happened that a friend of Frank's owned an island not too far from the mainland and about half-way between Rio and Santos.

One weekend Frank's friend invited both of us to be his island guests. Accepting enthusiastically, we piled into my four wheel drive and sped off to Santos.

From there we chose the open shore route rather than the inland road which recent rains had made all but impassable. The miles slipped by as we raced along one scalloped ocean beach after another. At times we motored along damp sand but when the beaches would disappear we found ourselves forced out into the shallow surf where our speeding tires would generate a rooster tail of salt spray.

Drained after this oftentimes scary driving experience, we finally pulled in to a humble, coconut-tree-shaded village on the shore of a river which emptied into the nearby boiling Atlantic surf.

It was there that we transferred all our baggage to a modest fishing craft. My camera gear was stowed in a duffle bag which I falsely assumed would provide ample protection from any possible sea water mishap.

Our prow was soon bouncing into the breakers and all of us became drenched. I crossed my fingers hoping that my photographic equipment would still be dry.

Tiny and blurred, our cone-shaped island destination was barely visible through the distant horizon haze.

Finally the engine was cut and we dropped anchor close in to this isle's shoreline. A dark-skinned canoeist came paddling out to meet us. Grabbing our belongings we gingerly stepped into the easily tippable dugout. Within minutes we were riding the combers between large rocks; then our hull scraped to a sudden stop on a pitifully small beach.

The island, very steeply sloped, was shrouded in dense tropical vegetation, covered but a few hundred acres. Our host's home, shaped like an inverted vee, encased the island's pointed summit.

I huffed and puffed up the numerous trail switch-backs, finally wheezing to a stop high above the ocean, and smiled at the architecturally attractive, flag-stone-faced retreat before me as I marveled over the sizeable effort that obviously had gone into its construction.

From the front garden we walked right into the door-less living room of this winterless hide-a-way. On the same floor level were the kitchen, living and dining rooms. The two flanking bedrooms, however, were one level down and clung like symmetrical saddle bags to the sharply angled bedrock on either side.

After touring the entire house, Frank and I easily concurred that the best view from the house was through one of the bathroom windows. I suggested that Frank sit on the throne and face toward the window that framed this dramatic vista while I photographed both him and what he would be viewing. His counter proposal suggested that we reverse roles.

Suddenly I gasped, "My gosh, did the salt water hurt my camera gear?" I rushed to my bag and, with heart in my mouth, quickly pawed through my wet clothes. In horror I slowly withdrew my sopping German Exacta Varex 35mm camera.

Upon returning to São Paulo, I called my insurance company and reported the camera accident, since the salt water had ruined it. The agent said that in such a case the company could not honor my claim. He told me that had the camera fallen overboard then I would have been covered.

So I replied, "Look, whether the camera had dropped into the drink or gotten soaked unintentionally as was the case, either way it was a total loss. Besides, I could have just as easily told you it had fallen overboard, but I chose to level with you."

He grinned, bought my logic and I was fully reimbursed, thus giving a happy ending to my unique island adventure.

*   *   *

Mr. Bankrupt

In Latin America, unlike in America, one's surname is the middle name, not the last name. My citizenship, however, being American, shows my passport name as Frank Bancroft Walker. Some Latins, unaware of this name sequence difference, have mistakenly called me by my middle name enough times that I was used to responding to Bancroft or Walker, or reasonable facsimiles of either.

Once on a routine business visit to Peru I was waiting for my name to be called by an airport customs official.

Presently I heard over the loudspeaker, "Señor Bankrupt."

As I made my way forward I muttered to myself, "He's not far off."

*   *   *

Parque Palermo Samples

One of my business trips to Buenos Aires coincided with Argentina's large annual agricultural fair held in that capital city's stately Palermo Park.

Our local Argentine company had a booth at this fair and we were providing free samples of one of our products as a promotional tool.

Lunch time rolled around and I found myself manning the booth while the others left to eat.

There were lots of kids roaming the fairgrounds and they just loved to fill their pockets with free samples, any kind of samples, regardless of whether they needed them or were even interested in the product.

Consequently our barrel of giveaways was depleting fast.

So I hit on an idea. "Kids," I intoned while summoning my most professorial stance, "we're going to do something interesting," whereupon I began passing out advertising fliers that listed the virtues of our product.

"Here's what I need from you. Study this sheet. When you have just half of our product advantages memorized, then you're to stand in line over there. I'll listen as you recite and give each of you that learns the lesson a free sample."

So with a suppressed smile, I watched their lips move in silence, their eyes either closed or looking pensively upward as they strained to learn their assignment.

My thinking was this: Maybe these children will help our sales by extolling our product's pluses to their parents.

Soon professor Walker began hearing their recitations and rewarding their performances with sample gifts and "Muy bien hecho" pats on the back.

*   *   *

Rio Negro, Victory from Defeat

The British were largely responsible for Argentina's railway system which today is essentially as it was originally laid out over 100 years ago, save for periodic equipment updates.

With Buenos Aires (or B.A. for short) as the hub, most of the railroad lines radiate out from there to various points of the compass.

Porteños (residents of B.A.) enjoy telling the story of how the B.A. to Rio Negro RR line began as an embarrassing fiasco only to become one of Argentina's more illustrious success stories.

Our narrative begins with engineers and their crews busily laying track, building bridges and engaging in the other needed myriad and costly activities associated with such a large project.

Many hundreds of miles later the final section of track was spiked in place at the shore of the Rio Negro way south in Argentina's wind-swept Patagonian steppes, ready to haul the planned tonnages of deciduous fruit back to Buenos Aires and from there to foreign markets.

The exhausted builders had no sooner wiped their brows and accepted the adulation of the crowds, the press and assorted government officials when an important detail was brought to their attention: the Rio Negro Valley soils, white hope for many awaiting farmers, were discovered to contain unacceptably high concentrations of salt.

So this rail line had suddenly gone from white hope to white elephant.

With egg masking their reddened faces, the fathers of this railway orphan hurriedly launched into a large-scale land reclamation program. It involved diverting part of the Rio Negro River in a controlled land-flooding operation. In this fashion the saline soils were repeatedly washed.

Finally free of harmful salts, this land was declared arable.

Today the Rio Negro Valley is a major exporter of deciduous fruit to many world markets and provides Argentina with sorely needed foreign exchange, with my employer reaping profits from the pesticides I would sell to those growers.

Thus, tainted reputations were washed as clean as Rio Negro Valley soil and this project's authors, albeit tardily, were finally able to bask in the limelight of their rags to riches achievement.

*　*　*

STIFF ANCHOVIES

During the years I was working for an international fishing company in Peru I became heavily involved in the manufacture of fishmeal. One of my responsibilities was the importation and sale of fishmeal plants. These plants processed anchovies into high protein fishmeal widely used in America as feed in the poultry industry.

On one occasion our company's purse seiners were bringing into port for offloading such large quantities of anchovies that the pier discharge facilities were simply not geared to handle with dispatch this unusual tonnage. At the time we were using the archaic system of hand shoveling this fish into 55 gallon drums which were then winched onto the pier.

(Regrettably it would not be until several years later before the technique would be commonplace of pumping water into the fish hold, with the resultant slurry of water and fish then being easily sucked out with great speed.)

Consequently, long lines of anchovy-ladened boats, which had no on-board refrigeration whatsoever, waited many hours in the boiling sun for their turn to pull alongside the pier and unload.

So large volumes of fish began to rot.

My boss struck on an idea to help alleviate this problem, and I was selected to carry out an experiment. He reasoned that, because formaldehyde could preserve cadavers from rotting, why not give it a try on anchovies.

I flew to Chimbote, a large fishing port north of Lima, and boarded one of our purse seiners. With me I carried a container of formaldehyde plus a bucket.

With each net-full of anchovies successfully captured, the brailing operation began. This entailed scooping out (brailing) the anchovies from the purse seine net, one brail-load at a time, and dumping same into the boat's hold.

After every brailing, I would slosh over those fish a bucketful of formaldehyde diluted in water.

I don't have to tell you that the result was the stiffest (and smelliest) anchovies you'd ever want to behold.

Rotting was out of the question. And, for all I knew, so also was the palatability of the chickens that ate the stuff.

But that problem was beyond my purview. It was for the bigwigs to sort out.

*   *   *

TOM COLLINS

It was the year 1952, part-way through my Peruvian residency, when I found myself taking a local two-week vacation from my work in the fisheries of my host country. That time frame saw Peru as the largest exporter of fish products in the world. My own part in that industry centered largely on the commercial aspects of an operation involving the harpooning, freezing and shipping of broadbill swordfish to eagerly-awaiting North American markets.

So, with a group of friends, I headed out of Lima for the lofty Andes mountains, our ultimate destination being La Paz, the better known of Bolivia's twin capitals, the other being Sucre. Ninety minutes later the tires of our plane, a piston-driven, WW II vintage DC-3, kissed Cuzco's landing strip in a puff of blue smoke. Our journey's first leg was now history.

Cuzco, at a thin-air elevation of over 11,000 feet, understandably had us huffing and puffing while lugging our travel gear over to the airport's taxi stand. After a bone-jarring if harrowing ride through stop-lights, lurching in and out of potholes, around buses while crossing over many a double line, our dilapidated car finally shuddered to a stop, its engine wheezing in what almost sounded like a death rattle before lapsing into silence.

"Veinte soles, señores," declared our driver as he extended his hand, a wide, toothy smile leaving little doubt over his tip aspirations.

Onto the train we piled and then made our way forward in search of six seats in reasonable proximity to each other. Most of the passengers were highlanders known as "serranos" and their baggage was a bit more diversified than ours, bedrolls to be sure, but also clucking chickens and an occasional oinking pig.

It was not long before our noisy, soot-belching train completed its clickety-clacking switch-backing climb to the altiplano, a vast, towering 12,500 foot-high, tundra-covered plain. This expansive prairie, with snow-capped Andean peaks dotting the distant horizon on all sides, supported long, cold-climate grasses which were rough to the touch. That coarseness had a purpose. This area's camel-related ruminants, the llama, alpaca, guanaco and vicuña, must constantly have their fast-growing teeth kept in check during grazing to avoid starvation. These sandpaper-like plants conveniently wear down the teeth at about the latter's natural growth rate, thereby preventing those teeth from growing so long as to make eating impossible. Mother Nature sure had her thinking cap on.

The railway line's terminus was Puno, a cold, wind-swept Peruvian port city on the shores of the massive lake called Titicaca which straddles the Peru-Bolivia border.

Peruvians like to say that the lake's Titi is on their side and the Caca belongs to Bolivia, while the Bolivians claim the reverse. This unique body of water, at over 12,000 feet elevation, is the highest steamship-navigated lake in the world. So large it is that it took our chugging ship most of the night before depositing us at the docks of Guaqui, Bolivia's main Titicaca port.

For many years that lake supported a thriving rainbow trout industry with any number of canneries dotting the shoreline. An American businessman living in Lima once took me to his freezer chest and showed me an 18 pound rainbow he had pulled out of Lake Titicaca. Unfortunately that trout canning industry later died when the fish succumbed to a rare disease that wiped out the lake's entire rainbow population.

Not far from the port of Guaqui is located another shoreline town called Nuestra Senora de Copacabana. And a very interesting story was once told me during my subsequent Brazilian residency. It seems that a wealthy Carioca (i.e. resident of Rio de Janeiro) owned a substantial stretch of beach property. On a trip he once made by ship from Rio to Buenos Aires and thence by rail to the Bolivian town of Nuestra Senora de Copacabana, his boat was threatened with sinking because of a violent storm. Dropping to his knees, he prayed to Nuestra Senora de Copacabana (Our Lady of Copacabana) that if she would intervene and help avert this impending maritime disaster, he would name his beach front in her honor. His prayers were answered. These beach sands at once became known as Copacabana, a name now familiar around the world.

During our Lake Titicaca crossing I developed an acquaintanceship which later blossomed into a lasting friendship. The name of this loving, gentle, man-of-the-cloth was Tom Collins, not to be confused with the gin-laced cocktail. Father Collins was a Maryknoll missionary priest who was returning from a stateside vacation to Bolivia where he had been working for many years. We met on that Titicaca crossing.

Much of his missionary work was along the Beni River deep in the Amazon basin of northern Bolivia.

Not uncommon, he told me, was it to see a boa constrictor hanging from a tree as a vine decoy, hoping to deceive a victim, or a jaguar or other prolific jungle fauna. He was also well aware of the huge Apazauca spider and its lethal bite to unsuspecting sleepers.

For many years I corresponded with this dear man. Yet because of his great humility it was only after he died that I learned he had been promoted to Bishop.

There are many saints in the remotest of places and Tom Collins surely was one of them.

*　*　*

<h1 style="text-align:center">MISCELLANEOUS BRAZILIAN REFLECTIONS</h1>

Our family's home from 1959 to 1967 was in São Paulo, Brazil. It was from that base of operations that my travels fanned out to cover the whole South American continent. This story, however, deals with miscellaneous Brazilian reflections, gleanings from my almost ten years of living and working there.

- - - - - - - - - -

Brazil's capital of Rio de Janeiro was moved to Brasilia during my long Brazilian residence. Juscelino Kubitschek, the president until the early 60's, was the prime mover of this massive undertaking. He created a completely new city in Brazil's hinterland. Its purpose was to draw the population from the coast to the interior to develop that country's vast untapped wealth.

In order to meet the planned Brasilia inauguration schedule, the final months saw planeloads of clay being flown to Brasilia to complete the final construction phase of key government buildings. I saw trucks and earth moving equipment everywhere. All wires, power and phone were underground. Nothing was overhead in keeping with that city's ultra-modern design.

Brasilia finally opened as Brazil's shining new capital, but a very real problem then faced the nation, viz. how to entice all the needed government officials away from fun-loving Rio and to their new isolated workplace deep in the country's interior.

- - - - - - - - - -

Presidential elections were held soon after we took up residence in Brazil. Janio Quadros, the highly successful governor of São Paulo, won in a landslide.

Honest, innovative and hardworking, O. Janio, as he was called, was soon stepping on lots of toes belonging to the status-quoers whose cushy lives resisted change.

So O. Janio, less than one year into his presidency, quit in a pique of disgust but believing that the people would rise up in his support and bring him back on their shoulders with an all-encompassing mandate to rule as he saw fit.

Well it didn't happen as he had hoped and his vice president, Joao Goulart, took over, ushering in devastating changes of the worst kind.

Goulart, the alleged illegitimate son of former dictator Getulio Vargas, began playing footsy with Mao Tse Tung. Communist cells slipped into cities throughout the country as China prepared to make Brazil her vassal.

164

Matters worsened. The U.S. Consulate warned all U.S. citizens to get ready to leave at a moment's notice.

Then came the famous "Marcha do Dilencio" (Silent March). Through the center of São Paulo marched in total silence many thousands of concerned citizens, fingering their rosary beads in hushed protest to Brazil's impending fate.

The military, interpreting this march as a national plebiscite against Goulart, deposed the president and spirited him to neighboring Uruguay as the nation sighed in relief.

Only then was the full truth revealed. Tons and tons of Chinese take-over literature in warehouses all over the country were found and destroyed.

One Sunday at our church we heard a high prelate speak from the pulpit while brandishing an edict. He told us this edict listed people to be summarily shot at China's takeover of Brazil. The speaker's name was on that list.

These were indeed exciting times for all of us residents.

- - - - - - - - - -

Many Japanese farmers, who bought our chemicals, populated Brazil. Entire towns seemed like transplants from Japan. Radio stations broadcasted in Japanese. Calendars hanging on restaurant walls featured Nipponese beauties clad in old world kimonos. Once my wife and I attended a large Japanese wedding celebration. We were among 200 guests. The newlyweds, dressed in the ceremonial garb of the old country, sat together at one end of a long table.

With everyone attentively listening, close friends would, one-by-one, rise to speak (fortunately for us, in Portuguese, as we did not know Japanese). Their subject matter touched on the private lives of the two protagonists, as well as "birds and bees" comments which produced, at times, two very red faces as well as titters from the crowd.

- - - - - - - - - -

I was to learn that Brazil's coffee trees were not infrequently subject to serious weather damage, despite being in the subtropics, due to their highland habitat. Growers who were caught unprepared could, and occasionally did, lose entire plantations. The problem was not so much because of the freezing temperatures at night as it was the rapid thaws soon after the sun came up. The latter could produce severe splitting of the trunk and limbs of the coffee tree akin to a cold drinking glass shattering when suddenly immersed in hot water. They solved this difficulty by using smoke. Strategically placed smoke generators would be employed to blow smoke through the trees at night. Then after sunrise, the trees would heat up but gradually, since the smoke only slowly dissipated, thereby saving the growers from otherwise severe tree-splitting and ensuing crop loss.

My involvement with the coffee growers was limited to two products. One was an herbicide and the other, an organo-phosphate insecticide that controlled the leaf miner. The latter, if unchecked, could rapidly defoliate vast acreages of coffee trees causing major tree damage and subsequent plummeting of crop yields.

- - - - - - - - - -

One of the most striking features about the huge city of São Paulo was its ever changing skyline. High rise office buildings and apartment complexes under construction were constantly seen dotting the horizon. To the uninformed visitor, such sights would often be taken as a sign of great prosperity, while the truth was quite different. You see, poor Brazil was plagued with great and constant inflation…… with equally great and constant corresponding new construction.

The unwise would leave their cruzeiros in the bank only to see their purchasing power quickly erode. But the savvy put their money into real estate since the value of such investments kept up with Brazil's galloping inflation.

- - - - - - - - - -

Soccer was Brazil's national passion. I recall, during one of its matches for the coveted world championship Jules Rimet Cup, seeing the entire city of São Paulo, normally seething with activity, come to a standstill. Strategically placed loudspeakers were busy broadcasting the live action. Fans, their fanaticism clearly showing, stood around in clusters, sipping their coffee demitasse "cafezinhos," while yelling encouragement to their heroes.

Near our home was the Pacaembu Soccer Stadium where we, on occasion, would go to cheer on Pele, later to be heralded as the greatest soccer player ever. He was then at the pinnacle of his career. That player was so adept at dribbling that it was not at all uncommon to see defenders being cleverly out-feinted by Pele to where they would literally lose their balance and fall without even being touched. The government, by decree, later declared Pele a "national treasure," so great was the glory his skills brought to his country.

- - - - - - - - - -

166

Once in downtown São Paulo I had fun taking a long-lens picture of a balloon salesman while he was practicing dubious business ethics, as later events were to confirm. He was standing on a corner behind a small folding table on which were piled un-inflated balloons.

In his hand he held a full-inflated, massive balloon, which the public was intended to presume had earlier come from that same table. Though I was some distance from him, his sharp, wary eyes saw me. Quickly he hid the balloon behind him. The only problem was that he was of a very lean build and his globe was much wider than he. So the inflated sample he thought was being concealed from my view was actually quite visible on both sides of him.

Clearly he feared his ruse was being documented and that he had better hide the evidence.

I say ruse because not long before this incident a similar one occurred in Montevideo during a routine business call I was making on our Uruguayan distributor, Eduardo Cabezas. We were walking down the street together when we both saw a balloon salesman, just like the one described above. Eddie turned to me and said, "Frank, watch me. I'm going to have some fun with this kid."

Approaching the skittish, unkempt lad with a runny nose, my companion opened with, "Say, muchacho, how much do you want for a balloon?" After Eddie got his answer, he continued, "Tell you what. I'll buy one, but since I don't have much time to blow it up, why don't you just sell me the one that's already inflated."

Quick on the draw, the urchin, after wiping his nose on his sleeve, replied, "Oh sir, I couldn't do that. It would not be hygienic."

As we walked away laughing, I turned to Eddie and said, "You know, we could have played a trick on him. After learning how much he was asking for a balloon, and it being obvious that his inflated decoy had to have cost far more than what he was pawning off as being identical, I could have accidentally (on purpose) bumped into his sample and burst it. Then after apologizing profusely, I would hand him his publicized price."

- - - - - - - - - -

It was not until long after I first met Otto Lohmann that I learned he had been a Nazi during WWII and had fled Germany. For many years he lived in Argentina and from there emigrated to São Paulo which was where I knew him.

Ours was primarily a business relationship. He worked as a salesman for the Brazilian distributor I had contracted to handle the farm chemicals of my stateside employer.

And on occasion I would talk business with him at his apartment. At the time he was divorced which helped explain, I suppose, the series of girlfriends he was constantly introducing me to.

Later he would explain that he was protecting his female companions from their abusive husbands, as he strove to convey the impression of "good samaritanship." And because he was my friend, I took him at his word.

I never saw Otto again, for I left Brazil behind me and moved back to the United States. Then years later while speaking with a former business associate who knew Otto, I inquired as to Otto's whereabouts.

"Hadn't you heard?" he replied. "Otto was beaten to death by the husband of one of the ladies he insisted he had been protecting."

So I grieved over my lost friend.

*   *   *

A Chance Meeting

In my late 20s I lived in Peru where I would date local lasses, but soon I grew discouraged over not being able to find the girl of my dreams. So I decided to go on a dating strike.

Now it so happened that one of my colleagues in Lima where I worked was another American, Jake by name, who was married to a Peruvian. She was Luchi and I was soon to learn that her abiding avocation was pairing people up, for she just loved to see the fruits of her efforts be rewarded with the tinkle of wedding bells. Her batting average, experience later told me, would not have earned her a spot even in the minors, until, that is, one very special day. But then I am getting ahead of myself.

I was humming away at my desk when Jake walks up and says, "Say Frank, Luchi has a girl she would very much like you to meet. Could you come to our house for dinner?" His faint smile told me he was party to a plot to end my blissful state of bachelorhood.

Thus it was that I was to fall victim to a whole series of Luchi's "perfect matches," none of which ever got past my seeing each potential bride to her front door the night of our initial meeting for the first (and last) time. The chemistry just was not there and some of these damsel hopefuls were absolute frights.

It finally got to the point where I pleaded with Jake, "Hey buddy, please let Luchi know that I am overdue for a breather."

Dutifully, Jake laid off, but only for a while.

Then, with my guard down, Jake announced, "Say Frank, Luchi is up to her old tricks again. This time she wants to see this French dentist fall head over heels for a German girlfriend of hers (an unlikely ethnic match at best what with the French and Germans, because of their historical conflicts, hardly on speaking terms).

"So that this encounter can be staged in the most casual of circumstances," Jake purred away, "she is planning a big picnic. Frank, we need about six cars. Do you think we could count on your car?"

I accepted and was given a list of names and addresses of those I was to pick up.

Well, the conspiracy to create a Franco-German alliance laid an ostrich egg while I wound up meeting and marrying one of the persons I had driven to the picnic that wonderful afternoon.

Indeed, so smitten was I over Isabel Castro that I proposed marriage one week after our first meeting. We were wed a few months later, and 58 years later we're still together.

And match-maker Luchi took all the credit, which was okay by me.

*　*　*

CICCILO

Periodically my bosses in New York City would visit me at my base in São Paulo, Brazil from where we would tour South America.

On one such visit, Len accompanied me to Montevidio, Uruguay where we were met by our company's charming distributor, Eduardo Cabezas Minetti. Eduardo's popularity was legendary, starting with none other than his country's president, to whom we were introduced. It was unusual for us to walk the streets of Montevideo accompanied by Eduardo without seeing him often tip his hat, smile and acknowledge his many friends.

This particular Sunday Eduardo picked us up at the hotel and inquired, "What kind of food would you like to have for lunch?"

Len was partial to Italian cuisine. With a name like Minetti, we knew Eduardo would know just the right place. Nor were we to be disappointed.

Soon we pulled up to Ciccilo's in residential Montevideo.

The shades were partially drawn. We peeked in and could see chairs piled atop the tables. Eduardo knocked repeatedly.

Finally a short roly-poly man, sporting a Ben Gurion pink with white fringe hair style, emerged from the kitchen in back, wiping his hands on his apron as he waddled to the door.

"Oh, Eduardo, I'm so very sorry," he lamented with crestfallen countenance, "but we don't open till this evening."

Eddy, his heart set on lunch at Ciccilo's, started pouring on the old charm. "Look, Ciccilo," he pleaded, "we have a distinguished visitor who is partial to Italian food, and I told him yours was the best!"

Cicclios' smile told us he was softening. "Eduardo, honest, I don't have any food ready, but you're welcome to come in," he replied.

Once inside, each of us outdid the other as we lauded first his fish net decorations, then the telegrams on the wall from such operatic notables as Lily Pons and Lauritz Melchior.

Ciccilo had clearly warmed to our presence. He rushed to draw the blinds. Then with the room darkened, he flicked a switch and soft star-like lights began to twinkle across a mural. "Mi Napoli," Ciccilo beamed as he gestured with great pride toward the city of his birth.

More exclamations of our ever-deepening appreciation for absolutely everything Ciccilo stood for caused his resistance, already badly shaken, to totally collapse.

"Say fellows," he enthused, "how would you like to try our house wine?"

We hastened to clear a table top of its chairs while our host hurried to the wine cellar.

Soon we were seated, purring like kittens, as we nibbled our hors d'oeuvres and sipped his very tasty wine. On several occasions Ciccilo arose from the table either to check on the progress of our gourmet meal or else to turn away would-be diners by pointing to the "closed" sign.

On Sundays Italian families love to gather together. So as we were eating, Ciccilo's brother let himself in and walked up to our table. Then Ciccilo's son, daughter and wife all arrived.

The next thing we knew the room had burst into song. Mama was at the piano, daughter on the drums, son on accordion while Ciccilo and his brother, seated at our table, and with their happy eyes sparkling, were busy singing and strumming their mandolins.

I started to whistle softly to a Puccini aria they were playing. With a laugh in his eye and a smile on his ruddy face, Ciccilo looked at me as he stood up. Clearly he had something in mind.

Mandolin in one hand and with free hand on his chest he began to whistle. It took very little discernment on our part to realize that we were witnessing a remarkable talent as Ciccilo would slide from a delicate canary-like tremolo to a vibrant, glass-rattling bass.

At one point his son worriedly cautioned his dad to be careful of his heart, for it seems Ciccilo had a cardiac condition and strenuous whistling aggravated this problem. Later we were to learn that Ciccilo was a TV celebrity and appeared often as a whistling soloist.

During that marvelous afternoon I was able to snap a picture of father-and-son looking with great love at each other as they played for us.

So on my next visit to Monty I presented to Ciccilo an enlargement of that father-and-son picture, nicely framed, as my thanks for our memorable lunch. His gratitude was actually embarrassing, for he attended our table to the neglect of the other diners.

Not long after I learned that Ciccilo had retired to his "Napoli of the twinkling lights." *(See photos.)*

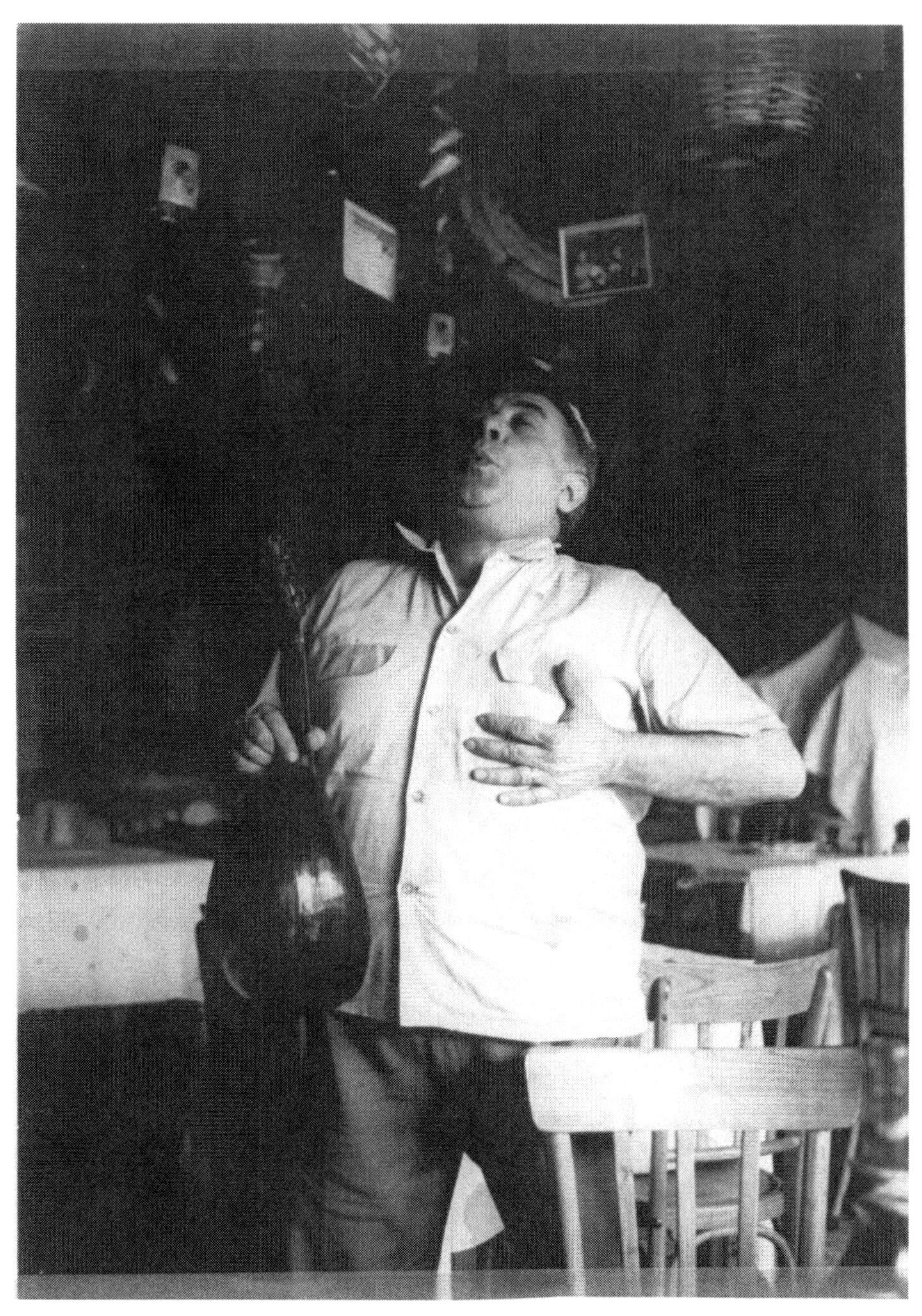

Whistling Virtuoso Ciccilo

Ciccilo and Son

*   *   *

CHAPTER 6

FAMOUS PEOPLE

-----

* See photo

MY ENCOUNTER WITH CHURCHILL

My encounter with one of the world's most famous men is something I will never forget.

It happened in Washington, D.C.'s Union Station in 1947. I was a student at Georgetown University. Our rifle team was waiting to depart for a scheduled match against West Point.

With target rifle slung over my shoulder, I stood on one of the train docks just inside the depot's metal gates. I could see nearby a waiting train car bedecked with flowers.

Suddenly I heard sirens wailing. The air seemed electric with anticipation.

Moments later a phalanx of motorcycles entered the dock area. Directly behind was a Rolls Royce.

The car door opened and a long cigar emerged followed by the old Bulldog himself, Sir Winston "Winnie" Churchill. He walked briskly over to the crowds, who were cheering from behind the gates, and waved with his famous "V" for victory gesture.

Then he turned and headed in my direction. As he approached, others nearby began to clap and Winnie took in this adulation with obvious satisfaction.

But I was not clapping, England's history of using other countries to further her own ends was on my mind.

Churchill stopped about ten feet from where I stood and looked me right in the eye, smoke billowing from his puro. He was clearly waiting for my applause. It seemed like an eternity as I looked at him and he at me. Neither of us budging.

So I asked myself, "Would there be any justification for my clapping for this man of history?"

Soon I had an answer. During England's darkest hours of W.W.II, Winnie's tenacity and guts had held his country together.

I smiled and began to clap. Churchill snorted his approval and then strode toward his flower-draped train car. *(See photo.)*

Winston Churchill

* * *

During my Florida residency I would sometimes team up in tennis doubles with Jim Pollard, the basketball Hall of Famer. Jim was a decent tennis player and we had some good matches together.

He told me of an amusing but also greatly satisfying experience he once had on the tennis court. His partner and he had been challenged by a couple of hot shots who soon were demolishing them.

A U.S. Coastguarder on liberty was leaning against the fence watching the slaughter. Finally he couldn't bear to see the punishment continue. So he approached Jim and said, "What say to our taking these dudes on?" Jim, even though he had never met this man before, agreed, figuring he couldn't do any worse.

The Coastguarder was all over the court, hitting winners at will. Jim was glowing with pride as he saw game after game pile up without the opponents being able to win a single one.

When it was all over everyone shook hands and exchanged names. The Coastguarder's? He was Jack Kramer, number one player in the world.

Epilog: Years later, while a staff tennis teaching pro at California State University at Northridge, CA, I invited Jack Kramer, then in his 60s, to be a guest lecturer during our university's annual "tennis day."

By then Kramer had become one of the key figures in developing professional tennis worldwide.

He graciously accepted, arrived in tennis togs ready to play and promptly refused our proffered honorarium. As we climbed the staircase together headed for the office of the university's Director of Athletics, I noticed Kramer wince. He confessed that arthritis was ravaging both of his hips and he was due soon to have them replaced. Yet he insisted on going onto the gym court where he proceeded to play very effectively to an overflow audience against our university's two best players.

At Kramer's request I provided a running commentary on his playing technique over the p.a. system, explaining what this celebrity was doing and why, as Kramer demonstrated the style which had brought him so much fame.

Quite a man was Kramer!

*　　*　　*

It was 1948. My father was Night World News Editor for Hearst's International news Service at their New York City corporate headquarters when over the teletype came the laconic flash that Mahatma Gandhi had just been assassinated.

This was a story of great international significance and no one knew this better than Dad, for Gandhi was world-renowned for his peaceful efforts to effect needed social change.

Now normally when a world figure dies the media carefully research first before doing a well-documented bio which often times then must be rewritten before it reaches its final, journalistically acceptable form. However, Father had a privileged memory and was a gifted writer, and this was a story that required uncommonly prompt action if INS was to scoop the competition (as they wound up doing).

He yelled out, "Get me live, quick!" which meant he wanted all the necessary switches thrown so that the story he was about to write would be received immediately and simultaneously by all of INS's many bureaus worldwide. Because of the great urgency of the moment, time simply did not allow for rewrites. The polished, accurate chronicle had to hit the wire at once.

Dad, seated before a Telex keyboard, while watching the unfolding and highly abbreviated message on the incoming Telex machine beside him, began typing Gandhi's complete, error-free bio as fast as he could (and he was a very fast typist).

When I first hear of Dad's dramatic and impressive handling of that electrifying story I was reminded of similarly unique skills I had been made aware of during my WWII stint in the Navy. When a communication of major military import was being relayed via semaphore (i.e., using hand-held signaling flags) down the column of U.S. naval war ships from vessel to vessel, normally each message would first have to be hand-recorded by the receiver while he faced the sender. Then he would turn to face the next ship behind him and relay with his two flags the message he had jotted down moments earlier, which procedure was repeated successively from ship to ship. However, uncommonly competent flagmen would be able to eliminate an extra step thereby relaying the message faster. The technique they would employ to accomplish this would be to face the sending flagman and virtually as fast as each letter was received it would be re-transmitted backwards (in mirror image) in order for the ship immediately to the rear to receive it forwards.

This superb handling of a great story serves to illustrate one (among many) of the reasons why my father was considered a top newspaper editor within the international community of professional journalists.

*   *   *

ADOLF EICHMANN

Until the early 60s infamous Adolf Eichmann was still at the top of Israel's most wanted list because of the millions of Jews he had sent to their deaths. It will be recalled that this man was a high ranking Nazi secret policeman who, during WW II, directed the deportation of millions of Jews to extermination camps.

When the Axis powers were defeated many of Hitler's henchmen like Mengele, Eichmann and numerous other notable Nazi offenders went into hiding.

Eichmann chose Argentina as his refuge. Mengele went to a remote town in the interior of southern Brazil near the Paraguayan border, while still others were scattered elsewhere in South America.

For years Israeli Intelligence did not relent in its crusade to find Eichmann and bring him to justice. History shows they were successful. A fascinating book, "The House on Garibaldi Street" tells the story of the hunt for and ultimate capture of Adolf Eichmann.

He was finally tracked down to a modest home on the outskirts of Buenos Aires. His pursuers then kidnapped him, drugged him and spirited him out of Argentina and back to Israel. There he stood trial for mass murder, was found guilty and hanged.

It was not until after Eichmann's execution that the location of his Buenos Aires hideaway was revealed.

To my great surprise I learned that my taxi route, each time I would travel from the country's Ezeiza International Airport to my hotel in downtown Buenos Aires, would take me right by Eichmann's home while he was still living there incognito.

You see, in those years Argentina was part of my South American beat.

*   *   *

Linda Ronstadt I first heard sing during a PBS television special. Prior to that I had not known what a truly special voice she possessed.

I sat totally engrossed while she serenaded her audience with a series of Spanish songs which later appeared under the label "Canciones de Mi Padre" (My Father's Songs).

Rapt as I rarely had been I shook my head in disbelief at her ability to toy with the notes she dominated as few I had heard before, or since for that matter.

A full orchestra accompanied her.

I could not help but reflect on what seemed quite obvious. So special was her talent, that all the musicians on stage with her, realizing the prestige she was bringing to them all, were giving 110% as they played their hearts out.

* * *

FRITZ KREISLER

My deep admiration for Fritz Kreisler began the evening my mother took me, then a teenager, to see and hear that world-famous violinist/composer perform at the War Memorial Opera House in San Francisco.

Hobbling onto the stage, for he had recently been run over by a car, that virtuoso, with great tenderness and feeling, held the audience spellbound as his Stradivarius made each piece come alive.

It was for me a memorable evening.

Years later I read a story about Fritz Kreisler that moved me greatly.

The lives of great musicians are usually a checkerboard of highs and lows, and Fritz Kreisler's was no different.

This particular incident occurred during one of his lows. Down and out, unshaven and in tattered clothing, but with his cased Stradivarius tucked firmly under his arm, Kreisler was wandering along the sidewalk in downtown Los Angeles. Suddenly he stopped to peer into the window of a stringed instrument store.

Then he walked in and approached the proprietor. "Excuse me," he spoke, "Do you have any Stradivariuses similar to this one," as Kreisler unlatched his case to show him his priceless violin.

This shop owner, even though he did not recognize this tramp-appearing person as Fritz Kreisler, was still knowledgeable enough to realize that the numbered violin he was being shown belonged to Kreisler.

"Just a minute," he shot back to Kreisler, "I may be able to find one for you."

He quickly disappeared to a back room and telephoned the police. "Please send an officer quickly. I have a man in my shop who has stolen Fritz Kreisler's Stradivarius violin."

The next scene is at the court house. Kreisler's accuser repeats his charge that this hobo stole Fritz Kreisler's invaluable Stradivarius.

"But your honor," Kreisler softly interjected, "I am Fritz Kreisler and this violin is mine."

The judge replied, "Well, even though you have no I.D., I believe we can settle this matter very easily. Mr. Kreisler, if you are who you claim to be, would you please play your instrument for us?"

After adjusting his bowstring tension and tuning his violin strings, Kreisler began to play.

His music immediately brought gasps of wonderment and deep appreciation from everyone present, but most of all from the shop owner who, with head bowed in shame, mumbled in between sobs, "Your honor, this man is indeed Fritz Kreisler."

This gripping story I have often told by way of introduction, as a harmonica soloist, before playing some of Kreisler's compositions.

*　　*　　*

SADDAM HUSSEIN

America remembers all too well *Desert Storm* and Saddam Hussein's despicable role in that Mid-Eastern conflagration. Unfortunately, that man's intense hatred for our country, so evident then, seethed and boiled for years to follow.

It will be recalled that when we and our allies brought Iraq to its knees, the United Nations established a free zone in northern Iraq to where Iraq's Kurds could retreat without fear of unprovoked attack from their arch enemy, fellow Iraqi, Saddam.

At the time my son, Frank Jr., headed up the emergency shelter program of a worldwide missionary organization, WYWAM.

Frank and an associate flew to southern Turkey and from there made their way overland to northern Iraq for the express purpose of establishing emergency shelters for the homeless Kurds in that cold, mountainous part of northern Iraq.

Their host was a Kurd who lived in one of the rare homes in that desolate area. Looking at Frank quizzically, that Kurd asked, "Why oh why did you Americans not take out that butcher when you had the chance?"

He then went on to relate that he personally saw Saddam on a prior occasion walk up to one of the Kurds and, not liking the expression on his face, remove a handgun from his holster, and at point blank range blow his head apart.

General Schwartzkoff, commander-in-chief of the allied forces during the *Desert Storm* conflict was deeply troubled over not being allowed to eliminate right then and there that absolute menace to the free world. Schwartzkoff knew far better than most just how depraved and dangerous that man really was.

* * *

JUSCELINO KUBITSCHEK

Shortly after my long residence in Brazil had ended and I was living once again back in the states, I had occasion to visit Houston, Texas.

That particular day, upon approaching the hotel concierge to retrieve my key, I noticed to my astonishment another hotel guest standing right beside me, there for the same purpose.

It was Brazil's much-loved, former president, Juscelino Kubitschek.

So I addressed him in Portuguese. His eyes brightened and I was instantly charmed by his smile, a legendary smile that I, and millions more in Brazil, had grown to love during Juscelino's presidency which was precisely during the period of my residency there.

He seemed most interested in learning how I spoke his language, a tongue very little-known in the United States.

Thus it was that we settled in for a delightful half hour of Brazilian recollections. I told him what a marvelous achievement his country's new capital, Brasilia, was, it being common knowledge that Kubitschek was Brasilia's author and finisher.

Juscelino Kubitschek

I learned from him that ever since his exile from Brazil following the military take-over in the early 60s (on the heels of President Joao Goulart's ostracism by Brazil's armed forces), he had been very active in foreign trade out of his offices in New York City.

Later, I was to learn, that Brazil's military had finally relaxed their stand against Juscelino, who then was allowed to return to his homeland. Earlier the military, knowing of Juscelino's enormous popularity, were uncomfortable over letting him return and possibly upsetting their benevolent military dictatorship. Not long after that Kubitschek died tragically in a motoring accident and the whole nation mourned.

That face-to-face encounter with Juscelino Kubitschek told me more about the man than a library of books could have.

He remains as one of the most captivating, fascinating, charismatic persons I have ever met. *(See photo.)*

* * *

One of my father's crack re-write men was a wordsmith named Thayer who became financially indebted to Dad while working at the San Francisco Call Bulletin, that city's leading daily newspaper.

Because of his fluency in Spanish and his love for Latin America, Thayer left the Call Bulletin and joined Drew Pearson, an internationally famous columnist, who then assigned Thayer to cover the River Plate countries (Argentina, Uruguay and Paraguay) out of Buenos Aires.

This was back in the forties when Juan Domingo Peron was Argentina's dictator and his wife, Evita, was the power behind the throne.

Evita, before marrying Juan Domingo, had been a cabaret dancer whose "leggy" posters had adorned many an Argentine billboard.

After she became Argentina's first lady, Juan Domingo ordered all undignified pictures of her destroyed and "Evita" was thereafter referred to, by edict, as "La Senora," a title more befitting her new, exalted status.

Remembering his debt, Thayer advised my dad that he had secretly acquired a banned cancanish photo of Evita which, if agreeable, he would smuggle out of Argentina in exchange for the cancellation of his financial obligation. Dad agreed.

With the picture in hand, Dad approached *Life Magazine* who, trying to get it for a song, claimed they already had one like it.

"Like fun you do," Dad responded as he snatched it back. Whereupon he turned on his heel and headed out the door ignoring their frantic attempts to salvage what they knew was a very big and exclusive picture slipping from their greedy grasp.

He wound up selling it to a delighted *Look Magazine*, *Life*'s arch-enemy.

Soon after the picture was printed, Thayer had to flee across the River Plate to sanctuary in Montevideo, just a step ahead of Peron's pursuing secret police.

During her time as a dancer, Evita's accouterment would have been considered risqué. By today's standards, however, what she wore back then many today would swear would have kept her warm in a blizzard. *(See photo.)*

P.S. A highly-touted and long-running Broadway musical, "Evita," heralded the life of dictator Peron's famous wife.

Evita in Her Pre-First Lady Days

*   *   *

Before the dawn of the 19th century Peru, South America, then a third world country, could boast of having built one of the highest railways anywhere on the globe. It was an accomplishment which, given that project's complexity and state-of-the-art demands, was heralded far and wide as an engineering feat of huge proportions.

Beginning at Lima near sea level, this railway zigzagged far into one of the world's loftiest mountain chains, the mighty Andes, in the process reaching just over 15,000 feet. That elevation compares with the U.S. mainland's highest point, before Alaska, namely Mt. Whitney, whose peak is recorded at 14,495 feet.

Thousands of Chinese coolie immigrants were employed for this massive undertaking which involved much blasting to create many tunnels, constructing numerous bridges while all the while fighting such severe hardships as soroche, a mountain sickness attributed to high elevations.

Henry Meiggs was this project's developer and chief fund-raiser.

But one of the brains behind the technical aspects of that railroad's construction was Francisco Talleri, a high ranking engineer. He was a Swiss Italian who immigrated to Peru for the purpose of paying a debt of honor owed by his deceased father.

Talleri's great railroad line achievement brought him both fame and fortune. Even a street in downtown Lima bears his name.

He became a large Peruvian landholder. And while he was mayor of Ancon, a beach resort town near Lima, the treaty which ended the War of the Pacific, a conflict between Peru, Bolivia and Chile, was signed in his home.

Many of the temporary immigrant Chinese laborers who helped build this railroad later opted to apply for Peruvian citizenship but they needed sponsorship, and Francisco Talleri was of great help to a number of them. To show their appreciation for Talleri's kindnesses, quite a few changed their names to Talleri. And so it is that today one can find in Peru, not only fair-skinned, European-appearing Talleris but slant-eyed Talleris as well.

An amusing story is told by my wife of Francisco and his young but sharp daughter, Paulita. It seems that Paulita had just lost a tooth. She knew that her father each night before retiring would place all of his pocket change on a table beside his bed. The coins would be neatly arranged according to their denominations and a number of them were valuable gold pieces.

So Paulita that night asked her father, "Daddy, do you think if I put my tooth somewhere that the fairy would reward me?"

"Yes, yes child, I am sure so," he replied. "Now run along to bed, dear. It is late." As she left his bedroom she quietly sneaked her tooth right into the middle of all her father's many coins.

Early the next morning Francisco was awakened by Paulita's squeal of delight. "Oh, Daddy, look at what the fairy brought me," as she scooped up all of her father's change. From his bed and with one eye open and a slight smile creasing his face, Francisco realized hc had just been had.

This short vignette of Francisco Talleri is accurate for, you see, he was my wife's grandfather.

*   *   *

THE OLD GOAT

Back in the years when Franklin Delano Roosevelt was president, and even after his death, there were two kinds of people, the ones who loved FDR and his memory, and those who couldn't stand him. My father was of the latter persuasion.

When my youngest brother was seven years old, my dad took him to visit Hyde Park, FDR's estate, where his crypt is displayed among flowers in the well-landscaped grounds.

Many other visitors were also wandering about Hyde Park that day in hushed reverence, especially when they passed our ex-president's resting place.

Suddenly a little boy's loud voice broke the awed silence, "Hey, dad, is this where the old goat's buried?"

Turning a bright crimson, dad whisked brother Mike from the scene. For as they say, "Out of the mouths of babes."

*   *   *

JOHN BARRYMORE

Stories are told of John Barrymore and his abiding love for the practical joke.

One afternoon a large group of Hollywood friends and celebrities were partying on the back lawn of Barrymore's estate.

A guest approached Barrymore. "Oh, Johnny, could you direct me to the lady's powder room," she cooed.

"Gosh, Mabel, I'm terribly sorry, but our plumbing is out of order. Would you be willing to use our temporary outhouse over there?" replied the host.

Dismissing the slight inconvenience with a magnanimous wave, off she hurried.

As soon as she latched the door behind her, Barrymore silently motioned for his friends to gather 'round the one-holer.

When it was time, Mabel pulled the chain and all four walls collapsed.

*　*　*

My Ancestors:

Dr. Frank Watts Bancroft,

H.H. Bancroft,

and

General William Albert Ryan

It was at St. Mary's Hospital in San Francisco back in 1924 when I filled the delivery room air with my very first yelps, yelps which have continued to this day.

When I was old enough to be inquisitive about my origins and how it was that my parents had come to name me Frank Bancroft Walker, my dad sat me down.

"Son," he quietly said, "you were named after a man I deeply admired. He was Dr. Frank Watts Bancroft, a noted research zoologist. He was your grandfather, your mom's father. You would have loved him but unfortunately he died soon after I married your mother. He suffocated to death due to cancer of the throat.

"I first learned of his greatness," dad continued, "during the early stages of my newspaper career when I was a reporter with the San Francisco Examiner. My city editor once gave me an assignment. It was to interview a key discoverer of vitamins and then do a feature story on that man.

"So I took the ferry across San Francisco Bay and taxied to the University of California in Berkeley where I met the man I was to interview. He was a biochemist and staff research scientist, whose name I can no longer recall.

"Knowing that most successful people have had, at one point in their lives, mentors who have helped them greatly, I innocently asked the question, 'To whom do you owe your success?'

188

"I was not prepared, however, for his answer which came back, 'To a man by the name of Dr. Frank Watts Bancroft. Have you ever heard of him?'

"With a smile I softly replied, 'I married his daughter.'"

Dr. Frank Watts Bancroft, the grandfather I never knew, was a PhD, phi beta kappa and full professor of zoology, within the University of California's teaching system. His earlier studies included stints in Germany where, as a necessary study tool, he acquired fluency in that language.

Among his many significant research achievements was the first recorded successful experiment known as "artificial parthenogenesis of the frog," an effort that found him teamed up with a very noted scientist, one Jacques Loeb. That body of work, which during my college years I read in a medical journal in the Library of Congress, was one of the essential building blocks for what is today known as artificial insemination, a current worldwide practice.

Because of important research that grandfather also did for the Rockefeller Research Institute, after he died that institute asked my grandmother for (and received) his brain. One day I hope to pay my respects to that most important part of what remains behind of grandfather, Dr. Frank Watts Bancroft. His phi beta kappa key I inherited and passed on to my eldest son, Frank Bancroft Walker, Jr.

Grandfather's wife, medical doctor Eleanor Stowe Bancroft, was one of California's early women surgeons. Widely traveled and extremely well read (she owned a very large library), in later life she became campus physician at Mills College in Oakland. Instead of a wedding ring she asked Frank, her husband-to-be, for a gold bracelet because, unlike a ring, she would be permitted to wear a bracelet during her surgeries. That bracelet my wife now wears since it too interferes less when, that is, she carves a turkey.

Grandfather's father was Albert L. Bancroft who, together with his historian brother, Hubert Howe Bancroft, owned an important publishing company in San Francisco, The Bancroft Publishing Company. Albert was the managing partner of that enterprise.

Hubert Howe Bancroft, a prolific writer of western American history, sold his sizeable library to the University of California at Berkeley. That collection, together with many other significant writings and important documents, is currently housed on that university's campus in a separate, internationally recognized library called the Bancroft Library, named in H.H.'s honor. An editor's copy of Hubert Howe's noted five volume work, *Native Races of the Pacific States,* dedicated, both in print and in H.H.'s own handwriting, to his brother, Albert, was given me by my mother. I in turn, gave it to my son William, when he was old enough to appreciate it. A main street on U.C. Berkeley's campus is named Bancroft Way in his honor.

After my father finished speaking of mother's side of the family and how I was named, he then launched into a fascinating account of his grand uncle, General William Albert Ryan.

In 1873 Ryan died a martyr in Santiago de Cuba while fighting for the Cuban cause for freedom. His life had been about as gripping as they come. During our Civil War, Ryan was an officer in the Union army, and had left behind a legacy of swashbuckling leadership. He was guided by strong convictions of basic justice for which he wound up giving his life at the hands of Cuba's Spanish conquerors.

I vividly recall an oratorical contest I once entered in high school. My father wrote the script of Ryan's Cuban exploits which I memorized. Part way through my delivery I momentarily stumbled over my lines which pushed me out of the running; yet my message about Ryan's heroics engraved in my memory to this very day the tremendous value of standing up for what one holds dear.

Here is that epic story of General William Albert Ryan.

At the North-South War's conclusion, Ryan was wrapping up mustering out matters preparatory to returning to the rich copper mines he owned in Montana when he was approached by several Cuban freedom fighters. At the time, the late 1860s, Cuba was suffering under the heavy yoke of pillaging and rape by her cruel Spanish overlords.

These Cubans had heard of Ryan's exploits and they were looking for an American with Ryan's qualities of courage, leadership and influence to help champion their cause, a cause much akin to the one that had precipitated our own revolutionary war.

So moved was Ryan by what he heard from these Cubans, that he abandoned his mining plans and devoted the rest of his life to helping Cuba in her struggle for freedom.

He organized numerous expeditions of American volunteer fighters. Led by Ryan, shiploads of these men would land on Cuba's shores and fight shoulder-to-shoulder alongside the Cubans against their Spanish oppressors.

Because of Ryan's great courage and leadership qualities, Cuba's government in exile, headed by his close friend, General Carlos Manuel de Cespedes, Cuba's revolutionary president in exile, made him a general in the Cuban army.

General William Albert Ryan, the Author's Great-Granduncle

On one occasion Ryan arrived with his usual shipload of freedom fighters only to learn of a particularly heinous wave of atrocities that the Spanish had been inflicting on their Cuban subjects. The Spanish army had just got through pillaging several towns, torturing and slaughtering men and children, and ravaging the women.

Livid, Ryan raided a Spanish military stronghold, captured its occupants, scalped them and then defiantly sent gunnysacks full of Spanish scalps to the Spanish military headquarters.

Seething with hatred for Ryan, Spain now plotted for his head. Spain's ambassador in Washington, under orders from the Spanish crown, implored President Ulysses Grant to stop Ryan's expeditionary force activities in Cuba. To his credit, Grant chose to ignore that plea.

Major U.S. newspapers gave heavy coverage to Ryan's Cuban adventures. They dubbed him "George Washington Ryan."

Then it finally happened. In 1873 the U.S.S. Virginius, loaded to the gunwales with volunteer American soldiers led by Ryan, was ambushed by Spanish war ships and captured.

Ignoring desperate high level American and English extradition maneuverings, a Spanish kangaroo court in Santiago de Cuba quickly threw the book at Ryan. Annals show that Ryan demanded his blindfold be removed. He then looked his firing squad in the eye before bullets took his life.

Not satisfied with seeing Ryan's lifeless body, his executioners then cut off his head, impaled it on a sword, lifted it high and marched triumphantly through the streets of Santiago while horses, dragging his bloody corpse, brought up the rear.

My admiration for these three (and many more) ancestors runs very deep.

Author's Note: Once on a business flight in Central America, while Fidel Castro was still in the Sierra Maestra preparing to dethrone dictator, Fulgencio Batista, I was chatting with my seat partner, a Cuban. After telling her the above story of General Ryan, she smiled and said, "My great grandfather, who was your outstanding General Ryan's great friend, was General Carlos Manuel de Cespedes. Not only was he Cuba's president-in-exile, but he, too, died a martyr's death soon after your dear General Ryan's execution. The equivalent to your *Congressional Medal of Honor* is Cuba's *Medalla de Carlos Manuel de Cespedes.* And to this day school children in Santiago de Cuba each year deposit flowers on Ryan's grave."

A book, *The Virginius Affair,* authored by Richard Bradford, goes into considerable detail on the international implications of Ryan's activities in helping the Cubans. I also have a biography of General W.A.C. Ryan written by his brother, a newspaperman. It is entitled *the Life and Adventures of General W.A.C. Ryan, the Cuban Martyr.* One of my twin sons, William Ryan Walker, my wife and I named in that hero's honor. *(See photo.)*

*   *   *

BOBBY RIGGS

In my mid-forties I radically changed professions and went from international market development of chemicals in Latin America to deep involvement in many phases of tennis in southern California.

At one time I sold tennis courts for a builder named George Peebles who earlier had been an accomplished tennis player. A close friend of his was Bobby Riggs, a name very well-known in (and even outside) tennis circles.

Riggs' trophy room was jammed with proof of his world-class court prowess.

It was during the annual National Seniors Invitational Tennis Championships being held in La Jolla, California that the setting of this story takes place.

Peebles and I were watching Riggs demolish a challenger with his pin-point lobs.

Later, George and I were seated outside the tennis stadium having a coke when Riggs walked up to greet Peebles, who then introduced me.

But to digress for a minute to provide a bit of background on Riggs and to set the scene for what was to transpire during our conversation.

Riggs was a delightful con man and a gambler at heart. One of his favorite bet-winning tactics would be to express profound if noisy dissatisfaction over his on-court performance, peerless though it usually was. Such trickery lulled many an unsuspecting opponent into fatal overconfidence by challenging Riggs to a match with money on the line. Customarily, Bobby would come from behind to *barely* eke out a last minute victory. Then shaking his head in feigned astonishment over his victory, he would *reluctantly* hold out his hand to receive his winnings.

And oh how he loved to talk. He was particularly noted for suckering others into unwittingly stroking his ego by ever so subtly eliciting their praise of his court skills.

Now back to the story of my encounter with this tennis legend.

No sooner had Bobby opened his mouth when I heard him, true to form, complain, "Gosh, I sure wasn't playing my best tennis today. I should have done this,

193

done that etc." as he droned on while sadly shaking his head in mock disgust over his alleged court failings.

To give him the satisfaction of yet another victory of deception, I played along. "Oh, I don't know, Bobby," I said in polite disagreement, "your lobs looked awfully good to me."

Riggs, nodding his head vigorously (while no doubt winking to himself) quickly gushed, "Say, they WERE quite good, weren't they!"

* * *

WILLIAM RANDOLPH HEARST

My father never graduated from college. But he excelled in English and, despite being blind in one eye, he was a prolific reader. Among his many qualities he was noted for his steel trap memory. With a gift for writing, he chose early in his career to be a newsman and rose in the William Randolph Hearst news empire to become one of Hearst's top editors.

Examples of his considerable accomplishments are the subject of numerous stories found elsewhere in this anthology, of which this story is but a small part.

While Hearst was still living at his San Simeon Castle, dad was invited to be "Citizen Kane's" week-end guest.

Upon arriving, dad was shown to a large, high ceilinged drawing room by a butler who, after motioning him to a couch, left to announce my father's presence.

As he waited for this man of history to appear, in staggered Hearst's mistress, one-time noted actress, Marion Davies, several sheets to the wind.

She plopped herself right beside Dad and began to snuggle. Large beads of perspiration began covering his forehead as father diplomatically edged away from this job-wrecking time bomb.

Not to be denied, she once again closed the gap with dad quickly moving away as before.

Just as he reached the end of the couch the Old Man strode up and this uninvited lady visitor weaved her way out. Fortunately, Davies' flirtatious ways were not foreign to Hearst so that my father's employment remained intact.

The two men then proceeded with their business.

* * *

A Night with Bob Hope

Back in the early '40s Bob Hope was at the peak of his career as America's premier comedian.

At the time my dad was editor of a large San Francisco daily newspaper. Every year at Christmas time Dad's paper would sponsor a large benefit for Catholic charities at the San Francisco Civic Auditorium.

One year Bob Hope agreed to donate his services as the master of ceremonies. Dad, wanting to be sure that Hope got there on time and in one piece, assigned one of his reporters to stick to Hope like flypaper.

I recall our family waiting by the stage for Hope to arrive, but when it was time for the curtain to go up Hope was nowhere to be seen. Lesser comedians took turns ad-libbing as they stalled for time. Still no Bob Hope. Finally Hope strolled onto the stage and, as usual, wowed 'em.

Later Dad took his reporter aside and asked him, "Why were you guys so late? What ever happened?"

"Fred, you won't believe this," he said apologetically, "but this guy Hope has a personality that just won't quit. First we had one drink, then another and before I knew it we were good and late."

*   *   *

CHAPTER 7

MIRACLES

-----

* See photo

AN ANGEL?

In Hebrews 13:2 the Bible reads, *Remember to entertain strangers because thereby some have unwittingly entertained **angels.***

Accordingly, I wish to relate an incident that occurred to Daryl Smith, the son of Mary Smith, a very dear friend of ours.

Daryl was in our local Bootjack Market ready to pick up some mushrooms when a total stranger walked up to him and said, "I just want you to know that everything's going to be just fine."

"But I don't even know you," Daryl responded.

Speaking again, she said, "Don't worry, everything will be fine, *and don't forget the mushrooms!"*

*   *   *

THE FRANKFURT MIRACLE

My wife and I, at the urging of our missionary son, went through the same evangelism school he had previously graduated from.

We were some 45 adults in our class at YWAM's university of the Nations in Kailua Kona, Hawaii. During that 3-month schooling period we were to change professors on a weekly basis since each instructor taught on his specialty and there were a number of distinct disciplines comprising our course of studies.

The following account, which astounded Isabel and me, we learned about while in Malaysia on Jesus' great commission mandate, "Go ye therefore into all nations," immediately following our Kona, Hawaii studies.

One of our University of the Nations instructors, whose field was prophesy, had kept us students spellbound during our time together. Then he flew off to other scheduled teaching assignments.

Some time later that very same instructor happened to be at an airport in Frankfurt, Germany. To purchase his ticket he handed his credit card to an airline agent. The agent, however, rejected his card and demanded cash payment.

Men of the cloth are rarely overburdened with cash and our hero was no exception. Dejected, he then shared his predicament with his wife and son who were travelling with him. The son said, "Dad, let's pray." And pray they did.

Then following the urging of an inner voice, our protagonist walked over in faith and stood in the same ticket line he knew all too well, an act which most would agree made no sense since he was devoid of the needed cash demanded of him moments earlier.

The man in front of him was a tall gentleman, likewise waiting to purchase a ticket. That person turned around. It was Jeff Coors, recent CEO and president of Coors Brewery, a fellow missionary classmate of ours and coincidentally a student of that very same professor.

Following their warm embrace, Jeff immediately solved our teacher's financial problem. Indeed, Jeff earlier had been that company's CEO, but following his conversion to Christianity, he had resigned to assume the directorship of the non-alcoholic portion of the Coors holdings.

How beautifully Our Lord protects His own, weaving into many situations His own miracles.

*   *   *

GIZELLE

It has now been many years since America became home to Hungarian immigrants, Gizelle and Paul Angeles. Today they are in their golden years.

Paul retired as an aeronautical engineer and has taken on a new role. He waits on stroke stricken Gizelle hand and foot, bathing, dressing and feeding her. Indeed, after he lifts a spoon to her mouth, he must gently coax her to swallow.

For hours Paul will sit on the couch, tenderly holding Gizelle's hand in his as he fondly looks into her expressionless eyes and softly speaks to lips that have not answered him for many years.

Paul says he is an atheist, perhaps because his mentors during his youth may have brainwashed him into believing there was no God.

One day four Christian neighbors asked Paul if they could come over and pray for Gizelle. Surprisingly this confessed atheist agreed.

So with Paul looking intently on, these visitors huddled over Gizelle while they praised Jesus in song and prayer and asked for His blessings on this tender, helpless soul.

Then suddenly Gizelle leaned forward and the same lips that had been silent for so long eagerly spoke out the words audible to all, "Jesus, Jesus." Leaning back, she then lapsed into her own silent world.

Everyone was astounded.

The four callers then bade goodbye, leaving Paul to ponder in the afterglow of that Divine encounter. It was an encounter between Gizelle and her Guest whom she had beckoned into her life during that brief window in time when she had called out, "Jesus, Jesus."

Little did she, or her husband for that matter, realize that those two spoken words guaranteed her an eternity of bliss in heaven. Our Lord's Word in Joel 2:32 unequivocally declares, *"All who call upon the name of the Lord will be saved."*

Author's note: these four Christians were Paul and Elaine Chappell and Isabel Walker and her husband (and writer of this article). This incident took place in Port Hueneme, California, on Thursday, November 29, 1990.

The awesome power of God brings a physical euphoria to each of us whenever we recall, as we often have, that memorable afternoon when Our Lord changed forever the destiny of a helpless and former atheist.

*   *   *

THE ITALIAN MOOSEHEAD

The only clan gathering I can remember our extended family ever having took place at Sequoia National Park's Cedar Grove high in California's Sierras. Our tents, to accommodate the 45 adults and kids in our group, were all pitched together in the same area of this inviting, evergreen-shaded campground. The refreshing sound of the crystal-clear Kings River added to the charm of this vacation setting.

My birthday was celebrated there. And knowing of my love for Saint Francis of Assisi, my wife presented me with a biography of that saint.

One of my young nephews, Peter Huttlinger, hunted around the campground for a gift. Soon he came up to me and said, "Uncle Frank, here is a present for you. It is a moose-head." Whereupon he handed me a small piece of tree bark.

I looked at it and yes, I could make out a slight resemblance to the head of a moose. But as I continued to turn this bark around and around in my hand to see what other shape it might also reveal, suddenly I saw a perfect boot of Italy.

Since Saint Francis was from Italy, I thought Peter's gift to be highly significant and I later framed it as a very special treasure.

Years passed. Then my family was invited to attend the induction of another nephew, Tony, into the order of Saint Francis as a brother. At this particular ceremony Tony took his first vows as a Franciscan.

The night before that sacred event I was scratching my head to try to come up with a suitable gift. Then the light went on… that little piece of bark!

It was not long after that I found it stashed away in a closet. But this time I scrutinized it more carefully than ever on a hunch, a long shot. In so doing I was rewarded with a startling discovery.

Whereas this piece of bark, as with many other similar pieces, contained a number of very small dot-like burn marks scattered in small clusters randomly across its face, there was still something special that caught my attention. One dot was all by itself.

"Could it be," I mused. "Oh no, it just couldn't be. But then it might be. I think I'll check it out."

Quickly I opened the World Book to the section on Italy and looked at the map of that country.

My face lit up. That isolated dot was precisely where Assisi was located!

Written on the back of this framed piece of bark, and presented to Tony, was the above story.

Some may say this was all mere coincidence, and … they might be right.

As for me, however, I have not the slightest doubt, and the laws of probability will surely corroborate, that this "coincidence" was more than coincidence.

P.S.   Pete Huttlinger, by the way, went on to become a world class guitarist with three appearances at Carnegie Hall during this century's first decade already to his credit.

*　*　*

THE GOOD SAMARITANS

My father was a heavy smoker, two to three packs a day every day of his adult life. In his 60s during a routine physical the doctor found a finger-size tumor on his lung. He was told he had "wild oats," one of the most virulent types of cancer known. Dad then confessed to me, "Son, I have no doubt that this was caused by my smoking." That problem spread and ultimately took his life.

Many years later, when I learned that my kid brother, likewise a smoker, was to be operated on for the identical malady my dad had faced, I drove at once to The Veteran's Hospital in San Francisco to sit in vigil at his bedside. Fortunately that operation, a lung removal, was successful.

As I was leaving the hospital for my home in Mariposa I thump-thumped to a stop on nearby Geary Street. My rear tire was very flat. It was Sunday and stores where I might find a phone to call AAA all were closed.

Thus I began ringing door bells of private homes hoping to find a kind soul that would lend me their phone. The first two turned me down flat as my tire. After all, I was a stranger and one can never be too sure about helping out someone you don't even know.

But the third home restored my faith in mankind and mankind's sometimes elusive quality of "Samaritanship." That lady had been Samaritan #1 of this narrative.

I then began what was to be a surprisingly long wait for the help I'd phoned for but that never came.

So I finally found myself having to rustle my 78 year old bones hunting for the jack and then the correct place to put it to where I would not collapse my fender.

Suddenly I was tapped on the shoulder. I looked up at a wide toothy smile and a pleasant, heavily accented voice asking to allow him to change my tire. I was flabbergasted, since minutes earlier other Samaritan hopefuls had passed by without so much as sniffing in my direction.

Soon my car was ready to go and this kind soul, on his own, had even put my demised radial in the trunk.

We fell to talking. In his very broken English I learned that this Good Samaritan (Good Samaritan #2 actually) had recently arrived from his native Kazakhstan. He was Russian.

And was I EVER impressed by this marvelously accommodating foreigner who certainly taught me a valuable lesson, viz. if someone needs help, then help we must give without regard to economic status, ethnicity, religious persuasion or any other condition that otherwise might serve as an excuse for looking the other way.

*   *   *

A Lost Cashier's Check

While my wife and I were still living in the San Fernando Valley situated along the northern rim of greater Los Angeles, I once had occasion to withdraw $2,200 from our savings account in the form of a cashier's check and then deposit it in our checking account at another bank.

I stuffed the check into my shirt pocket, fastened my seatbelt and took off. En route to the second bank, I had several intervening stops to make. The first was to buy gas, then it was for a haircut (or more accurately, because of my great baldness, a neck trim), followed by some shopping my wife had charged me with doing.

Finally I pulled up to the drive-in teller. I reached into my shirt pocket only to find to my horror that the check was gone.

"Yipes," I exclaimed, "whatever could have happened?" I then thought that it probably brushed out of my shirt pocket when I had removed my seat belt while alighting at any one of the several places I had visited earlier.

That day it had been extremely windy meaning the check could have blown away absolutely anywhere.

Worriedly I began to retrace my steps. Hopes of finding that lost money were, I reasoned, dim at best.

No, the gas station manager had not found my check but he promised to keep an eye peeled and he took down my name and phone number.

Next I walked up to my barber, but he too had not seen it.

With mounting gloom, I trudged across the street to where I was parked. I was about to open the car door when I realized to my embarrassment that I had not prayed to The Lord for His help.

So I stepped over to the gutter, knelt down and lifted up a short prayer of supplication. No sooner had I said my *Amen* when an inner voice told me to look down. So I did and saw a nondescript piece of paper, partially covered with mud, right beside where I was still kneeling. It had dirty tire tracks across it. Picking it up, I turned it over.

My eyes widened to rival old "Banjo Eyes" himself, Eddie Cantor. It was indeed my lost check, a bit the worse for wear but still legible.

I made a beeline for my checking account bank where I approached the manager. She motioned for me to sit down and I, all smiles, began to unfold my unlikely story.

Her face was radiant. She kept nodding and saying, "I believe every word you're saying."

"We will certainly honor this check," she gently spoke and as I departed I just knew that she, as did I, clearly believed in the wonderful power of prayer.

*　　*　　*

Drugs and Salvation
(Or How I Became a Jail Chaplain)

This story began when my wife, Isabel, who is fluent in Spanish, was temporarily on staff at a nearby elementary school. Her ESL (English as a second language) assignment was to help several Mexican immigrant students whose knowledge of English was very limited.

More than half of those pupils were members of the large Vargas family.

Shortly after Isabel had completed her teaching contract and left the school, she learned through a fellow teacher, Carol, that Mrs. Vargas had suddenly and inexplicably withdrawn her children from school. Deeply concerned, Carol asked Isabel if she would accompany her as an interpreter on a visit to the Vargas' home. What they learned was shocking.

It seems that Mr. Vargas had overheard drug-dealing conversations and witnessed four skittish men, all trespassers, removing white powder-filled plastic packages from an abandoned well on the same rural property where he worked as caretaker.

When the traffickers saw Vargas eavesdropping they shot at him but missed.

Vargas fled and went into hiding, leaving his family behind. Alarmed over the possibility that her children might be either kidnapped or otherwise harmed by these men, Mrs. Vargas withdrew them from school.

Later on that family became reunited at a secret location.

During this entire episode many people were praying for a happy ending to these disturbing events. Concurrently, several calls were made to Drug Enforcement Agency officials, one of whom was my nephew, who gave assurances that they were already working on this very case and that a raid was imminent.

Not long after my friend, Rocky, who is a prison chaplain, called to ask if I could serve as a Spanish interpreter since a drug operation had just been closed down and its members, who knew very little English, were now behind bars.

So it was that I met face-to-face with those who had tried to kill Vargas.

As the weeks slipped by at the jail I saw, under the skilled and loving hand of Rocky, each of these felons, one-by-one, turn his life over to Jesus Christ.

However there was a hold-out, Pedro, who was cocky, self-assured and who appeared to be the ring leader of this busted drug ring. He was not taking Rocky's message of salvation all that seriously from what I could observe, until, that is, one particular evening.

Rocky had just passed out a brochure on salvation in Spanish and each inmate was taking turns reading aloud from it, while I, following along in English, was checking for translation accuracy.

Finally it came Pedro's turn to read. And so, matter-of-factly, Pedro droned on when suddenly he fell silent, closed his eyes and began to weep. The room hushed, for we all instinctively knew we were privileged observers to a mighty conversion move of God's Holy Spirit. After Pedro had regained enough composure to speak, through a voice that cracked with emotion, but through lips that smiled, he gently intoned, "I'm sorry. I'm too choked up to continue."

During that serene and sacred interlude we all approached Pedro and each in turn joyously hugged his new fellow brother-in-the-Lord.

Another prisoner, Lupe, then resumed reading where Pedro had left off. Lupe later softly confided that he and a fellow inmate had been privately praying for Pedro………. and God had honored their plea.

Even though Pedro might not have been dramatically knocked off a horse by Jesus on the road to Damascus the way the Apostle Paul was, he was nonetheless zapped by the same Holy Spirit. When Rocky could not make it to jail, I would replace him. I thus began my work as a chaplain which this year will be 18 years helping inmates find Jesus as their Savior. *(See photo.)*

And during my witness of this beautiful event, my mind raced back twenty years when, at age 47, I found my Lord and Savior, Jesus Christ, at a religious retreat known as a Cursillo. I remember bawling like a baby while basking in the spectacular elation and grace that enveloped me. It was then that I realized beyond all doubt that I, through faith, had just been saved for all eternity by the sheer mercy and goodness of God, for I knew I had certainly not earned any right to be saved.

I recall vividly on the Monday following that retreat arriving at work still in the afterglow of my heavenly encounter of the previous day. As I made my way past our secretarial pool, I observed all eyes lift in unison and turn toward me. Each face wore an unusually beautiful smile.

That salvation experience, by the way, resulted in a radical change for me. I left a top position in international sales management in Latin America, where heavy travel had been badly straining my marriage, to become a simple low paying tennis teacher in obedience to God's beckoning.

I have never regretted for a moment that decision to ask Jesus into my heart and its consequences, consequences oftentimes involving outright miracles.

Inmates with Author

Then there was the time I was attending the funeral of a dear little nephew. One of my sisters approached me as I stood beside the casket. My arm was in a sling. "Frank," she said, "how is your arm?"

"Mizzie," I told her, "it's been two months now since I've had to abandon my tennis teaching because of severe tennis elbow. I can't even shake hands it pains me so. Cortisone shots did nothing for me."

Miz softly said, "May I pray for you?"

"Be my guest," I answered.

Next thing I knew she was touching my elbow while asking Jesus to heal me.

As she spoke I felt a wave of heat surge through that arm. I removed my ailing limb from its sling, opened and closed my fist, straightened and doubled my arm. All pain had left.

That afternoon I was serving cannonballs serves, just like old times.

Now it is up to the reader to conclude whether or not prayers have power.

As for me, it's no contest.

*   *   *

The Fire

Much of my youth was spent in San Francisco. On our block lived my friend, Gerry Flaherty. His dad was a fire chief. In later years Gerry was to follow in his father's footsteps.

When WW II came I joined the Navy and lost touch with many of my friends, Gerry included, who had joined the Air Force and served with distinction in Europe.

Years later our family moved back to San Francisco to a totally different neighborhood from the one we had left many years earlier. While my sister was unpacking she found a picture of me in a navy uniform which she promptly placed on the mantle-piece.

Shortly thereafter one of the packing crates caught fire and 911 was called.

The firemen bounded up the stairs with hoses and axes. As they burst into the living room one of them, Gerry Flaherty of all people, noticed my picture and quickly said to his men, "Fellows, I know these people. They're the Walkers. Let's take it real easy with the axes."

* * *

God Means What He Says

One day, just after our Sunday church service had concluded, I was standing outside the sanctuary chatting with friends, Frank and Betty Cooke.

"Since I have done a lot of writing," I told them, "I have this burning desire to visit missionaries all over the world to glean from them the miracles they have witnessed while serving The Lord. Then I would plan to write and publish such a collection as a means of bringing glory to God by showing that He indeed is alive, that He cares and that He rewards those who believe in what His Word says."

I noticed a faint smile crease both of their faces, and Frank spoke up. "I believe we have a story that could be of interest but I will let Betty tell you."

And so it was that soon I found myself marveling at the words that flowed from her lips as her eyes flashed in excitement during those few moments when she ventured into her past.

Frank and Betty had just completed a stint as Mission Builders at Youth With A Mission's large missionary training center at Kailua-Kona, Hawaii. On a subsequent mission outreach, they found themselves in distant Fiji on one of that archipelago's many South Pacific islands.

Surprisingly there are still extremely backward areas in Fiji where tribes even today practice cannibalism. And it was precisely to one of those villages that the Cook's footsteps had been directed.

Because Frank and Betty were able to relate to me their Fiji experience, it is to be surmised that white missionaries were not on these natives' menu the day of their visit.

As they entered the cannibal compound a funeral service was in progress. A corpse, swathed in a shroud, lay atop a pile of wood since the custom was to cremate the deceased.

This couple, surely at the urging of the Holy Spirit, stepped forward, laid their hands on that inert body and, in a test of faith, began praying to Jesus Christ.

Those words must have been found pleasing to God since only moments later those same four praying hands began to move uncontrollably as the corpse stirred from beneath and then sat up to the incredulous gasps of the crowd.

God is constantly proving the reliability of His Holy Word. In the book of John, chapter 14, verse 2, He says: *"Most assuredly I say to you, he who believes in Me, the works that I do he will do also; and greater works than these he will do, because I go to my Father."*

This was a crystal-clear example of God meaning what he says simply because two willing souls took Him at His Word and stepped out in child-like faith.

How many more miracles is God holding in the wings awaiting but similar acts of complete trust?

*   *   *

JESUS, OUR CO-PILOT

Ever since my wife, Isabel, and I gave our hearts to Jesus Christ by inviting Him to take control of our lives, we have had simply marvelous experiences.

This narrative deals with some of the R and R trips my wife and I have taken together, with Jesus as our Co-Pilot.

First off, we must say that we have tried to begin each sojourn by remembering to ask Jesus to accompany us, to show us the things He wants us to see, to meet the people He has planned for us to meet and to enjoy the surprises He has in store.

Never have we been disappointed.

Take the time we trailered to Vancouver, B.C. for the 1986 Expo. We pulled in to an RV park on the outskirts of that delightful city, left our home away from home in the trailer spot assigned to us and then took off looking for a family-type café to slake our hunger.

Isabel turned to me. "Honey, let's pray that we find a place run by Christians." With that prayer lifted heavenward, we then began a watchful eye for a clean and hospitable-appearing diner. Soon we were drawn to a place.

We parked and walked in. An Asian lady showed us to a table. We could see another Asian, the cook, doing his thing. Clearly this was a mom and pop operation.

As Isabel perused the menu, I looked around and saw posters, artistically painted, hanging on the walls. Each had an encouraging Biblical scripture located unobtrusively at a lower corner.

"Are you Christians?" I asked the waitress. Her nod and sweet smile was all the answer we needed.

That entreaty to our Co-Pilot had surely been answered. Mere coincidence then or since never crossed our minds. "Thank you, Jesus," Isabel and I softly said as we bent in prayer over our awaiting meal.

- - - - - - - - - -

Our only daughter, Anne, at age 19 had just died in a tragic motorcycle accident. So, following the burial, my wife and I took off for a much needed change.

After visiting lofty Crater Lake in Oregon we were headed down to lower elevations when Isabel, my most competent navigator, suddenly said, "Would you believe it? The map shows that we will soon be passing Annie's Creek. We must stop there."

And stop we did where we beheld the most crystalline stream we had ever seen. What an absolute treasure, for that pure water completely mirrored our Annie's character. Her heart had been just as pure, not an ounce of guile.

The picture we took of Annie's Creek hangs in our home as a reminder not only of our Anne, but, even more importantly, for us to recall Jesus' faithfulness, our inimitable Co-Pilot.

Coincidence to some, perhaps, but certainly not to us.

- - - - - - - - - -

On another occasion we were off on a short vacation which was to take us from our home in Mariposa, a small hamlet near Yosemite National Park, north to Seattle.

Pulling away from our driveway, we, as always, asked Jesus to take over.

Our base of operations during our stay in Seattle was the home of a lovely American missionary and RN, Barbara O'Conner. She had lived for many years in Korea where she won souls the soft-sell way, as a volunteer tending to the health needs of that host country.

She told us that she had developed a particularly strong bond with one of her small Korean patients who had a severe eye problem. Later she was to sponsor that Korean girl enabling her to immigrate to America. But over the ensuing years, our hostess told us with sadness coloring her voice, contact was lost with her little Korean friend.

Now it so happened that our son, Frank Jr., who had been a full-time YWAM missionary for many years, asked us to look up his dear missionary buddy and best man, Jim White. He gave us Jim's Seattle address and phone.

We called Jim who, happy over our arrival, said he would drive over to see us, a considerable distance in this greatly-spread-out city, Jim living way at Seattle's southern end while we, some 25 miles away, were about as far north as you could get and still be in greater Seattle.

I put our hostess on the phone so she could give Jim directions. It wasn't long before her jaw sagged in utter disbelief. Jim knew precisely where she lived because he, in earning sorely needed monies for his sustenance as a missionary, was doing a remodel of a home whose back yard abutted the very home where we were staying!

But that wasn't all. After Jim walked in and our hugs and greetings finally gave way to conversation, Barbara found herself repeating for him what she had earlier related to us about her close Korean friend with whom she had regrettably lost contact.

"What is her name?" Jim asked.

When she told him, Jim then said, "She is quite fine. I know her very well. Saw her only recently. She calls me 'Uncle Jim.' Presently this girl lives in Alabama with her adoptive parents."

Jim smiled while the three of us, eyes bugging out, remained speechless.

Coincidence? Hardly. Jesus' fine hand was there with yet another cheerful and, in this case, astounding surprise.

We encourage our readers to invite Jesus to come along the next time they travel. They won't regret it if our experiences mean anything!

*　　*　　*

JOE

My New Orleans telephone rang. Miz, my kid sister, was calling from Alexandria, Virginia.

"Frank," her voice quivered, "My Joe is dying in the hospital. Can you come?"

Soon I was winging my way eastward.

She led me to her husband's bedside. With all the machines that were hooked up to him it was obvious that medical science was keeping him alive artificially, and that Joe was in big trouble.

The doctor shook his head sadly as he spoke of the gloomy prognosis while we both gazed in deep pity at the unconscious patient.

I learned that Miz had been incessantly praying for Our Lord to heal Joe of his hopeless condition.

Then Joe unexpectedly bolted upright, bright eyed and ready to take on the world. In no time he was back at work.

The doctors, astounded, stammered in their amazement.

With a gentle smile, Miz confided, "Frank, I know exactly what happened. For the longest time my prayers had been focusing on Joe's recovery. But I finally realized that I was being terribly selfish.

"So I sorrowfully came to God," she confessed, "with this amended prayer, 'Lord Jesus, I must apologize for pleading for Joe's life when you probably have other plans for him. So I now yield to your wishes and ask that Your will, not my will, be done. I give you my Joe if You wish to take him.'

"It was right after that new prayer on that wonderful day that Joe was miraculously and instantly healed," Mizzie confided through a radiant smile.

And it was then that I too learned the very same lesson my sister had learned, viz. *When you pray, ask that God's will, not your will, be done,* because in so doing you may be in for a most pleasant surprise as certainly happened on that momentous day.

*　　*　　*

Our lovely nineteen-year-old daughter had just died in a tragic motorcycle accident and our youngest son had run away from home.

Grieving and broken, Isabel and I took an R and R and trailered to Oregon. Soon we had found a delightful spot just beside the scenic and fish-filled Umpqua River.

We parked our trailer at a well-maintained park facility amidst evergreens. The air was pure and fragrant and we were filled with the wonderment of God's marvelous creation.

It wasn't long before my artificial flies were hitting pay dirt. But my goal was steelhead and not the smaller rainbows and browns that were filling my creel.

So when the park ranger stopped by our home on wheels I recall asking him what the secret was to catching the elusive steelhead. "Well," he said with a twinkle in his eye, "if you promise to watch your language I'll introduce you to a neighbor of yours right over there. He's a pastor and a superb steelhead fisherman."

Before I knew it this fine man of the cloth, with me right behind him, was wading chest high in the mighty Umpqua, showing me where the big ones were by gracefully arcing his fly toward his favorite holes and riffles.

I found myself confiding a sorrow over my son's running away from home. "Let's pray," he softly said.

With water rushing around us, we tucked our rods in our armpits and, holding hands, he lifted up a beautiful prayer to the Lord beseeching the return of our son, Marc.

Later, our day's fishing done, I saw Isabel running from the trailer to greet me. "Guess what," she enthused, "I just called home. Marc is back!"

Wide-eyed, I asked, "When did he return?"

The time was precisely when we had been praying, right in the middle of the Umpqua's majestic waters that momentous Oregon afternoon.

But that uplifting experience was not all that Our Lord had in store for us because, anxious to do battle with the fabled Umpqua steelhead, the very next day I made a beeline for those river hot spots my mentor had shown me earlier.

In no time my line snapped taut. My streamer had fastened onto what, because of his aerial, tail-walking displays, I could easily see was a VERY large steelhead.

For the ensuing 45 minutes he took me downstream, repeatedly breaking water and stubbornly refusing to succumb to the pressure of my severely arcing ten foot 7-2/3 ounce H.L. Leonard split bamboo salmon rod.

Finally my adversary decided to sulk behind a rock in midstream some 35 yards away in water far too deep and swift for wading.

Then it was suddenly over. My line had gone slack. That trophy fish had won. I stopped to applaud for he indeed had earned his freedom.

Still filled with the high emotion of the moment, I temporarily placed my fishing vest, which contained all sorts of valuable tackle, on top of my truck's tool box and, completely forgetting it was there, I drove off.

No sooner had I arrived back at the trailer when my palm slapped my forehead. "My fishing vest," I gasped. But too late. It had blown off the truck.

I retraced my route but no luck. Someone had picked it up.

Next I found myself doing two things in an effort to retrieve my lost treasure. First I prayed asking the Holy Spirit to touch the person who found my vest with the desire to return it. And secondly I placed an ad in a local paper in nearby Roseburg.

Two weeks later back in our Los Angeles home far to the south I answered a long distance phone call. "Did you lose a fishing vest?" the voice asked.

Once assured that I was its owner, this model of honesty confessed that he, quite frankly, had been tempted to keep it, but then his conscience got the best of him.

True to his word, he mailed me the vest with nothing missing inside its many pockets.

That trip to Umpqua was indeed memorable for the things, of course, that vacationers customarily enjoy, but those two highly unique bonuses, bouquets I prefer to call them, from Our Gracious Lord who had blessed that R and R with very special meaning.

*   *   *

MIZZIE'S DOVE

My sister, Mizzie, has had enough tragedy in her life to keep Job company. Two of her eight children died early. Then her husband succumbed tragically, leaving Miz with six young ones. Later two of her adult sons died by their own hand.

Ultimately she became an alcoholic. Fortunately she did something about her problem and joined A.A. That was many years ago and she has not touched a drop of liquor since then.

Attending A.A. meetings several times a week, Miz became an accomplished speaker and brought comfort and hope to many.

One particular A.A. evening after she had spoken to an assembly of alcoholics she felt a strange urge to approach a visiting married couple. "Could you help me?" she implored. "I've had this cloud of gloom hanging over me now for many years."

They immediately responded to Mizzie's plea and invited her to their home.

When Mizzie arrived next day, she was asked to go back to her earliest childhood memory and try to recall from that moment forward all the times people had injured her feelings. She was to state each offense and then to vocalize her forgiveness of all persons involved.

She began the torturing assignment while her hosts read from the Bible in another room.

This exercise took one full, heartrending evening as she recalled such incidents as when a man of the cloth had violated one of her young sons. There were numerous other moments equally as devastating.

When finished, Mizzie thanked them and left, feeling a certain sense of relief.

The following day while in the kitchen, she had the inexplicable desire to step out onto the back patio. No sooner had she done so when a white dove from out of nowhere lit at her feet. At once Mizzie said she began to experience an upwelling of enormous joy that swept through her entire body.

She called her sons out to see this cooing dove that would not budge from her side. Forty-five minutes later the phone rang and Mizzie went in to answer it. Minutes later she raced back out to be with her feathered visitor, but the bird was gone.

However its gracious calling card of great peace and joy has stayed with my dear sister ever since.

How wonderful indeed is Our Lord's Holy Spirit.

*   *   *

I Never Left You

Our youngest son, Marc, was 10 years old when a landmark event took place. We were living in Woodland Hills, California at the time.

Marc and his circle of friends were not much into things Biblical.

Then something quite significant happened whose full import I was never to appreciate until years later. Very early one morning Isabel and I were shaken awake by a euphoric Marc. "Dad, mom!" he yelled excitedly, "I've just got to tell you about a dream I had tonight. Aunt Sheila and I had gone to the Fallbrook Shopping Center where we noticed a crowd gathered around a man. When we got closer I saw that this man was Jesus. And oh, dad, oh, mom, his eyes were so beautiful and full of so much love."

We bolted upright in bed for Marc now had our complete attention. He was truly ecstatic and his eyes were wide open and fairly glistened with excitement.

"I heard someone from the crowd yell at him, 'Jesus, why did you take so long to come back?'" Marc continued.

"And dad, mom, do you know what Jesus answered?

'I never left you'."

When this occurred, through our ignorance of the Bible, we did not attach too much weight to the vision experience Marc had just shared with us.

But as Isabel and I got deeper and deeper into God's Holy Word the significance of Marc's vision started to take on great meaning.

And today, many years later, there is no doubt in our minds that Marc had received, and was unwittingly passing on to us, a message from God, a message out of Joel 2:28, whose importance at the time Marc had been totally unaware of, a message that says, "Young men shall see visions."

And equally dramatic was the second Biblical message from Matthew 28:20 where Jesus promises, "I will never leave you nor forsake you."

Marc today, at 39 years of age, is on fire for the Lord and is very much into His Word. And his father was to become a jail chaplain.

How faithful indeed is Jesus who never gives up knocking on our hearts. May His name be praised forever!

*   *   *

THE PRISON MIRACLE

While still a tennis teaching professional, I remember going to San Luis Obispo with my dear wife, Isabel, on a weekend R and R. Actually a collateral reason for that trip was to visit Charles, the son of one of our neighbors. Charles was doing time for seven counts of armed robbery in a nearby maximum security prison known as California Men's Colony or CMC for short. Many inmates there were in for heavy offenses and included members of the infamous Charles Manson Gang.

As we were leaving the prison, I spoke with a prison official about my possibly engaging in a voluntary tennis teaching program there. That conversation ultimately led, following routine clearance checks, to my being accepted and an all-day tennis seminar was scheduled.

I later learned I would be host to a group of inmates, tennis enthusiasts that affectionately dubbed themselves, "The Racketeers' Tennis Club."

Upon arriving with racket, balls and much instructional paraphernalia, I was met by my sponsor who helped me through various security checks. Following routine paperwork, we were driven in a state car around to a massive two-story-high side gate. It closed behind us, and after more routine inspections, a second and equally imposing gate swung open.

Finally we were within the prison's inner sanctum and moments later our car pulled up to a classroom where I was helped in with my gear.

The class was some 25 strong, all tennis buffs. A prison reporter and cameraman were also present.

Over the next eight hours it was strictly tennis and I must say those students were among the most attentive I have ever taught.

During the morning session a few in the audience had to leave the classroom. They must have spread some kind of word that I had passed their test, because when we later broke for lunch, prisoners who were not even in my class were smiling and waving in my direction.

Because I had asked the Lord for help in preparing for this session, all glory and praise I give Him for whatever favorable acceptance may have resulted.

At noon my sponsor took me to the staff dining hall and over lunch explained, as he apparently was required to do, that the inmates all know full-well that if any visitor is taken hostage during a breakout attempt, the guards are under orders to shoot regardless. I gulped and thought, "Hey, thanks a lot!" But I figured the odds of my being so involved were slim.

Class then reconvened and we went to one of the prison's four quads, which are outside recreational areas. This one had a baseball diamond, two tennis courts and vast amounts of wall area ideal for tennis ball hitting practice.

The lesson I chose to give was on the serve. So I first demonstrated and then one-by-one I had each inmate execute while I dictated my correctional hints to a

216

scribe. That way the student would have a written Rx for future reference as a self-help aid.

One student, a massive and muscular type, ran up panting. He was late. Soon he was demonstrating his serve to me. His form was close to being perfect and his power awesome, but all his balls were hitting the tape. I said encouragingly, "That is very good," not wanting, for self preservation reasons, to incur his wrath. Then I offered a few suggestions. He listened intently and resumed serving. I was amazed. They were now all going in and with a velocity that touring professionals would have envied.

There is indeed great talent behind prison walls.

From the court we returned to the classroom. At one point one of the students, a man in his thirties, remarked that what I was saying was all well and good but he was too old to learn.

That then gave me the opening I had been hoping for, so I explained that I got into tennis late in life, at age 47 to be exact, made possible thanks to Jesus Christ. Previously I had worked for many years in Latin America developing farm chemical markets. I commented that if I could learn this sport with our Lord's help at such an advanced age, certainly they, who were younger, could at least do likewise but probably a lot better.

Just before the day ended, the president of the Racketeers Tennis Club invited me to return as keynote speaker at their upcoming annual banquet and I accepted.

Back home I began preparing for what I would speak about and decided on the title, "How Jesus Christ Got Me Into the Tennis Business."

The day of the banquet came. I arrived early so I would have time to visit my friend, Charles, beforehand. To gain entry into the prison one must go through a metal detecting frisker. During that probe it was necessary to remove my keys, belt, coins and even my shoes because of the metal lasts. So while holding up my beltless pants I finally made it through without sounding the alarm.

After seeing Charles I waved at my guard friend, the one who had frisked me, and left the prison since I had a couple of hours to kill before returning for the banquet.

I headed for a local hotel, sat down in the lobby and wrote out my speech notes onto small crib cards, while Satan (I was later to realize) was looking over my shoulder at what I was penning while plotting a way to foil my plans to glorify Jesus.

With the dinner commencement hour fast approaching I drove back to CMC and noticed that many visitors by then had arrived to attend this same tennis banquet.

I was the last to go through the security frisker, everyone before me having breezed by the detector without incident. Before attempting to walk through the hoop detector I said to my guard friends, "Fellows, I know what I have to do," since I had done it only two hours earlier.

So off came my belt and shoes, and my coins and keys I withdrew from my pockets.

With supreme confidence I started through the hoop. To my amazement the bell rang. I turned to the guards and said, "I can't understand this at all. I repeated the identical procedure that got me through a short time ago but now the bell is sounding.

One of the guards suggested that I run through. I tried that. No luck. More alarms.

Finally a guard approached with a hand-held detector and began passing it over my body. He started high and worked his way down in a zigzag motion.

It was only when he got to my shins that the warning bells began clanging. He looked at me quizzically and remarked, "Do you think you might have metallic thread woven into your pants?"

"Beats me," I said. "Let me roll up the bottoms." But once again the familiar warning sounded.

We looked at each other speechless. I then proceeded to remove my socks and once more neither could believe his ears when the room again filled with ringing.

This led him to ask, "Can you recall having had any operation on your shins where metal pins may have been implanted?"

"Never," I replied.

Shaking his head and with a smile he waved me on through.

Delighted over Satan's failure to stop me, I went in and witnessed for Jesus Christ.

At the banquet's conclusion I approached that same guard who earlier had used his detector on me and asked if anything like that had ever happened before.

Shaking his head he replied, "I've worked here for twenty years and this is the most baffling case in my memory."

However, had that guard known of my intention to extol Jesus at the banquet and of Satan's utter hatred for the Savior of the World, then the reason for all that bell ringing would have become as obvious to him as it was to me.

*　*　*

A Spectacular Healing Miracle

I had just pulled up to my sister Miz's home in Danville following a seven-hour drive from southern California.

As I stepped from the car, I noticed Miz, arms ladened with dresses, emerging from her front door.

"Oh, Frank, how wonderful to see you. I am on my way to deliver these dresses. Could you please accompany me while we talk," she said with a smile.

As we drove, a fascinating story began to pour from her lips.

The person we were headed to see, Marion Burgio, was to select one of these dresses to wear during a guest speaking engagement at an upcoming Katherine Kuhlman revival and miracle healing in Los Angeles.

What now follows is this lady's story as initially told to me by my sister Miz, and later embellished by 60-year-old Marion Burgio herself with further details by Marion's husband, as I sat listening, totally rapt.

For sixteen years crippling arthritis had confined Burgio to a wheelchair, culminating with her doctor's prognosis that she had but two weeks to live. Legally blind and with severely impaired hearing, this pitiful creature, her face ashen with skin hanging in loose folds, was then told that her faltering heart would probably give out in two weeks.

Realizing he was on the brink of becoming a widower, her husband was now desperate. He had read that a Katherine Kuhlman miracle healing service was scheduled soon in his area.

The day of the service saw dying Marion Burgio being pushed by her husband into the absolutely packed auditorium and over to the wheelchair section.

Numerous healings were occurring that evening. Suddenly Katherine Kuhlman's voice dramatically announced that a woman in the wheelchair section was at that very moment being cured by Jesus Christ of crippling arthritis.

As Kuhlman spoke, Marion Burgio felt a warmth sweep through her body. This was followed by the uncontrollable urge to get up. Completely dumbfounded, Mr. Burgio then witnessed his wife bolt from her wheelchair, run down the aisle and up onto the stage.

She had been instantly and miraculously healed.

Miz eased to the curb just as she was concluding the above story. "Frank, could you wait here for just a minute. I'll be right back," she assured, while leaving with her armload of dresses.

In no time Miz and a spry, radiant Marion, arms locked together, to my utter astonishment, came skipping toward the car. After introductions were complete, Miz and I were invited in.

Her husband entered the living room and soon both he and the protagonist took turns recounting, as well as elaborating on the other's statements, all that had transpired during this astounding transformation. So excited were they during their telling that each would sometimes unwittingly interrupt the other in their enthusiastic determination that no detail be left out.

The lady I saw and heard and speak was so strikingly different from Miz's description of how she had looked before the Kuhlman experience, that quite frankly I was both flabbergasted as well as deeply honored to hear all of the particulars. God had obviously done a simply awesome body overhaul.

The woman I saw was vibrant and appeared easily able to do battle on a tennis court. Her skin was smooth and fairly glowed. Her once blind eyes now clearly saw and, although she had been practically deaf, I witnessed a woman who had no difficulty in hearing everything that was said. And no longer was her formerly distressed heart condition a problem.

Thus, it was anticlimactic for me when my wife, my sister and I attended a subsequent Kuhlman revival at the large Shrine Auditorium in Los Angeles and, along with ten thousand others, heard Marion Burgio's testimony in person, a testimony which by then had become very familiar to me.

And on stage she was wearing one of the dresses that Miz had brought her.

In retrospect, I feel certain that the great key to Kuhlman's phenomenal success as an instrument of God's awesome healing powers was her deep faith in and unwavering acknowledgment of Jesus Christ, not herself, as The True Healer.

* * *

OUR RETIREMENT MIRACLE

At one point in our life our family's finances were doing so poorly that we were two months away from being out in the street, literally. My building business had been struggling. We had to sell our home to gain working capital just to stay afloat and now all that money was gone. Our church pastor even took up a special collection for us.

Within that same time frame I awakened very early one morning and was on the verge of dozing off when I had a vision. I saw a freshly plowed field of rich brown soil and in that field were many green shoots sprouting all over. As suddenly as this picture flashed before me came its immediate interpretation. The caption below it read, "I will make all things new." Later I was to learn that this message was right out of Holy Scripture's Book of Revelation.

Then things began to happen. Overnight my handwriting, which for sixty years had been almost illegible, changed to copperplate calligraphy.

Not long after, during a Sunday morning service in our newly-found church, Jack Hayford's Church on the Way, a member of our prayer circle gave my wife and me a scripture for our financial plight. It was Joel 2:25 and 26. We started to pray this daily and slowly our poverty-headed worm began to turn.

Within a year and a half we were able to make a down payment on a modest Los Angeles home. Providentially, that seemingly mediocre piece of single-dwelling property was located in an area which the city's master plan (we were to learn) had slated for rezoning to permit apartments.

So I began the long process of trying for a rezoning which, if successful, would allow me to add four apartments to the rear of our dwelling.

My first hurdle was overcome when the city's zoning commission gave their approval. I figured (erroneously I was to learn) that the rest of the red tape would be a piece of cake and I fully expected my councilman to give his okay rubberstamping the zoning commission's previous green light.

Much to my surprise this did not happen. I appeared before that councilman during a public, full council hearing in L.A.'s downtown city hall. His voice boomed out over the p.a. system. "Mr. Walker, you will have to come up with better arguments than these or I will reject your petition."

My case was then continued and I returned home, concerned but bound determined to give it my best try.

My efforts had me going to neighbors and getting their signatures of approval.

But my biggest argument was to be the nearby university's endorsement. My plan was to have them give me a letter stating that they heartily favored low cost off-campus rental housing which mine planned on being.

When I told them I needed this letter to strengthen my arguments to my councilman in order to gain his nod for my rezoning project, I was momentarily puzzled over their refusal. (Later, however, that puzzlement was to be amply clarified.) Nonetheless, the university did say that even though their enrollment was

30,000 students, they only had on-campus beds for 650. This was an argument I was later to use.

The morning of my continued case arrived. Well before the session began I found myself saying a brief prayer asking the Holy Spirit not only to guide me as I committed my arguments to paper but also to make my councilman receptive to them. Then I dashed off some twelve points designed to bolster my position.

Once in the expansive, marbled, high-ceilinged meeting room I approached my councilman's assistant. I read him my arguments and he told me to be sure to read them when my turn came.

Soon I found myself again on the hot seat, eyeball-to-eyeball opposite my chief stumbling block.

I inhaled ready to start reading my points when I was abruptly cut short. "Mr. Walker," he intoned. "Don't read a word." Heavens, I thought, I'm sunk. He won't even permit me to present the arguments he had previously instructed me to prepare.

Just then his assistant approached, leaned over the councilman and said, "Mr. Walker has some points he would like to bring to your attention."

"Oh, very well," he sighed impatiently, "Proceed, Mr. Walker."

No sooner had I finished reading the one dealing with the university's serious lack of student beds when the councilman bellowed his interruption, "Mr. Walker, if you think you have enhanced your cause with that argument you are sadly mistaken. It so happens that I have repeatedly tried to help that university with its student housing problems but they would not listen to me."

It was then that I realized I had unwittingly placed myself in the middle of an ongoing battle between the university and this man.

After he had vented his anger and his facial color had cooled from bright crimson down to pink, he, clearly still quite irritated, said impatiently, "Please continue, Mr. Walker."

When my presentation ended I looked up knowing full-well that I had lost. However our eyes never met. His were strangely cast down at the table.

Then I received the shock of my life. "Mr. Secretary," he uttered in a whisper, "I wish you to record my approval of this project."

I was flabbergasted. At once I said a silent prayer of thanks to the Holy Spirit who obviously had been in full control without my councilman even realizing it. For all the world it seemed as if this man had just been led, like a bull with a ring in its nose, against his own will.

The end of this saga saw our property rezoned and sold at a very handsome profit which allowed us to retire sooner than we had planned and to enroll in YWAM's missionary school.

Clearly there is a God who is faithful to His Word, His Word which says *"You have not because you ask not."*

May His name be praised.

*　*　*

GOD STILL SPEAKS

Our son, Frank, once told us of an incident which occurred while he was a missionary doing volunteer construction at Youth With A Mission's world headquarters in Kona, Hawaii. The project Frank was working on was the erection of an important Christian university. And now, years later, that seat of higher learning, known as The University of the Nations, has graduated many students who have gone on to do Our Lord's work in the missionary field all over the world.

However at some point during that construction assignment Frank agonized over whether or not he was in God's will.

One night quite late Frank was tossing and turning, not able to sleep. So he decided to dress and take a walk.

Presently he heard a voice calling him by name. "Frank, look up."

Frank obliged.

While his head was tilted skyward, his eyes contemplating the star-lit heavens, the voice asked, "Frank, do you see those stars?"

"Yes," Frank replied.

"Well," the voice from above continued, "I placed each one where I wanted it and you I have also placed where I want you."

CHAPTER 8

JOURNALISM

-----

* See photo

SILENT CAL

My father, after having established an outstanding track record as a young newspaper reporter first in Oakland and later in San Francisco was hired by International News Service (I.N.S.) to be their man covering the White House and the Hill. At the time I.N.S. was a William Randolph Hearst world-wide wire service and a major competitor of both U.P. and A.P.

Shortly after my father arrived for his new assignment, the dean of Washington, D.C.'s Press Corps put his arm around dad who, at 23, was among the youngest newsmen in our nation's capitol.

"Freddie," he said, "How would you like to meet President Coolidge?" Dad, of course, was flattered and readily accepted.

As the two walked into the Oval Office and up to Coolidge's desk, the older press man addressed our country's leader, "Mr. President, I would like you to meet …….." but he never finished his sentence.

The president looked up, saw dad, and enthused, "Why Fred Walker, how in hell are you?"

Then he buzzed for his press secretary who immediately appeared and heard Coolidge say, "Please meet Fred Walker. He knows what news **NOT** to print."

It seems that dad had been among the bevy of newsmen following Silent Cal during his re-election campaign. And although muckrakers were busy writing derogatorily about Coolidge's private life, father had chosen not to stoop to that level.

Coolidge never forgot that. Indeed, not infrequently the President was to call dad into his office. On one such occasion as my father approached his desk, Coolidge, whose feet were on the radiator that wintery day, motioned for Dad to sit down beside him.

"Fred, put your feet up on the radiator," he began. "I know what you guys are writing about me, but tell me, what are you **saying** about me?"

Coolidge was smart enough to realize that the press at times omits important items from their stories, just as he remembered dad had previously done (to the president's eternal gratitude).

Was dad merely lucky to have enjoyed Cal's friendship? Or does the following of higher principles have its reward?

(See Coolidge's autographed photo plus a letter from that president.)

*   *   *

Picture and Note from President Calvin Coolidge to Author's Father

THE WHITE HOUSE
WASHINGTON

August 16, 1923.

My dear Mr. Walker:

Of course, I remember you and the
incident connected with my visit to San
Francisco. It is a pleasure to know that you
have some ties which bind you to the western
part of Massachusetts, and I want to extend to
Mrs. Walker and yourself my sincere thanks for
your good wishes.

Very truly yours,

Mr. Fred J. Walker,
Cosmopolitan News Service, Inc.,
21 Spruce Street,
New York, N. Y.

National Press Club of Washington

THIS CERTIFIES THAT

Mr. _______________________

has been elected an ______________ Member of
the National Press Club of Washington.

_______________________ President

_______________________ Secretary

Letter from President Coolidge

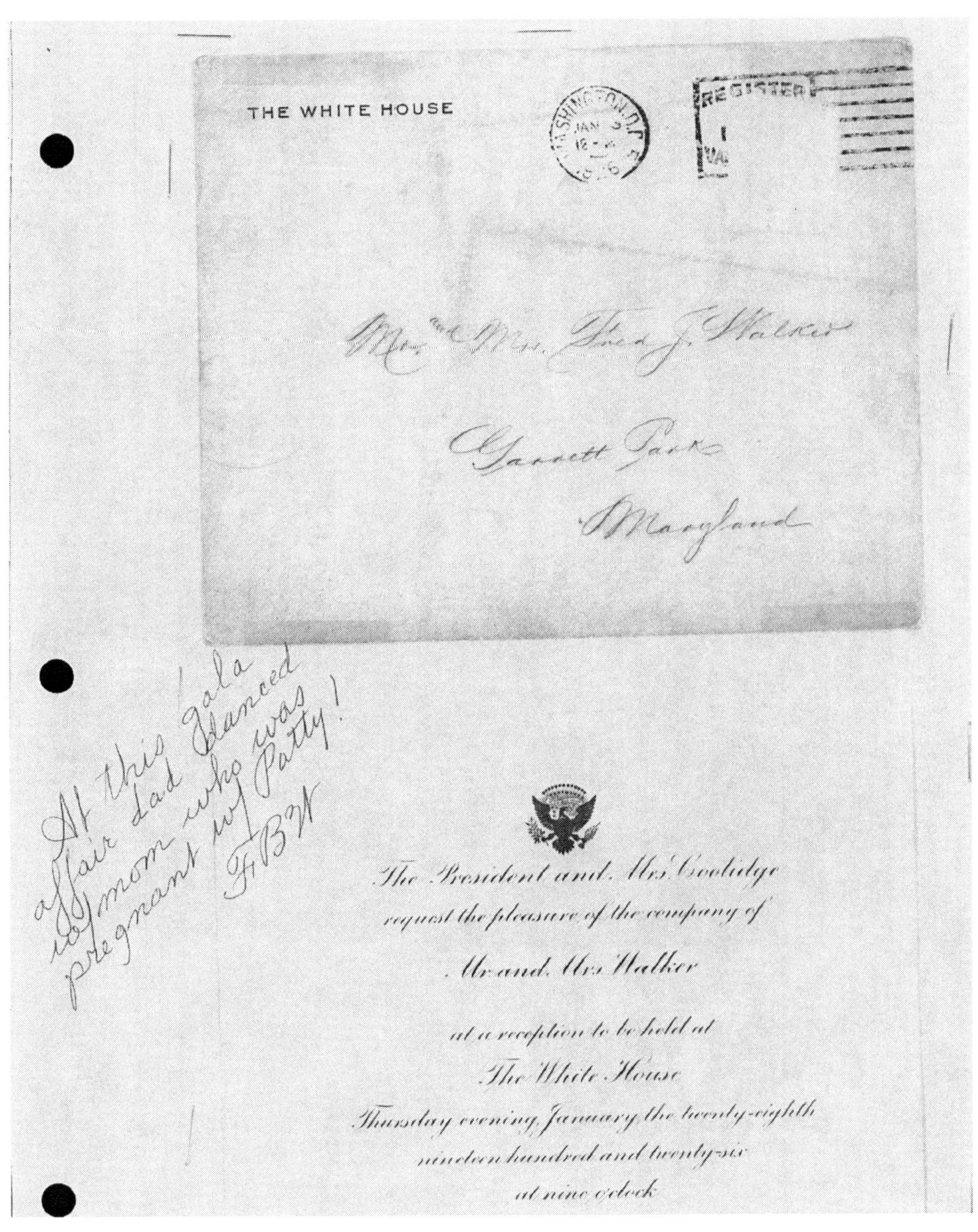

White House Invitation

With my father, Fred Walker, in the middle, standing. Gable on right.

Clark Gable with Author's Father, Fred Walker (standing)

During the 20s my father was International News Service's Washington, D.C. correspondent, covering the White House and the Hill.

In that period a story of international importance broke. It was the famous Billy Mitchell court martial. Newsmen from around the world covered this breaking story.

General Billy Mitchell had become one of the most controversial figures in American military history, primarily because he had the audacity to insist that air power was destined to compete on an equal footing with that of the army and navy. Subsequently history overwhelmingly validated Mitchell's position.

Jealousies within the armed forces set the scene for court martial proceedings against General Billy Mitchell on the grounds of insubordination. Among those sitting on the court martial board was General Douglas MacArthur who, to his credit and despite his famous ego, voted for Mitchell's acquittal.

Dad was familiar with civil courtroom language, as were the other numerous reporters, but not with military parlance. So he researched it and in the process found a major difference between the two which was to result in a world-wide news scoop, later to be written up as journalism at its best.

In civil court if the defendant is guilty the jury spokesperson so reports using the words, "We find the defendant guilty." But during a military court martial, a guilty verdict is announced differently. "Are there any prior convictions to the accused?" are the tip off words preceding the announcement of a defendant's guilt.

During Mitchell's trial the result right up to the end was too close to call. Dad, therefore, wrote two separate stories, one, he's guilty, and the second, he's innocent.

He handed both stories to his teletype operator down the hall from the courtroom. By prearranged signals, the operator would send the guilty story if Dad wiped his brow and the innocent version if he scratched his ear.

The courtroom was absolutely jammed with reporters, both domestic and foreign, as all awaited the verdict with pencils poised.

At the instant Dad heard the words, "Are there any prior convictions to the accused?" he wiped his brow and the guilty story hit the wire.

As the clock ticked away, all other pencils remained at the ready without anyone else in the press corps realizing that Mitchell's guilt had, in so many words, already been declared. Later when a translation of the court martial findings was made for the laity, the reporters dashed for telephones while dad smiled over his huge scoop. *(See photo.)*

Billy Mitchell Standing at His Court Martial. Author's Father, Third from Right, Hair Parted in Middle, Covering this Blockbuster Story for International New Services.

* * *

THE CHASE

It was the fall of 1945 in San Francisco. World War II had ended earlier that same year. One hundred and twenty-seven countries had just signed the final document that brought the United Nations into existence and ushered in what was designed to be an era of world peace, security and the betterment of mankind.

So justifiably it was time to celebrate. And San Francisco had just the place for the gala event of the century, the stately, world famous art museum, the California Palace of the Legion of Honor.

Long lines of Rolls Royce's and vehicles of like opulence waited to discharge their heads-of-state and jewel laden, be-furred companions.

Inside, the clinkings of stemware rang out everywhere, along the marbled floors, under the Rembrandts, Rubenses and Picassos that graced wall after wall.

Secret Servicemen were out in force to provide security for this unusually large gathering of world leaders to say nothing of the high society and Who's Who top names adorning the guest list.

The press, both domestic and foreign, was well-represented.

My father, then City Editor of San Francisco's leading newspaper, the Call Bulletin, had sent his crack rewrite man and cameraman, Johnny Keyes and Murray Fay, to cover this international event, thereby adding two more clinkings to this august occasion.

Keyes was conducting interview after interview to the company of Fay's frequent flashes. Suddenly they both stopped right in the middle of a routine interrogation and quickly excused themselves.

For there, only partially concealed behind a potted plant, was a Secret Serviceman, taking an unauthorized recess from his duty of guarding a foreign president, in a passionate embrace with a woman.

Off went Fay's flash. Our casanova, no doubt fearful of losing his job (and possibly a wife) as well as causing bosses several levels above him to pound the pavement with him, yelled frantically, "Give me that film!" and the chase was on.

Picture if you will this glittering setting with the world's crème de la crème standing around in small clusters while two newsmen, running in overdrive, are careening around corners, knocking down Lord knows who, with oodles of vintage champagne spilling down many a gasping royal bosom.

Just as lover boy would almost catch up with Fay the baton would deftly be passed to Keyes. And so it went.

Along the way other Secret Servicemen joined in the pursuit.

At one point Keyes grabbed a priceless Crusader's sword from a wall and held off (by then) the not-so-Secret Servicemen in order to buy time for Fay who was dashing pell-mell for the exit.

The next morning Ed Coblenz, the Call Bulletin's publisher, called my dad into his office. "Say, Fred, what's this all about? I got a call from the Secretary of State all hot and bothered over a picture."

*　*　*

The year was 1945. The place, San Francisco. The United Nations was in the process of coming into existence.

Up for consideration was whether or not to admit Poland, a Russian satellite, with full voting rights. Those who opposed argued that Russia would receive an unfair voting advantage if Poland were admitted with separate voting rights.

So during the lengthy debate on this issue the world press correspondents (and they were many) filed their daily stories. Most of them were copying the prestigious New York Times which pontificated its conviction that Poland indeed would be admitted with full voting privileges.

At the time my father was city editor of the San Francisco Call Bulletin. And each day the headlines of his paper would blatantly insist that Poland would not be admitted.

The reason for the Call Bulletin's unwavering position was due to the homework my father had been doing in anticipation of this crucial question. He knew that historically the British were masters of diplomacy and international savvy.

So Dad cultivated a friendship with Great Britain's delegate, Francis Thompson.

Now it so happened that in the marketplace bananas were in short supply and Thompson just loved bananas. And just as coincidentally he would often find bananas on his doorstep, courtesy of the Call Bulletin.

Father, deeply respecting Thompson's views on the Poland matter, kept asking him how he thought it would turn out. Each time Thompson would reply that a snowball in hell would stand a better chance than Poland.

Deeply troubled with the Call Bulletin's position going counter to most of the other newspapers, publisher Ed Coblenz would call Dad into his office and grill him, "Fred, are you absolutely sure of what you are doing?" To which father would reply, "Cobby, just wait and see. Our pipeline is lots better than that of the New York Times and its numerous copy-catters."

The Poland decision was finally announced. Their voting rights were denied. Hastily most of the red-faced correspondents were forced to issue retractions, while the Call Bulletin buffed its "I told you so" nails.

Frequent scoops like this one helped explain how it was that the Call was number one in circulation among its San Francisco competition, The S.F. News, S.F. Chronicle and S.F. Examiner.

*   *   *

THE MURDERESS

One of the reasons, I'm sure, why my father became such a good newsman and editor, apart form his considerable innate skills, was because he settled on a career very early in life, and then stuck to it.

In his late teens dad left home, largely due to incompatibilities with his new stepfather, his own father, an inventor, having died when dad was but a boy.

From early youth dad had a flare for writing yet he never was to graduate from college. His very first newspaper job he got while in his late teens as a cub reporter with a Portland, Oregon newspaper. However, lack of experience got him fired after but one week.

His second job episode at another daily met with the same fate.

However by then he had gained enough savvy to where the third time around his employment stuck.

But, longing for bigger city action, his itchy feet soon landed him in San Francisco in the early 20s where he attempted to join the San Francisco Examiner. "Not enough experience," the city editor told him.

Not to be deterred, he traveled across the bay and called on the Oakland Tribune where he was hired as a cub reporter.

Shortly thereafter a big story broke in San Francisco. A notorious murderess, one Winnie Judd, had escaped prison back east and had fled to the west coast only to be recaptured. She was being temporarily held, incommunicado, in a downtown San Francisco jail. This woman had been guilty of multiple killings. Her homicidal m.o. was somewhat unique, especially for a woman. One by one each of her several husbands she would murder, stuff each body into her car trunk and then dump it at a lonely spot.

A Chicago sheriff had flown in to San Francisco to bring her back to prison. He was there just long enough for the extradition paperwork to be finalized. While seated just outside that prisoner's cell door, this lawman was flatly refusing all interviews by the clamoring press.

Undaunted by that obstacle, dad got permission from his city editor to buck the odds and to try anyway to interview this murderess. Still smarting from his job rejection by the San Francisco Examiner, dad was eager to scoop the Examiner on this story in that paper's very own backyard.

A gift of gab is an asset in this business and my father had that talent. He approached the sheriff and, appealing to that man's sense of self-worth, introduced himself as a writer who wanted to tell the story of his heroism.

In the scene that followed, dad had talked the sheriff into releasing the killer and then he accompanied both prisoner and captor to a nearby photo studio to be photographed.

Next, he taxied them to dinner at a fancy nightclub, where dad wound up dancing with this assassin and getting her complete story.

Well, imagine what must have hit the fan when the next morning the San Francisco Examiner saw they had been scooped on this blockbuster story by the very man they had earlier refused to hire.

It was little wonder, therefore, when the Examiner subsequently lured my father away from the Oakland Tribune where he continued to make a name for himself with the same resourcefulness, drive and writing skills his new city editor had previously learned about the hard way.

Dad's star was rising fast. And it was not long before he was approached by George Holmes, a top executive with International News Service. Then a major wire service, INS was part of William Randolph Hearst's news empire, as was the Examiner.

The job he was offered, and which he wound up taking, was to be INS's correspondent in Washington, D.C. covering the White House and the Hill.

He continued to distinguish himself, not infrequently with scoops of great international import to include the world-famous Billy Mitchell court martial where he got the drop on every single one of the many papers and news agencies, both domestic and foreign, covering that extremely high profile case. President Coolidge used my father as one of his press confidants.

But the launching of his success-studded career he owed in no small measure to a dance he once had with a murderess back in San Francisco.

*　　*　　*

A Police Reporter

During my grammar school days how well I recall looking up at the towering frame of my dear father as he shaved, and listening, rapt, to his exciting tales as a police reporter with the San Francisco Examiner.

236

The following accounts come to mind.

Back in the 20s the Chinese Tong Wars were still aflame in San Francisco's Chinatown. Since my father's assignment was, as a police reporter, to accompany the police during their raids and investigations of reports of violence or other public disturbances. Father was given a police badge plus a key to the police phone boxes and a 38 automatic, some of which I inherited and then passed on to my sons.

In those years secret, mafia-type Chinese gangs thrived in San Francisco. They dealt in white slavery, racketeering, gambling and narcotics. Frequently warfare would erupt between competing gangs for this lucrative underworld business.

Dad described to me the amazing network of underground tunnels lacing that San Francisco district known as Chinatown. Often father would follow close behind the police as they answered a report of a shooting. Not infrequently they would pull a rug away in a living room to expose a trap door leading to a tunnel and then make their way, sometimes for blocks, before emerging through a second door into another home during their pursuit of criminal suspects.

Once, dad, who was quite fearless, was along with the police chasing a killer. With gun at the ready he kicked down a door ready to shoot it out if necessary, only to see a curtain fluttering in the breeze. The suspect had fled.

Those were indeed exciting times and were part of dad's early training as a reporter, training which ultimately lead to his becoming a nationally known and respected editor within the William Randolph Hearst newspaper empire.

*   *   *

THE *CALL BULLETIN*

Back in the thirties my dad was West Coast Editor for International News Service (INS). His office was in the same building occupied by a sister William Randolph Hearst news-gathering organization, the San Francisco Call Bulletin.

At the time, dad was a well-seasoned newsman with a long list of credentials to include much reportorial work for a number of newspapers during his early career, to wit INS's correspondent covering the White House and the Hill; owner-publisher-editor of Pittsburg, California's only newspaper, the Pittsburg Post Dispatch; city editor of Hearst's large Chicago daily, the Herald American; West Coast Editor simultaneously for King Features Syndicate and Central Press; and night world news editor for INS at their corporate headquarters in New York City.

He was very well-read, had a steel trap memory and I recall his awakening every morning at 4:30 a.m. to devour all of San Francisco's newspapers cover-to-cover before leaving for work despite being blind in one eye.

Dad had been groaning for some time over the Call Bulletin's constant muffing of big news stories, a key reason why that paper was fourth in circulation among San Francisco's four daily newspapers. One day after noticing a particularly painful mishandling of an important story, he could no longer keep silent. So he called up Lee Ettleson, the Call Bulletin's Managing Editor, and said, "Boy, Lee, you guys sure dropped the ball on that one!"

Lee, still smarting over what had happened, and knowing of dad's background, growled, "Well, Fred, do you think you could have done any better?"

"With my eyes closed, Lee," he confidently retorted.

That very day dad was offered, and accepted the job of city editor of the San Francisco Call Bulletin, in the process leaving his INS post. Within one year he took that paper from last in circulation to a dominant first. His competitors at the time were the San Francisco News, the Chronicle and the San Francisco Examiner. And the Call Bulletin remained the top paper for the ensuing period of his editorial direction, some seven years.

There were many facets to his success. A few, of which I am aware, include: a sound knowledge of what is news; integrity; outstanding writing ability; dynamism; extreme loyalty to and appreciation for his staff; an unusually keen ability of sizing up people; and the acquisition and skillful directing of top writing talent.

Unlike too many executives who, perhaps because of their own insecurity, shy away from hiring people whose skills exceed their own, dad's philosophy was much different. He was drawn to all who had the potential of making his paper a success.

In the process he acquired great writers. One of these, Jack MacDowell, was awarded the Pulitzer Prize and went on to be press secretary for the then California governor, Ronald Reagan. My father favored those whose education was strong in English and history. Journalism majors oftentimes made him wince because, he would sigh, "I not infrequently would have to undo some of that learning and replace it with *school of hard knocks* journalism. So, much better is for me to mold a well-educated person, who never formally studied journalism, to my journalistic ways."

Writers that my father had trained were in demand nationally and readily found work in such cities as New York and Chicago. One of his talented rewritemen, Thayer Waldo, went on to become a writer for Atlantic Monthly and subsequently joined the internationally famous, syndicated columnist, Drew Pearson, as

238

correspondent covering the River Plate countries of South America (Argentina, Uruguay and Paraguay) with base in Buenos Aires.

He always told us (we were six children), "Kids, never get into this business. It's not for you." However we all grew up with certain writing proclivities and most of us have been published.

My admiration for my dad will continue until the day my final curtain goes down. *(See photo.)*

Author's Father, Fred J. Walker, at Work as City Editor of the *San Francisco Call Bulletin*, Defending one of His Reporters

* * *

A San Quentin Execution

San Quentin Penitentiary near San Francisco had scheduled a gas chamber execution and each newspaper was allowed to send two reporters, but cameras were forbidden.

A photographer for the San Francisco Call Bulletin owned a special spy camera made to look like a pocket watch. Its lens was innocently located at the center of the winding stem.

My father, then city editor of the Call Bulletin, thought this would be a marvelous opportunity to smuggle in a forbidden camera and scoop the other papers by running an exclusive picture of the condemned as he was inhaling the deadly cyanide gas fumes.

So the reporter, and the cameraman who would be posing as the Call's second reporter, began practicing until they had their bit of deception down pat.

The day of the execution arrived. Reporters were crowded around the small, octagon-shaped, amply windowed death chamber, which chamber I personally happened to have seen on a subsequent occasion and can attest to its chilling, pale green colored eeriness.

The protagonist was lead into the chamber and then strapped to one of the two death chairs. When the warden nodded, the pellets were sent sliding down a tube toward their lethal destiny, a container of sulfuric acid.

Soon the condemned's head jerked backward. At that precise moment the Call's reporter, on cue, coughed to mask the click of his cohort's hidden camera whose tiny lens was barely visible as it poked through the buttonhole of the photographer's coat.

Next day the Call was ready to run the exclusive picture when dad had second thoughts since the warden, Clinton Duffy, was his personal friend.

He picked up the phone and called Duffy. "Clint, this is Fred Walker. I've got a picture of the execution which we are planning to run. But if it will hurt you, I won't print it."

"Fred, it would hurt me," Duffy replied, his voice a blend of sadness tempered with gratitude.

"Enough said, Clint. Consider the picture killed," sighed my dad… and he was true to his word.

* * *

THE PARTY

My father, a newspaperman, once wrote me about a San Francisco party he had attended. His humor shone through many of his writings, this one included.

"We were invited to the Mitchells for a musicale and drinks, arriving at 5 p.m. Mitch had two punch bowls working. One was authoritative, consisting of X gallons of whiskey, brandy, rum and sulfuric acid. The other was a champagne deal suitable for delicate old ladies and there were plenty of them present.

"I fortified myself with three slugs of Old Taylor beforehand and approached the punch bowl in the calm manner of Casey stepping up to the plate --'There was ease in Casey's manner, etc.' Well, Sir, that first jolt just about ripped off my head three minutes after it went down. It was a delayed reaction. A guy named Kelley, and whose nose testifies to his skill at bellying up to the bar, confided later that Mitch really had something. It developed that Mitch's formula was one gallon of hundred proof to one drop of water. Mitch explained modestly that a punch was no better than its ingredients.

"Outside there was a colossal jam of Rolls Royces, Bentleys, Mercedes in their private driveway, two stories above Broadway, with Cadillac relegated to the street. Looking down to the driveway below it seemed to me I saw chauffeurs shooting crap but this was after several drinks and I could be wrong.

"Anyway, the director of Rome's Sistine Choir (it was that fancy a shindig) sits down at the piano and a medium sized dame stands up and announces her first number. Pianist glares at her occasionally but she manages to complete three or four songs and then starts to retire. I clapped like mad figuring Mitch's punch deserved that much of an accolade. She cheerfully returned and then confided to the audience that she was suffering from a cold. Sistine Choir wearily hauled out another piece of music as she announced the final number."

*　　*　　*

JAPS SINK OUR TANKER

One week after the Japs bombed Pearl Harbor a Japanese sub sank an American tanker just off the coast of Santa Barbara.

The accompanying Call Bulletin second front page award winning picture records the high drama rescue effort of survivors of that sinking who were still struggling in the boiling surf.

This spectacular, exclusive picture was obtained thanks to the resourcefulness and ingenuity of my father. The laconic teletype flash of this torpedoing received by the Call Bulletin in San Francisco provided no time for this huge breaking story in order to be able to rush a cameraman all the way to Santa Barbara.

So by phone my father located a Santa Barbara photo studio proprietor and contracted him to close his studio long enough to rush to the shore and capture this one-in-a-million picture.

Thus it was little wonder when the Call Bulletin was awarded the coveted Hearst award as the nation's best illustrated newspaper. *(See photo.)*

Sinking of the Montebello

* * *

CHAPTER 9

NON LATIN AMERICA

A Paris Hotel
Pierre's Fangs

A Paris Hotel

Pierre, a Parisian artist, is my wife's brother-in-law. While still residing in Brazil, our family decided to vacation in Europe. So Pierre wrote to say he would line us up with a few rooms in a small family-style hotel near their apartment just off the Etoile.

Now you have to understand the kind of guy Pierre is. Generous to a fault, loving and one who goes out of his way to be helpful.

But he does have his moments of distraction and therefore is not always as thorough as he could be, and this story is about one such time.

So here we were, eight strong, five young children, Mamena our duenna, Isabel and I, at Orly, tired and scruffy as we piled out of our plane following the long flight from São Paulo, Brazil.

Once through customs and after a taxi ride into town, we pulled up to our hotel.

No sooner had we entered the lobby when our eyes snapped to twice normal size as they followed scantily clad men and women, in a steady stream, scurrying from one room to another.

Clearly poor Pierre in his haste had unwittingly booked us into a hotel with brothel overtones.

We strained to suppress our smiles as Pierre, red-faced, hastened to find us more appropriate quarters elsewhere.

* * *

PIERRE'S FANGS

Two of my sons and I were being driven by my French brother-in-law, Pierre, from Paris to Switzerland.

Our mission in Switzerland was to arrange for hotel accommodations for our two families as well as to reserve space in a nearby Swiss health spa for my ailing father.

Pierre was behind the wheel, happy and carefree. He is a real joy to be with and our memories of that trip are pleasing ones.

With all of our goals accomplished, we headed back to Paris to pick up our respective families. Pierre was once again at the helm. Through the countryside we motored, singing or in animated conversation with Pierre the perfect Dr. Jekyll.

That is, until we hit the outskirts of Paris.

Then the dog-eat-dog traffic started to swirl around us and we observed a sinister Mr. Hyde transformation take place before our very eyes.

Pierre's smile began drooping. His shoulders uncontrollably hunched over the wheel. His eyes closed to mere slits while his incisors we expected to grow into Dracula-like fangs at any moment.

As we looked around us, we saw that all the other cars were steered by Pierre clones.

We were back in the mad car jungle. We were back in Paris!

*   *   *

CHAPTER 10

WWII

* (Photo only) – Father and Son
The General's Birthday Dinner
Mother Martin
The Navy Joker

The Author, Home on Leave after WWII, and His Father

*   *   *

It was at the close of World War II in Manila. My U.S. Navy boss had just left for home and civilian life leaving me, a fresh ensign, in charge of the Navy's cargo office.

Navy ships in that bustling port had to be constantly loaded and unloaded. Stevedores had to be arranged for and my checkers I finally was forced to arm with .45s to thwart the theft-designs of gangs that had been bullying my crews and making off with cargo I had been charged with protecting.

These were tough times in post-armistice Manila where ruin and poverty were rampant. It will be remembered that the Japanese, in conquering the Philippines, had severely bombed Manila. Later, during Uncle Sam's successful liberation efforts, our forces were obliged to bomb heavily leaving poor Manila, already badly shaken, virtually devastated.

Thus many were left homeless and had to scrounge just to survive. Makeshift huts were everywhere. One of the government warehouses overnight lost two of its corrugated iron walls to such scrounging. It was a rectangular building located on a remote peninsula with only two of its walls being visible from the road that passed in the distance.

The remaining two walls could not be seen and hence were fair game for marauders alert to the flawed protection system in place at the time.

The ritzy jockey club fronting Manila Bay had been wiped out. It was there that the U.S. Navy had subsequently built its Philippine Sea Frontier headquarters and where my navy officer colleagues and I were housed.

We ate quite well since our base commander was a close buddy of the admiral charged with supplying all navy troops in the Pacific war theater. "Hey, Joe," his message would read, "Can you divert another reefer? We're getting low on prime rib." White vested Filipino waiters, towels draped over their forearms, served us in the officer's mess (Navy lingo for our dining room). Our tables, covered with starched white linen cloths, had everything but candles and chilled champagne.

I remember our officer's club calling me one day and ordering an LCM full of booze. So I contacted our supply depot in Subic Bay and before long those happy hour refreshments were on their way. But just before this precious cargo was to be offloaded the order was cancelled. Apparently somebody had goofed since it had been finally discovered that the officer's club already had plenty in stock.

So the LCM, with me standing nearby watching, did a 180 and headed back to Subic. Next to me was Bill, a visiting friend, drinking all this in. He was an old high school chum who was then an army officer barracked near Clark Field not far from Manila. "Frank, how is this possible?" he moaned, salivating and watching with pain written all over his face as the LCM departed. "Liquor on our base is in real short supply and here you guys are turning it away because you have so much. One of history's great injustices!" he groused.

"Bill," I said, "I hope you can stay for dinner." He readily accepted. After finishing our gourmet meal and while over coffee and cigars he stammered, "Fffrank, I'm not at all sure that you realize how privileged you really are. It's not that I wish this on my worst enemy, but I'd like you to be my guest for dinner just so you can better appreciate your good fortune."

"Any time, Bill. Just say the word."

A week later, Bill called with the invite. I piled into my Jeep and sped off to my dinner rendezvous with Bill.

"I'm sure glad to see you Frank. Just wait till you taste our slop. It will probably include horse (next word censored)," Bill intoned, his jaw firmly set and mouth drooping in disgust.

Into the mess hall I was ushered with Bill bringing up the rear.

Now it so happened, much to Bill's incredulity and chagrin, that it was his base commander's birthday and the general's staff had ordered all the usual slop put away and in its place as a surprise to all, we were served one of the most sumptuous meals I could ever recall savoring.

"Boy, you guys sure live it up, Bill," I exclaimed with tongue in cheek. "Why this food is absolutely marvelous, ambrosia fit for a king. You lucky devil, you. What's the idea of putting one over on me like that?" I continued, delighting in every minute of my contrived soliloquy as I simply poured it on.

"But Frank, honest, this meal is terribly unusual. Why I'll bet we aren't served something as nice as this but once or twice a year at the very outside! You gotta believe me," he apologized, furrowing his brow purposely to stress his sincerity.

"Yeah, Bill, I'll bet," I chortled as I swung into my Jeep.

"Thanks a million, Bill, for a memorable evening of simply superb food," I shouted back through a wide smile while taking off in a cloud of dust leaving poor Bill shaking his head and muttering to himself with words that must have gone something like this: "I just don't understand it. We were supposed to have the customary swill. And to think that Frank has now left, convinced that all of our meals are Michelin four star like tonight's."

*   *   *

MOTHER MARTIN

My long-time pal and college chum was Jack Unsinn. He was a delight to be around and his ingenious mind was always coming up with unique pranks to pull.

He once talked me into being his accomplice in probably the most exciting escapade of all.

During the initial stages of WW II we were attending a U.S. Navy V-12 college study program at Gonzaga University in Spokane, Washington. One of the campus dormitories, De Smet Hall, had four floors. Jack and I roomed together on the second deck (we called the floors "decks" and used other navy terminology as sort of a warm-up to our impending war-time overseas assignments).

Each deck had one of its own residents, called a "mate," assigned to keep the rest of the guys in line.

Many of us were just dying to put a fast one over on Martin who was mate of the fourth deck. Martin was so motherly that he early on became known as "Mother" Martin. He would practically tuck each of his men in at night.

Then one evening after taps had already sounded and lights were out Jack and I crept up the "Ladder" (stairs) bound for the fourth deck. Our navy caps were tightly pulled down to help conceal our identity and we wore long black G.I. issue raincoats to complete our disguise.

Slithering into the "head" (bathroom) we filled a large bucket with water and, staggering out with it, headed for "Mother" Martin's room. We then carefully leaned this five gallon container against "Mother's" inward swinging door.

Next, Jack lit a firecracker and tossed it through Martin's transom. The explosion was deafening.

We bolted for the ladder barely ahead of that deck's occupants who had already begun to pour from their rooms and mill about along the hallway, while "Mother," sopping wet, was angrily barking orders.

In no time we emerged at the second deck only to hear voices from above crying down the stairwell, "They went to the second deck!"

248

Knowing we had to protect our fellow second-deckers from being tainted with the guilt from our dastardly deed, we quickly sent up a buddy to the fourth deck to confuse our identity. He walked up and down the hall whispering, "They came from the third deck."

Next morning at 5:30 a.m. we were all lined up to begin our customary calisthenics. The Chief Petty Officer barked, "Okay you wise guys, who did it?" For you see, dear "Mother" Martin was frightfully upset and in matronly fashion, with hands on hips and nostrils flaring, had reported the incident to higher authority.

Most everyone knew that Unsinn and Walker were the culprits but no one so much as let out a peep.

The Chief Petty Officer issued dire threats of cancelling liberty unless and until the guilty ones stepped forward.

Silence reigned (but liberty grounding happily was never imposed).

It was only on the eve of our graduation that lips were unsealed. By then, "Mother" Martin had regained his composure and --- even cracked a smile.

*　　*　　*

THE NAVY JOKER

During WW II I was in the U.S. Navy, shore-based in Manila, working out of the Port Director's office.

That city had suffered greatly, first when the Japanese bombed and captured it and again when the U.S. liberation forces drove the enemy out.

Because of such devastation, we largely had at our disposal only make-shift latrines.

One particular day with dysentery being rampant, saw long queues of desperate Navy men anxiously awaiting their turn outside our latrine.

Inside was a long plank with a series of holes in it that served as toilet seats. Beneath the plank was a trough of running water.

Now the Navy would not be complete without at least one practical joker. So by that definition, our Navy was complete indeed.

Waiting his turn at the trough's upstream end was one such wise guy. When the seat vacated he quickly lit a large wad of paper and stuffed it through the hole.

As the fiery ball traveled down the trough and under the bottoms of these deeply concentrating GIs, in rapid sequence almost reminiscent of the military order to "count off" they bolted into the air with assorted yells of "Whoops, ouch or hey" which conveniently helped to mask the snickers of our joke perpetrator.

What happened to the prankster after he was discovered is another story.

CHAPTER 11

PATHOS

The Flower Girl
Silent Dialogs
The Fleeting Castle
Lung Anybody?
Thank you

THE FLOWER GIRL

My little 5-year-old granddaughter, Megan, was in her room sobbing away. Worried over her daughter's wailing, Renda rushed to Megan's side, put her arm around the tot's heaving shoulders and tenderly asked, "Dear, what seems to be the matter?"

With tears rolling down her cheeks, Meggie looked searchingly into her mom's eyes and replied, "I want to be a flower girl. Do you know anybody who is getting married?"

It was not long after that incident that her favorite uncle, William, a bachelor, came to visit Meggie.

Running up to William, Megan blurted out, "Uncle Will, when are you getting married?"

*   *   *

SILENT DIALOGS

My son, Will, and I had pulled into the Clovis Community Hospital parking lot where we soon were asking our way to the admitting desk.

Then while Will was busy being processed for his scheduled medical procedure, I found a comfortable sofa in an adjacent lounge area and began studying the operation manual for my newly-acquired portable scanner. This little electronic marvel, about the size of an overgrown pen, amazingly can scan up to 1,000 pages of text before needing to be down-loaded to a computer to make room for the next scanning foray.

After a few minutes into my learning assignment I chanced to look up. Two ladies seated close by were in animated conversation. Their facial expressions, alternating from joy and silent laughter to commiseration to deep interest, easily spoke to the close friendship they enjoyed with each other but without an audible word being heard during their all-consuming tête-à-tête.

Focusing on their hands, I noticed their fingers were going a mile-a-minute, like miniature whirling dervishes, as they carved into the air their noiseless comments. Presently the sofa opposite me received three visitors, a father and his two hamburger-clutching tots.

While these kids munched away, dad was talking to them, but despite my hearing aids turned up full blast, I couldn't hear a thing. The little girl was juggling her hamburger in one hand with its meat, onions and tomatoes oozing out and ready to fall. The nimble fingers of her free hand were dancing in response to her daddy's finger-spelling message.

Suddenly, the other kid's deportment had incurred his father's displeasure. Shifting his attention to the offender, pop started lecturing him with scowls and blurring fingers of admonishment, as any caring parent is want to do. Matters were set straight right then and there.

And had I not looked up when I did I would have missed this delightful interlude, this peek into the silent world of the deaf.

*　*　*

THE FLEETING CASTLE

We had just left Biscarosse in southwest France and were headed back to Gourbera, our temporary vacation headquarters located two motoring hours south of Bordeaux and but a short distance from the Pyrenees. Pierre de Gasztold, my wife Isabel's French brother-in-law, a professional artist, was driving.

"Say, Frank," Pierre asked, "could I impose on you to take some photographs of a series of murals I recently did at a castle not far from here?"

Immediately I responded, "Pierre, I'd be delighted. And I'm sure Isabel and our son, Will, would be equally happy to admire your work."

It was not long after that we pulled up to a locked gate which opened, following Pierre's brief words on the intercom.

The long driveway, shaded from the hot mid-summer sun by two rows of massive oak trees whose branches interlocked over us, led to a three-story castle that fronted on the wide and quietly flowing Adour River.

Presently we were climbing the ancient stone steps to an imposing and equally ancient stone castle.

The owners, a retired couple, showed us into a high-ceilinged drawing room which had been Pierre's work place for some two months of full time effort. We all gazed in open-mouthed admiration at Pierre's four-wall masterpiece which I then proceeded to photograph in great detail.

Next we were given a tour of the downstairs whose furnishings, room after lavish room, virtually oozed affluence.

Our excursion ended in a hunting room on whose walls hung, among other trophies, a massive boar's head.

The heat that day was muggy and oppressive and all of us were terribly thirsty. One in our party finally asked for a drink of water and our hosts, with seeming reluctance, then brought a much welcomed tray with drinks.

As we drove off there was a sad emptiness that pervaded our car and for the longest time no one said anything. The utter materialism, the inordinate attachment to things temporal had been so totally obvious to all of us. I, for one, asked myself, "Do these people believe in the eternal tomorrow? They certainly are wealthy, but then so was Howard Hughes and look at how he spent his last years."

Isabel, whose French is absolutely flawless, was the first to speak. "How pathetic," she mused. "Earlier I overheard our hosts whisper disparagingly about our group with condescending remarks and intonations."

"Pierre," I said, "during those two months when you were creating your showpiece at the castle you must have savored some very tasty meals."

Quickly, he responded with sadness in his voice, "Frank, not once was I ever offered anything."

I looked back for a short moment at their "fleeting you-can't-take-it-with-you," castle which housed a fortune in objet d'art.

If ever there was a need to weep it was then.

*   *   *

The beeper my 62-year-old brother, Jim, had been wearing for the longest time finally went of. He picked up his oxygen bottle and, on lungs that were barely working, he huffed and puffed his way on level ground out to his car.

A lung donor had just been found.

Following more than four hours of surgery at San Francisco's U.C. Medical Center, Jim was wheeled into the coronary section of intensive care sporting a new lung received from a 21-year-old donor.

Two days later I visited Jim. He was seated in a chair beside his hospital bed, rosy cheeked and wearing a broad smile. I had not seen him looking so good for years. My amazement showed as I, wide-eyed, smiled right back at him.

Presently a nurse entered and asked Jim to put his finger into a device she carried which measures oxygen content in the blood. "Completely normal," she happily announced.

Then Jim said, "You know, Frank, the other lung from the same donor went into a woman who, by the merest coincidence has the same identical birthday as mine, Feb. 18, 1932!"

Later I called Jim and learned he had returned home. "Frank," he enthused, "I'm off oxygen now and the oxygen content in my blood registers 99, even though 97 is considered normal."

"Praise the Lord," I said to myself, "another miracle of medical science in cooperation with the life-saving generosity of a donor."

Then my mind raced back to 1978. On the phone was a staff physician at the San Bernardino County Medical Center announcing that our 19-year-old daughter was in the I.C. unit in critical condition.

Our family piled into the car. Shortly after arriving we saw that her severe head injury required that she be on a ventilator and other life-support systems.

It was then that we learned the devastating news that her EEG which measures brain activity showed straight lines. In other words, she was brain-dead. We soon had a second EEG performed which confirmed the prior test.

Gently, the doctor told us that Anne's driver's license indicated she wished to be an organ donor in case of her death.

The hardest decision we ever had to make as a family now confronted us.

But we all knew we had to respect our daughter's wishes.

And so it is that parts of our dear Anne live on in the bodies of others and we are just as proud of her as we know the family of the lung donor must be by unselfishly allowing brother Jim and his birthday twin to receive new leases on life.

*   *   *

THANK YOU

This is a story about a cat, just an ordinary nondescript cat. We first saw it at our front door, scrawny, all its teeth weren't there and fur was missing in patches. The poor thing looked like death warmed over.

My dear wife simply could not ignore this feline's plaintive mews that asked for help.

Almost at once "Billy Boy," as we dubbed him, had become an official member of our household and was loved by all.

He ate like a horse but never gained the weight we were hoping would hide his pitifully prominent ribs. When we took him to our fine vet, "All Creatures," his skin and bones appearance was diagnosed as thyroid-related and medicine was prescribed.

But the very next day, to our shock and great sorrow, dear Billy Boy we found dead, lying in the street near our home, the victim of a car or perhaps an unfriendly animal. Exactly how he died we'll never know, nor is it important that we do.

At least we were comforted with the thought that he had spent his last days knowing he was loved.

Billy Boy we then buried, shed a tear over his grave and prayed a prayer of thanks to our God for bringing him into our lives.

Since his thyroid medicine bottle was still unopened, we took it back to All Creatures where Dr. Eileen Bissmeyer, gave us a full rebate.

And now for the heart-warming finale to our Billy Boy saga. In the mail we received a lovely card of condolence from "All Creatures" with touching notes not only from Dr. Eileen Bissmeyer, but also from each member of her staff.

Such compassion came as a most welcome surprise. It made our day and the sweet fragrance of its impact still lingers.

CHAPTER 12

TENDER

BABY ON THE WAY

I was waiting at the Ewing Wing's nurses' station at Mariposa's Fremont Hospital for the convalescents to finish up their bingo so I could play my scheduled medley of harmonica tunes for these dear shut-ins.

Near me was an elderly man in a wheelchair rolling quickly toward a restroom while repeatedly shouting, "Hurry, another baby is on the way."

One of the nurses soon approached him, gently placed her hands on his shoulders and, while locking her eyes onto his, ever so tenderly told him that he was having a dream.

Then with the bingo game finally over and the cards collected, I proceeded to belt out a series of tunes ranging from church, to old favorites to classical.

Later, as I was leaving, I couldn't help but reflect on the demanding life of a hospital nurse and how I admired their dedication, their kindness and devotion to duty.

How fortunate indeed are these convalescents to be blessed with such loving care.

*   *   *

THE ORAL HOOP

We had just pulled in to UC San Francisco's sprawling medical center after a three-hour drive from Mariposa.

While my son, Will, was tending to business there, I plopped into a lounge chair to wait for him.

Nearby sat two medical-smocked Asians in animated conversation, which they frequently interrupted with boisterous guffaws as they contemplated their soon-to-be-revealed dastardly plot.

One of them held a wadded paper ball. A few feet away, slouched and snoring loudly, was the object of their scheme, a woman, face pointed ceiling-ward, her gaping maw, like a basketball hoop, inviting a free throw.

The ball-wielding prankster made several warming-up, pumping motions with his missile, sighting in each time on his target in anticipation of letting fly with a potential one-pointer.

Clearly he was encouraging his growing number of tittering spectators to dare him to consummate his evil intent.

So I stood up, fished in my pocket for a coin, found a dime and defiantly tossed it onto the carpet. More giggles.

Not to be outdone, another observer immediately upped the ante by letting a $5 bill flutter to rest beside my measly ten-cent piece, whereupon the whole place erupted in peals of sustained laughter.

But all that happy noise came to an abrupt halt.

Our snoring oral hoop had awakened!

In a sense it was true that our fun had been interrupted, yet something far more important had occurred. A camaraderie had been born among people who, moments earlier, hadn't even known each other, nor cared, and all because of a snoring oral hoop.

*　*　*

OH FOR A CAMERA

Our seven-year-old grandson, Nick, was in children's court together with his grandmother, his uncle, his parents and custodial lawyers.

The judge, a kindly soul, was reviewing the case. Finally he pronounced that Nick could return to his mommy and daddy. Then, excusing himself, his honor retired to chambers.

Soon he returned with a fluffy teddy bear which he handed to Nick. The little lad, overjoyed, cried out, "Oh, thank you," as he threw his arms around the magistrate in a hug of gratitude.

The judge beamed, the bailiff beamed, the lawyers beamed, the entire court was beaming.

….. and no one had a camera to capture that precious moment.

*   *   *

EUNICE

This is a story about a friendship. Eunice is a nurse working at Mariposa convalescent facility known as the Ewing Wing at John C. Fremont Hospital. We first met her after she had befriended our esteemed, longtime companion, Mamena.

Mamena was 97 and a cripple when she first entered the Ewing Wing. At once a close bond between Eunice and Mamena was established as that dear nurse lavished her love on our ailing nonagenarian, who responded in kind. We saw this very special relationship blossom during our frequent visits.

Because Mamena only spoke Spanish and Eunice but fractured Spanglish, a new language developed between the two. Mamena had difficulty saying, "Eunice," so the closest she could come was "Lunes," a name Eunice grew to cherish. My wife and I then began calling Eunice "Monday" because that is what "Lunes" means in Spanish.

Once, as my wife and I were entering the Ewing Wing, Monday ran up to us excitedly, hardly able to contain herself. "Do you remember George, one of our mute patients?" she asked.

"Why sure we do," we replied in unison.

Monday went on, "Well, just a few minutes ago as I was hugging him I was dumbfounded to hear him speak while looking at me with completely transparent love.

"He said, 'You are an angel sent by God.'"

Yes, Monday did indeed pour out her love indiscriminately.

Then one day right after lunch, Mamena, as was her custom, had her hands folded in prayer for her Ewing Wing fellow patients when a nurse noticed that one of those hands, wrinkled from age and faithful service, had dropped to her side.

Mamena, in that unique atmosphere of love and caring, had, at age 99, quietly slipped into eternity while the Ewing Wing sorrowed, and Lunes grieved for her special friend.

*   *   *

PAT, OUR GREYHOUND

When mother married dad she brought with her to that union an adult pet greyhound named Pat that she had raised from a puppy.

Actually, Pat was a greyhound whippet cross and as such was a startlingly swift runner.

During my preschool years our family lived in the country near Pittsburg, California where father ran the only newspaper in town. So Pat had lots of room to romp and chase jack rabbits.

A neighbor of ours loved to hunt with bow and arrow and apparently he had his eye on Pat. Then one day he approached mother and asked if he could borrow our dog to help him flush out rabbits so he could get a clear shot at them. She agreed and the two left on their quest.

Later that day the hunter returned Pat. "How did it go? My mother asked.

"Frankly, Mrs. Walker, we got lots of rabbits today but I didn't shoot a one. That dog of yours was so terribly fast that he would run down, grab and shake each rabbit before I had time to string my bow and draw a bead," he replied quietly if somewhat somberly.

*   *   *

MARNE LA COQUETTE

Nestled among the trees on the outskirts of Paris is the small town of Marne La Coquette. Its cemetery is very private and charming (to the degree that any graveyard could be considered charming). Miniscule and hidden, it would be easy to miss unless you knew your city geography well.

My wife took me there during one of our trips to Europe, for her dear mother, Lucila, as well as her cherished sister, Lucy, were both buried behind Marne La Coquette's graveyard gates.

During her last months of life, Lucila was a resident at a retirement home in Paris run by the extremely loving Sisters of Charity who cared for her with the tenderness a mother does for her child.

When Isabel learned of her Mother's passing, she flew to Paris and, after the burial, visited that same retirement home. The sister who had had Lucila under her wing related that her sweet charge kept to herself a lot and spent long hours in the chapel. With great love this nun said that Lucila was her "little bird."

I knew Lucila for 19 years and felt richly blessed by such a delightful mother-in-law. She was always thinking of others and went out of her way to be loving and caring.

In the very same postage-stamp-size cemetery, the famed French actor and entertainer, Maurice Chevalier, was also laid to rest.

Chevalier is in very good company!

*   *   *

MY STEERING WHEEL BATTLE

It had been a long, emotional and exhausting day. My wife had fallen that morning in our Mariposa driveway and, I was later to learn, broken her hip and left arm. Soon an ambulance, responding to my 911 call, was en route to our home. Meanwhile I prayed and, to bring limited comfort to my writhing spouse, placed a pillow under her head, not daring to move her for fear of making matters any worse than they already were.

At the emergency ward of our small, local hospital x-rays were taken and arrangements made for her transfer to a much larger, more adequate medical facility, Modesto's Memorial Medical Center. It was there where she was to receive a new hip plus a metal plate implant in her arm.

Many hours after our Modesto arrival, Isabel, now loaded with morphine, was finally wheeled from emergency to a semi-private room, while scheduling was being finalized for her surgery.

By then I was fagged, frazzled and flustered. So when the nurse in attendance leveled her know-it-all remarks at me I let her have it. Was I being kind? Heck no. I was burned up, unjustifiably I might add. So now there were two of us bent out of shape.

Then, remembering what the Bible had to say about love, that it was "kind," I soon became awashed with guilt. The angel atop my left shoulder was engaged in prolonged sparring with the pitch-forked one on the other shoulder as I resisted the apology that I knew had to come sooner or later depending on how long my stubbornness was to hold out.

Well, surgery was performed by a superbly skilled orthopedist, followed by Isabel's prolonged, week-long hospital stay there until her blood viscosity was stabilized.

Later, as I was leaving the Modesto rehab hospital where Isabel had subsequently been transferred to, my steering wheel and I had become engaged in a titanic battle. I wanted to head for highway 99 and my 80 mile journey home, but my steering wheel was saying, "No way, buster. You are going back to the hospital and apologize to the nurse you made miserable. So we are turning east, not south the way you planned. Are we clear??"

I grumbled, but the steering wheel won. East I turned. I parked at the hospital. Not knowing whether the offended nurse was on duty, I prepared a letter for her just in case. It was a letter, not of justification for my uncalled for remark, but of humble apology.

As it turned out, that nurse was off duty. At the nurses' station, since I did not remember the name of the nurse in question, I read to the nurses crowded around me and wide-eyed in amazement, my letter of apology. Some of them bore looks that said, "This guy has to be some kind of nut." Others smiled.

The head nurse then said, "We will place your letter on the main bulletin board and surely the right person will find it."

With my soul now bared to the quick, I departed. But my heart was singing for I was now at peace. The devil had slunk off, and my steering wheel was smiling as it winked at the angel.

* * *

THE HOLE

I was resting on one of the benches that Pioneer Market has thoughtfully placed for the weary.

Then a gentleman of some vintage eased himself down beside me.

"Nice day," said I hoping to open a dialogue.

After a low growl he allowed that the heat was terrible. Then for the next 15 minutes I was his audience while he ticked off reason after reason why everything could be better than it is.

"All the deer we used to see are gone because of the explosion in the mountain lion population," he muttered.

"And what's more, too many trees are being logged and soil erosion has become a major problem."

I looked like a yo-yo as I nodded to each of his maledictions.

While he inhaled in preparation for his next salvo, I slipped in a silver lining comment, sort of a donut to hem in the hole he had been constructing.

"You know," I said with a smile, "the lupine that carpeted this area earlier in the year were simply beautiful."

That threw him momentarily as he fumbled for a way to re-group.

Presently my wife approached with her cart of groceries.

I bade my bench partner goodbye, leaving him to ponder his "hole," but hopefully the donut that surrounded it.

*   *   *

LAUGHING IN LOVE

For the past 18 years, as a volunteer chaplain at Mariposa, California's County Jail near where I live, I have been called on to tend to the spiritual needs of both the English and Spanish-speaking inmate populations.

This was how I got to know Ramón and his sidekick, José.

At first these nominal Christians were a bit leery of my purpose, but with each of my subsequent visits I began noticing a marvelous change come over each man.

Their initial boredom and suspicion soon gave way to tenderness, a desire to mend their ways and an eagerness to know more about Jesus the deeper they got into the Spanish Bibles I had provided them.

Early in our relationship they had said the sinner's prayer, inviting Jesus into their hearts and from that moment their maturity in the Lord grew by leaps and bounds.

Soon what once were dour expressions gave way to constant smiles.

I met with them on the eve of their departure to resume life out in the real world. "Ramón," I said, "I would just like you and José to know that I have noticed a simply wonderful transformation take place in you, clear evidence that Jesus does indeed live in your hearts."

He beamed and then replied, "You know, Pancho (my Spanish nickname), José and I just today were talking about you and we concluded the very same thing about you."

Together we laughed a hearty laugh, a laugh of pure love that said reams. A laugh that needed no explanation, for Our Lord was present.

*   *   *

LAWRENCE WELK

Mamena, our ageing, faithful Peruvian companion and governess to our five children, for years would religiously watch the Lawrence Welk show every Saturday night on TV.

Once we read where his show taping would be open to the public at the CBS studios in Hollywood.

So we took Mamena there and sat in the audience.

To be present during such a performance is quite different from watching on TV. For example, the voice of Welk's gifted tenor, Joe Feeney, had such a wide volume range that much of what we heard live simply could not be reproduced electronically for TV as we were later to realize when we watched on screen the very same program we had witnessed in person during the earlier live taping.

And frankly, that day at the CBS recording studio, Feeney's rendition of "Danny Boy" literally brought tears of appreciation to my eyes.

During a lull in the action, Welk walked over to the audience and began chatting with people at random. So I got up from my seat, made my way down onto the floor and approached the star.

"Mr. Welk," I said, "There is an ailing, elderly lady with me who thinks the world of you and she would like very much to meet you."

"But of course," he replied with a most gracious smile. "Where is she?"

I led him up the stairs to where Mamena was seated. He leaned over, took her hand in his two hands, looked into her eyes and with great tenderness told her how delighted he was to meet her.

When he learned that Mamena only spoke Spanish, he told me to tell her that he would very much like to have introduced her to his star female vocalist, Anacani, who was Mexican, but he regretted that she was absent.

It is redundant to say that Mr. Welk and his great charm made Mamena's day (and mine too!).

As we filed from the studio following the show, I felt as if I had to look up at Mamena despite her 4'-10" height, for she was truly on cloud nine!

*   *   *

PSALM 23

On occasion Isabel and I would visit the L.A. County jail in downtown Los Angeles and provide whatever comfort we could to some of the inmates.

Charles was one we would see on a weekly basis pending his reassignment to a more permanent correctional facility. He was up for seven counts of armed robbery.

Happily Charles said the sinner's prayer one day as we listened to him by phone while watching him through the thick glass that separated us.

As our friendship grew, our visits would involve giving each other Bible memory assignments.

During one of these Bible sessions I was to recite Psalm 23. So with Charles listening, his eyes twinkling, I began, "The Lord is my shepherd, I shall not want…" and I then faltered.

A voice behind me continued, "He makes me to lie down…" I whirled around to see a smiling, handsome black lad.

Then I looked back at a laughing Charles. There I was between two wonderful, happy souls who clearly were at peace.

What a beautiful experience.

*   *   *

THE MARLIN

This is a story that amazed many, but to some was accepted with a quiet, knowing smile and a heavenward glance of appreciation.

Brenda Mallaburn is a single parent who was attending University of the Nation's missionary school in Kailua-Kona, Hawaii, as were my wife and I.

It was Sunday afternoon and Brenda was on the Kona pier with her two young children watching the sport fishing boats pull up with their marlin catches.

Her young son, Christopher, excitedly said, "Mom, let's go marlin fishing." Not an unusual request, really, since the Kona waters are world-renown for their many trophy-size bill fish.

"Oh, hush, Christopher," she gently admonished, "you know very well we have never tried to catch anything larger than a mackerel and besides we don't have the money."

Not to be deterred, Christopher proceeded with his plan. "Aw come on, Mom it'll be so much fun," he whined.

More resistance by Mom.

After about the third round, Brenda was finally nagged into action. She sighed, "Oh, very well, Christopher, let's talk to someone."

So Brenda approached the skipper of one of these sport crafts and inquired what the cost would be to go fishing.

"Who wants to know?" he asked.

Shyly Brenda replied, "A single woman with two children and very limited means."

"Just a minute," he shot back and then proceeded to consult with his partner.

Soon he turned to her. "Be here Tuesday morning, you and your children, as my guests."

Brenda's jaw sagged in disbelief. Later it was to drop even lower when she learned her host was none other than the president of the International Marlin Fishers Association.

Bright and early Tuesday morning the three Mallaburns piled aboard and were soon fishing for tuna bait to be used in attracting the much larger marlin.

Brenda's rig was a light rod with 50# test line suitable for the smaller bait fish she was after.

Suddenly everyone aboard was electrified as they stared at a 400 pound marlin exploding from the water, hooked on Brenda's flimsy rig.

"Quick," the captain barked at Brenda, "into the chair with you!"

Frozen in horror she wailed, "I can't. I'm scared. He's too big."

They plopped her into the fighting chair anyway and hastily strapped her in.

And the war began, Brenda pumping her rod and reeling the slack in like mad.

The seasoned crew were buzzing with excitement and disbelief.

Her light rod was bent almost in a full circle. The captain and his assistant, afraid the light line would snap at any minute, put their hands between Brenda's rod and her face. This precaution was to prevent the severely strained rod from whipping back and slicing into her in the event the line were to break.

Christopher, frightened that his mother might be yanked from her chair and hauled out to sea, instinctively stuck his thumb in his mouth.

After ten grueling minutes, this petite British mother, out of sheer exhaustion, was ready to throw in the towel.

She prayed, "Lord, I've had it. You have to take over. I have run out of strength."

No sooner had she said her "Amen" than the billfish quieted down and Brenda's strength miraculously returned.

Ten minutes later her prize was on board with captain and crew shaking their heads in stunned silence. They knew full well that a fish of that size historically takes two or three muscle-wrenching hours to boat. Yet the clock didn't lie. She had done it in a scant twenty minutes.

The next morning her host drove up to the University of the Nations.

As he presented her with the large certificate of accomplishment, he smiled and said, "Someone up there likes you!"

*   *   *

GLIMPSES OF MY DAD

Two stories come to mind regarding my dear father which I've always cherished. In both cases they occurred in Los Angeles during my grammar school years.

The first one involves the then super movie star, Freddie Bartholomew, who was my hero, as my parents knew all too well. At the time this star's popularity rivaled that of Shirley Temple.

I had just seen Freddie Bartholomew in the movie, *"Captain's Courageous."*

This particular day I was carrying out my daily routine family chore, watering the lawn, when a chauffeur-driven Rolls Royce pulled up to our house.

Out stepped my father, a newspaperman, who, with a beaming smile, introduced me to the other occupant. "Son, I'd like you to meet Freddie Bartholomew. Freddie, please meet my son, Frankie."

To say I was flabbergasted would not do justice to this momentous event. Stunned would more accurately reflect how I felt.

Soon all my classmates learned in great detail about the day Freddie Bartholomew visited me.

What a blessing was my dear, dear father.

- - - - - - - - - -

The second story happened on one 4th of July. You see, there was a lady up the street that none of us kids really liked because she was mean. So we nicknamed her Mrs. Meanie.

What better person to pull a trick on than Mrs. Meanie on July 4th, mused I.

So a dastardly plot was hatched when my firecracker exploded right at her front door.

In no time Mrs. Meanie loomed at her doorstep and screeched, "Just you wait till I tell your father, you naughty boy!"

I raced in panic for home with Mrs. Meanie, hands on hips and jaw firmly set, marching behind me.

"Dad, mom, quick, I need your help," I panted to my parents, who were already well apprised of the multiple reasons for why Mrs. Meanie had earned such a nickname.

"Son. Mrs. Meanie will be here any moment so this is what we're going to do," my dad's soothing words pronounced.

"After she tells me what you did then I'll tell her I'm going to punish you right away.

"And here's where you come in. I'm going to pretend I'm whacking you real hard but I'll only be hitting the floor.

"Each time you see me whack I want you to yell really loud, you know, like it hurts.

"You got that?"

Bathed in enormous gratitude I replied, "Don't worry, pop. I won't let you down."

On our front porch Mrs. Meanie's harrumps told us that father's deception, executed behind our closed front door, had been victorious.

Our father-son deep friendship was thus sealed forever

CHAPTER 13

MISCELLANEOUS

Our Only Time-Share Experience
Our Miami Menagerie
Mariposa, Not Merced, Gateway to Yosemite
Hitler and the Berlin Olympics
Polls Tampering
Tattoo Shops, Not a Good Thing
What's in a Name
Double Date, Anyone?
How to Instruct Tennis
O.J. vs. Clinton
The Aborted Ticket
Louisiana Recollections
* Top Rifle Marksman (Our Nation's Top Scoring High School Rifle Marksman)

-----

* See photo

OUR ONLY TIME-SHARE EXPERIENCE

We had left our Mariposa home to enjoy an R and R at Lake Tahoe. While there, my wife and I decided to visit nearby Squaw Valley, a famous ski resort and one-time site of the Winter Olympics.

It was a lovely, picturesque location, a valley surrounded by majestic Sierra Nevada mountains.

As we approached the heart of this resort village, we saw a cable car terminus and decided to take a ride up the adjacent mountain.

But before we could open our car door, an athletic type pulled up on his bicycle. He was promoting time-share for one of this valley's main hotel-apartment complexes. We were offered a free lunch and a gift of our choice if we would but listen to their sales pitch.

By then it was lunch time, and besides, we had always been curious about the time-share concept and how it really worked. So we accepted.

The dining room ceiling was two stories high. One whole wall was floor-to-ceiling glass, enabling an impressive panoramic view. And we ate well, with enough left over to serve later as our dinner.

A very sharp saleswoman from New York was then assigned to us for the ensuing two-and-a-half hours. She showed us the apartments which were for sale. What we saw were several variations on one basic floor plan. The furnishings and interior decorating were in excellent taste. Outside we were led past free-form pools, attractive landscaping, tennis courts and golf course, all obviously done by pros.

Following the tour we were ushered into an informal sitting room where the sales pitch began in earnest. As the saleswoman talked, I was mentally calculating how much this investment would cost us per square foot.

Based on my experience as a one-time general building contractor, I could not see where their construction cost, land and profit included, could have exceeded $150 per square foot. Yet at the $1,000 a square foot they were charging, it was clear that they were enjoying a whopping profit.

When we hesitated over signing up, she called in the reinforcements. An oily smooth super-salesman then approached our table and proceeded to work us over for the next 30 minutes.

We were still not convinced, so it was suggested that we retire to their small projection room where we could talk things over and watch a movie about this time-share program.

No sooner had we entered, closed the door and sunk into the overstuffed chairs, when Isabel turned to me and, in Portuguese, as English or even Spanish would have been too risky, said, "I'm sure this place is bugged. Let's be careful what we say." So we stayed with our Portuguese.

When we emerged, our hosts had the strangest looks on their faces which lent credence to Isabel's earlier suspicion.

"We've decided to think it over," I said, "but we will take the portable TV gift."

"Are you sure you wouldn't like a lovely cable car ride instead?" they responded, their voices dripping with hope.

"Thank you, but the TV would be just fine," was our resolute reply, devoid of all wiggle room as we left with our doggie bag and one new portable TV.

*   *   *

Before retiring to Mariposa, our family at one point lived in greater Miami, Florida.

One day early in our residency there, my wife was at the kitchen sink when she heard a loud metallic thud outside. Looking from the window she saw an iguana on the hood of our car, staring her in the face.

Apparently that large lizard had dropped from a nearby shade tree. "Welcome to Miami," I mused when Isabel told me what had happened.

Not long after that incident I was introduced to the tree-climbing land crab, a frequent visitor, neighbors later told us, to residential Miami and environs.

Through the kitchen doorway leading to our open garage, I did a double take when spying a crab in the driveway just beyond our car. I moved to get a closer look. Our eyes met for an instant before it dodged behind a rear tire, so I quickly side stepped to get a better look at our visitor.

Once again he sidled from view, and I responded as before. So there we were playing hide and seek, with our crustacean pal probably having just as much fun in eluding my gaze as I was having in trying to get a clear view of him.

But the funniest Miami animal episode I can recall involved a monkey. Above our backyard, one fine day our son, Frank, then a young teenager, spied a monkey walking along an overhead telephone wire. From there he hopped onto one of our trees.

Frank rushed into the house. "Dad," he yelled excitedly, "there's a monkey in our tree and I'm going to capture him. Where is our crab cage?"

Soon, armed with a banana and our crab net, a wire mesh cage with hinged walls that can be made either to open or close, he rushed to the tree.

He put the cage down and, getting the attention of the monkey by waving the banana ostentatiously at the primate caller, he then proceeded to peel it for his intended victim who by then was salivating in anticipation.

Frank placed the banana inside the open cage whose four walls were designed to lock shut when an attached cord was pulled. With cord in hand, he proceeded to back toward the house while playing out the cord. Soon Frank, while spying from behind a curtain in his bedroom, was ready to jerk the rope at the instant his distant cousin grabbed the banana.

It wasn't long before hunger replaced the animal's better judgment.

"Dad, dad, I got him! I captured the monkey," Frank exulted as he proudly strode up to me, his prize screeching away, not liking his confinement one bit.

"Boy, dad, he's going to be so much fun. I'm going to build a cage for him and show all my friends. Wow!" Frank bubbled away. Clearly that was a high-water mark in his thirteen years of planet earth living.

My wife looked at me and I at her. Our eyebrows communicated our thoughts without a word being said. Never were we in more harmonious accord than at that moment. We needed a monkey like we needed a hole in the head.

So I spoke up. "Okay, son. You can keep the monkey, but we're going to have to lay down a few ground rules. First off, your little friend will need a cage that is large enough. Let's do a little research."

Once we determined the appropriate cage size, I said, "Frank, let us now make a materials list like wood for the frame, wire mesh and so on."

I got Frank actively involved in drawing up that list. "Now, son, we have to determine what all this is going to cost. I want you to call up a builder's supply house and price everything out."

After he was done, he brought me the fruits of his assignment, $64.50.

"Do you have $64.50, Frank? I don't. Your allowance is only $10.00 a month, so what are we going to do?"

"Maybe, dad, we could just give the monkey away. What do you think?"

"Son, I think you've made a very wise decision. Tell you what. Why don't you get the SPCA on the phone and tell them they can come and pick up the monkey?"

So ended our saga of "Frank and his monkey."

Then there was the time a python had found its way inside the stuffing of a couch we had in our garage and had bit another son of ours, Peter, while he attempted to extract it. But that is another story.

To tell the truth, I don't mind pets like dogs and cats. Iguanas, crabs, monkeys and pythons, however, I prefer just visiting at the zoo.

*　*　*

MARIPOSA, NOT MERCED, GATEWAY TO YOSEMITE

Have you ever noticed that Merced's city vehicles have the words, Gateway to Yosemite, emblazoned across their doors? And Merced's Chamber of Commerce gives strong coverage to that claim in literature available throughout Merced. Now I don't know about you, but for me, them's almost fighting words to this resident who loves his Mariposa, the true gateway to Yosemite.

My heavens, it takes almost an hour more to Yosemite from Merced than it does from Mariposa.

Indeed, if Merced's claim is valid then so could Fresno's or even Stockton's.

And while we're at it we mustn't forget San Francisco.

For that matter, how about Tokyo?

*   *   *

HITLER AND THE BERLIN OLYMPICS

In 1936 the World Olympics were held in Berlin during Adolph Hitler's dictatorship. The two stories that follow will serve to illustrate another of the many unfortunate facets to Hitler's severely blemished character.

Back in the late 30s I was visiting my grandmother, Dr. Eleanor Bancroft, at Mills College where she was campus physician. When I walked into her office I found her conversing with a petite muscular woman, one Helene Mayer, to whom she introduced me.

After her guest had left, grandmother turned to me and said, "The woman you just met has a most interesting background. She is a German Jew, an immigrant who teaches here at Mills College. She is considered by many to be the greatest woman fencer in history. She was forced by the Nazi regime to return to represent Germany in the 1936 World Olympics held in Berlin, even though she was a naturalized American citizen at the time. The reason why she agreed to join Germany's Olympic fencing team was out of fear of reprisal since her family lived in Germany.

"Then Hitler, after learning of her Star of David ethnicity, sent instructions for her to lose to her German teammate in the finals. So she dutifully lost.

"However, the following year to underscore her fencing supremacy, and to place in serious doubt the validity of her loss in the Berlin Olympics, she won the world fencing championship held in Paris. Her other fencing accomplishments include: National German Champion at age 13; Olympic Champion, 1928; European Champion, 1929, 1931; World Champion 1937; U.S. Champion eight times from 1934 through 1946."

When I told my Peruvian-born wife this story, she said, "Well, I have one for you. My brother, Victor, a Peruvian as you well know, was a student in Germany at the time and attended those Olympic games. He told me of another account very similar to that of Helene Mayer.

"Victor witnessed Peru's soccer team defeat the Austrians in the Olympics final only to see Hitler, who clearly favored Austria, the country of his birth, call foul and force the two teams to replay their match but this time without spectators. And, you guessed it, Austria won."

Is it any wonder that Hitler, facing defeat in WWII, committed suicide? He simply could not stand to lose.

*　*　*

POLLS TAMPERING

Just how neutral are our national polls, and is it important that they be scrupulously unbiased?

Are we, the citizenry, expected to believe, indeed expected to accept the spoon feedings of our nation's pollsters simply because the system they employ to sample public opinion goes unchallenged and is considered, on blind faith, to be pure as the driven snow?

How terribly easy it is for deceptively slanted public opinion samplers to ask questions in such a way as to elicit the answers they seek. Thus, "Mr. John Q. Public, sir, don't you agree that the nation's business can be hurt if all this anti-sex-oriented nonsense is allowed to distract our Washington leaders from more important things?" Well, put that way, of course people are going to answer in the affirmative, just as they would if asked, "Do you agree that forest fires should be put out before they burn down your house?"

If those same people on the street were queried by strictly truth-seeking pollsters would not their questions be more like, "Sir, don't you believe that the people we elect must uphold the law and that if they don't, there will be an important price to pay?" Or, another questions, "Ma'am, don't you think that if one of us common folk breaks the law and is put into prison for it, that an elected official who commits the same crime should not get off scot-free, but rather be obliged to suffer the same consequences?"

274

Senator "X" or Representative "Y" thinks, (innocently, I hope) "Gosh, the polls tell me that the people that voted me in don't want me to kick Clinton out so I'd better compromise with my "justice-at-all-costs" conscience and instead vote the way the polls say I should because I sure don't want to lose my cushy job."

But, you see, the impartiality of many polling companies has been so compromised that they, acting under imagined impunity, oftentimes become guilty of serious wrong-doing and hence should be more strictly regulated and prosecuted at the mere suggestion of impropriety. Such could greatly help to avoid the terrible miscarriage of justice we now find ourselves in with W.J. Clinton on the brink of walking away with a mere slap on the wrist while other felons languish behind bars for the same crime.

So, using those slanted polling results, our lawmakers then pontificate on national TV, "The American public is telling us, the duly elected, to stop all of this prying pettiness into the president's private life and get on with running the government."

As a member of that same American public, I thoroughly resent the dishonesty of being told I said something I did not say, and I know my resentment is shared by many.

A very strong case, I and many others feel, can be made that important laws have been broken by manipulators of the polls. They obliquely yet purposely tamper with the judicial process by their skewed presentation of voter opinion (for example, largely limiting their questioning to those geographic areas that historically vote a certain way, a way they, the pollsters agree with). That, coupled with their endless repetitions of such dishonest results (e.g., Tell a lie enough times and people will accept it as truth), have resulted in the obstruction of justice.

Let these pollsters and their backers be called on the carpet and be obliged to stop their thinly veiled programs of molding public opinion and, instead, begin to act in unbiased fashion.

*   *   *

TATTOO SHOPS NOT A GOOD THING

This deals with the controversy surrounding the Merced city council's recent rejection of a permit that would have allowed a new tattoo shop on Main Street.

I feel that those voting in favor of such a shop on Main Street may be missing a very essential point, which is this: More often than not we find that tattoo shops, adult bookstores, massage parlors, bars, drug dealers and prostitution all tend to attract each other.

So if a precedent is established today that allows a tattoo shop on Merced's presently most inviting Main Street, then tomorrow, with that precedent already established, in will come the girlie shows and all the rest.

When that happens, then the prestigious and long-established shops will move away from what they deem to be a contaminating, business-wrecking influence and Main Street will then revert to being a seedy place that attracts the wrong kind of citizenry. Not only that, but Merced's already overworked police force will moan the blues over all the extra work they'll be saddled with.

I well remember what happened to what was once a simply lovely, high-end Hollywood Blvd. in the greater Los Angeles area. Tattoo shops and the aforementioned marginal businesses entered. And now its city fathers are fighting tooth and nail to restore the elegance that street once enjoyed.

Even today cop cars spend an inordinate amount of time patrolling Hollywood Blvd. breaking up fights, loading drunks into paddy wagons, picking up prostitutes and all the rest. And the very same thing could easily occur to Merced if allowed.

This danger had to have been on the minds of those on the city council who recently voted down that tattoo shop three to two but still makes one seriously wonder what those two who voted in favor were thinking.

I have been a jail chaplain now for many years and I see a far higher percentage of people wearing tattoos within prison walls than without. In the larger correctional institutions many inmates get tattoos for survival in a prison environment of violence and sometimes even murder. Their tattoos are meant to say, "Don't mess with me 'cause I'm tough!"

Nationally recognized studies show that many employers, albeit illegally, shun applicants who brandish tattoos, even if it means their having to choose someone with lower test scores.

It has been said that many of our fighting men and women proudly sport the fruit of their visits to a tattoo shop, the suggestions being that to be tattooed is a glorious thing to be emulated by all wishing to be looked up to.

Well, one of my sons got one when he was with the 82nd Airborne and today kicks himself just as so many more who bear tattoos do. To have a tattoo laser-erased costs big bucks, meaning that most who no longer want their tattoos simply have to live with their mistake.

I must admit that some tattoos are most tasteful and even attractive. But when a guy, three sheets to the wind, staggers into a tattoo shop and picks out a design, he's more likely to emerge sporting a skull and crossbones than he is a rose.

*   *   *

WHAT'S IN A NAME

My wife and I had just landed at Honolulu after being in Malaysia for two months of missionary work. Consequently we had to pass through immigration and customs.

When my turn came, I handed my passport to an official who then inputted certain information into her computer.

Presently she raised a tall, red flag high in the air and asked me to please wait.

A large lump grew in my throat as I thought, "What did I do now?" Soon a higher authority approached, looked at me then at my passport while studying his computer screen.

I found myself sighing with relief when he finally said, "You may go."

Highly curious as to what exactly had happened I asked, "Was there a problem?"

He replied, "A person with your identical name is wanted for a serious crime."

*   *   *

DOUBLE DATE, ANYONE?

While still in college I once went on a double blind date. My sightless date was one of two sisters. The other sister's partner was a fellow who, by the merest coincidence, bore my very name, Frank Walker. No relation whatsoever.

So the two of us met for the very first time at the sisters' home. That evening, when one of the gals would speak out, "Frank," we'd both look up and when she would correct herself, "I mean Frank Walker," Frank and I would look at each other, smile and shrug.

It was an okay evening, I guess, but nothing to crow about, except for the friendship that Frank Walker and I struck up, for we both loved to fly fish for trout.

While our relationship with these two girls was limited to that one evening, our fishing friendship flourished.

Oftentimes Frank and I plus two friends, Dave Ducey and Art Scotfield would cut classes to enjoy a long weekend. Taking off in the wee hours of a Thursday evening from Washington, D.C. we would arrive at New York's Catskill mountains in time to start whisking our flies over the Willoweemock River by midmorning.

Thus, two girls' loss is a couple of blind date fishermen's gain.

*   *   *

HOW TO INSTRUCT TENNIS

At one point in my adult life I was a tennis instructor. As such I found myself teaching first on my own private tennis court. From there I moved to being the pro, during separate periods, at two different tennis clubs. My final years in this profession found me teaching advanced tennis in the daytime as an assistant professor at California State University, Northridge, California, while evenings I taught at Santa Monica College.

Concurrent with that teaching I became deeply involved in researching and developing instructional systems based both on the application of unique mental techniques as well as the utilization of newly-discovered streamlining of body motions employing kinesiological principles.

A part of that era found me as a board member of the California chapter of the prestigious United States Professional Association, America's largest tennis teaching organization, where I chaired its education committee.

One of the most valuable tools I used during my tennis-teaching career involved a revolutionary mental exercise first developed by a man named Tim Gallway, whose seminar series at UCLA I felt fortunate to attend.

An essential premise of proper instruction, of course, must always be to demonstrate correct execution. This is a universal given. But from there, instructional formats then branch out into a jillion different approaches.

Mine stressed:

1. Creating a focused awareness by the student on what he has done during the execution of each stroke, since the correction of any fault is made much easier once that error is clearly recognized. Progress from that moment of awareness then comes rapidly. It is somewhat akin to the recovery system AA uses wherein each alcoholic must acknowledge that he is indeed an alcoholic before he can make progress toward recovery.

2. Encouraging the student not to override or, frankly, to meddle with the body's innate ability, to execute a stroke beautifully. Indeed that particular mental exercise was always received with gratitude by my students, and I found it even of deep interest by San Fernando's Mensa organization during my guest lecture appearances before that group.

This teaching system worked for me.

*　*　*

O.J. vs. Clinton

The U.S. Senate has rendered its predictable "not guilty" verdict in the impeachment proceedings against William Jefferson Clinton, so it seems to me that a few comments are in order especially as they relate to the striking similarity in the very high profile trials of both O.J. Simpson and Clinton.

It will be recalled that O.J. Simpson got off scot-free in his criminal trial. He averted prison and possible execution because he had the big bucks needed to hire the nation's best lawyers. The latter successfully diverted attention from damning DNA evidence and instead directed it to anti-black bias which the mostly black jury bought.

But in a subsequent civil trial O.J. was found guilty as sin with the overwhelming DNA evidence being a major reason for that outcome.

Coincidentally we have Clinton who was nailed dead-to-rights by the blatant DNA evidence on Monica's dress that forced him to reverse his prior insistence of innocence, to "guilty as charged."

Yet in the hallowed senate chamber Clinton was found not-guilty with only lip service being paid in the form of "naughty, naughty finger wagging." As in the O.J. trial, Clinton's lawyers cleverly diverted attention from the facts to other things like "how bad prosecutor Ken Starr was," etc. …and regrettably it worked.

Undeniably our senators did not vote their conscience, in spite of what they were elected to do. Instead they voted along party lines. How weak, how immoral, how unstatesmanlike.

So if you're rich or powerful that's too often enough to tip the scales of justice (?) in your favor. As to the guys in prison for the same crimes Clinton committed. Well, clearly they were neither rich nor powerful enough to beat the rap.

Now as we, in our beloved nation, try to put this unfortunate adventure behind us, it is the hope of many that our leader will turn over a new leaf and begin to respect the high office he holds by, among other things, starting to follow the White House's time-honored dress code of keeping his pants on.

*   *   *

THE ABORTED TICKET

I had left my Mariposa home for Merced where I hopped into my dear friend and high school classmate, Ad Canelo's car.

With Ad at the helm, I was in the middle of a story about how an ancient Chinese remedy had stopped my kidney stone attack dead in its tracks.

He seemed intensely interested in what I was saying until, that is, I noticed him ease his sleek Lincoln Continental from the fast lane over to the shoulder.

Soon a highway patrolman approached and inquired if Ad realized he was going faster than the posted limit. He then asked for the car registration and driver's license, the usual prelude to a speeding ticket.

At that point I spoke up apologetically, "Officer, I have to tell you that this was all my fault. You see, my friend was truly engrossed in the story I was telling about an ancient Chinese remedy that had cured my kidney stone attacks.

He looked at me, looked at Ad, and possibly surmising that Ad also might have been a candidate for my Chinese remedy, handed the registration and license back. With a kindly remonstrance, we heard him say, "I'll issue you a warning this time. Please be more careful in the future."

Turning to me with a smile he then commented, "That must have been quite a Chinese remedy!"

"Officer, it really was," came my response, dripping with gratitude, while I heaved a sigh of relief.

*   *   *

Back in the fifties I lived in New Orleans developing markets for a large farm chemical manufacturer. What now follow are vignettes from that period in my life.

- - - - - - - - - - - -

My boss was George Voss. He was a wonderful guy, a total extrovert and a natural born salesman. So good was he that upon his retirement many years later he confided that he had difficulty spending the twenty grand a month he received in retirement checks.

- - - - - - - - - - - -

George told me of the time a young man applied for a salesman position. Always looking for ways to cut corners, George wanted to get this promising lad for a song.

"How much would you be willing to take?" George asked him.

"Oh, I was thinking around $400 a month," which back then was a decent wage.

To that George commented, "I was thinking more along the lines of $200."

"Well," the applicant responded, "are you more interested in getting $200 worth of effort from me or $400?"

He was hired at $400.

- - - - - - - - - - - -

Alexandria is a town that sits in the middle of the state. It is an old place with architecture and charm that reflects its antiquity. A to-the-manner-born hotel, The Alexandria, fronts the town square where concerts from its pavilion would fill the early evening air.

In order to gain entry to that hotel's high-ceilinged plush dining room, gentlemen were required to wear ties and jackets.

One day a cowboy, dressed in a shirt typical of his trade, bandana around his neck and sporting dusty boots, strolled in and, without waiting for the maitre d' to seat him, found a table and plopped himself down.

Soon he was confronted by an indignant head waiter, "I'm sorry sir, but you will have to leave. We only allow diners who are appropriately dressed," was his snooty edict.

With a glare the man rose and stomped out.

One week passed. Then the same cowpoke returned. Entering the stately dining room dressed as before, he once again chose a table to his liking.

Quickly appearing from nowhere was the same maitre d', "I thought I told you we only permit properly-attired guests to be served here."

"That's right, you sure did say that," he drawled. "But you see, I just purchased this hotel and I believe you just lost your job."

- - - - - - - - - - - -

Bogalusa is a wood pulp manufacturing town and you can smell it miles before you ever get there. You see, Louisiana is, as are a number of Gulf states, a large grower of pine trees, sources of wood pulp used to make paper products.

One day I recall asking one of the local wood pulp factory engineers, "How can you guys stand the stink from these plants?"

"Friend," he replied with a wry smile, "when your paycheck depends on it, that smell is more like the fragrance of perfume."

- - - - - - - - - - - -

I used to sell temporary soil sterilant called Vapam to the McIlhenny Co. of Avery Island, bottler of its world-famous, fiery Tabasco Sauce.

Old man McIlhenny who founded that establishment many years earlier, was a personal friend of President Theodore Roosevelt, a conservationist and nature lover as was McIlhenny.

So between the two they cooked up a plan to import the fur-bearing nutria, a rodent noted for its rapid-breeding penchant. After all, in those days the ladies enjoyed mincing along Crescent City's Canal Street wrapped in furs, so why not feed that market?

It was not long before the sugarcane-addicted nutrias were overrunning that part of Louisiana and absolutely devastating that important cash crop, much to the woe of Teddy and his hot sauce producing buddy, whose nutria plan laid a huge goose egg.

*   *   *

TOP RIFLE MARKSMAN
(OUR NATION'S TOP SCORING HIGH SCHOOL RIFLE MARKSMAN)

My high school years took place during the period of WWII. Three of my four high school years I was required, as were all high schoolers across our country, to take ROTC (Reserve Officers Training Corps). Each of these three years I was ranked top shot.

A number of us ROTC cadets developed considerable rifle marksmanship skills.

In 1943 during our national ROTC William Randolph Hearst shoot I was fortunate enough to tie with one other for top honors. We each scored 192 out of a possible 200 for four positions. *(See photo.)*

That 1943 Small Bore Rifle Championship was nationwide and sponsored by William Randolph Hearst. My score of 192 tied for 1st place among all ROTC high schools nationwide. The other winner was from Austin, Texas. In 1942, in the same championship shootout, my score was 195, the nation's highest.

CHAPTER 14

SATISFYING

Oh Really, A Riley?
Please Pay or Leave
Tail Wags Dog
Voss and His Gun

OH REALLY, A RILEY?

While still living in Peru as a happy bachelor I acquired a brand new, sparkling English sports car known as a Riley. It was a junior version of the Jaguar, and virtually as fast. Masterfully designed, it sported a long hood that concealed a huge engine. This vehicle's interior boasted tasteful appointments like burl hardwood dash, green leather bucket seats – the full on, as they say. So streamlined was its appearance that standing still it looked like it was going 100, a speed it could handily exceed.

I had this car shipped to the states and my Peruvian bride and I traveled in it on our California honeymoon.

One Sunday morning, as we were cruising along at an easy 65 headed toward Los Angeles on Interstate 5, a lady in her large four hole Buick (in those days it was Buick's most powerful car) passed us like we were stopped. Her patrician nose was high in the air, no doubt sniffing at our much smaller vehicle and its plebeian occupants.

Deciding I would have a bit of fun, I gently pressed the foot pedal just enough to close the gap between our cars and then I maintained a fixed distance behind her Buick.

She wouldn't have any of that so she put her pedal to the metal. But still the distance between our two cars, much to her consternation, strangely remained the same. We chuckled at her worried glances in her rear view mirror, since it was obvious she was by then going flat out.

Turning to my wife I grinned, "Honey, could you please pick up the comic section of the newspaper and start reading it in plain view."

With that, I applied a bit more toe pressure (with lots more pedal still left) and zipped by her, as we exchanged smiles and I nodded to her salute.

Moments later her Buick was but a speck in our rear.

The above story I later told to a family friend. Somewhere in his mid forties, he was a highly successful New Orleans ship's chandler. We were sitting on his attractive patio in a fashionable district of the Crescent City. Nattily dressed in tweed and smoking a pipe to add to his distinguished air, our host was the epitome of an ultra conservative British country gentleman.

While I was unfolding my Riley honeymoon experience I observed frequent, ever so quiet chuckles, coming from him, while he drew pensively on his aristocratic meerschaum.

When I was done he said, "Frank, would you like to come with me? I have something to show you."

Excusing ourselves to the ladies, we both left. He stopped in front of a car parked nearby. It was a dingy, nondescript Ford, a two-door sedan, maybe five years old. One of its windows was cracked.

"Shall we go for a spin?" he asked casually.

I responded, "Why, of course," but not quite sure what this was all about.

He swung into the driver's seat. I climbed in beside him. Then he reached over in front of me, opened the glove compartment and threw a hidden switch to activate his ignition.

When he turned the key, I jumped. It sounded like a dozen caged tigers had just come to life, all roaring at once.

Incredulous, I asked, "What in heck did you do to this car anyway?"

Obligingly, and while wearing an ever so faint grin that all but masked the keen satisfaction that glowed from within his chest, he lifted the bonnet. I let out a low whistle as I beheld so much engine that any mechanic who had to work on it, I mused, would find it a nightmare. There was hardly any working space left because of the size of his wall-to-wall power plant.

Soon he was reeling off, with obvious pride, all the things he had done to his car: Cadillac's newest, largest and most expensive engine, whose head had been shaved, twin carburetors, dual pipes etc. His long list clearly pointed to state-of-the-art, power-boosting modifications.

Purring in response to my numerous exclamations of wonderment, he then suggested, "May we go for a spin?"

"Deeelighted," I quickly said, anxious to see what this sleeper could do.

Well, he started off rather slowly until, that is, he reached high gear when he suddenly punched it and my back was immediately pinned to the seat. Outside a blue cloud of burned rubber hid where we had come from and the squeal that our acceleration made opened my eyes wide as saucers.

Frankly, I was glad it was Sunday and traffic was light, because in seconds we were doing 80 down a residential street.

Without slowing, he hit the horn just before reaching each cross street. The ear-splitting blasts sounded like a diesel locomotive.

I expected neighbors to be ringing 911 right off the hook followed in short order by a phalanx of cop cars, sirens blaring, bearing down on us.

Later, with the joy ride over and my goose bumps mostly subsided, I was thoroughly entertained by his account of a trip he once made on the turnpike from New Orleans to Baton Rouge in this very vehicle. His account was reminiscent of my honeymoon highway duel with the gal in the four hole Buick.

His Ford had just been passed by a youngster in a brand new Pontiac Firebird, then touted as the hottest thing on wheels. "I noticed the lad smirking," he said, "while picking his nose to add insult to injury."

"Frank, he chortled, "In the twinkling of an eye I sped past my startled competitor, practically sucking him up the exhaust pipe of my ho-hum Ford."

Shortly thereafter, my friend told me, he pulled up to a roadside café. A while later the lad in the Pontiac reverently eased to a stop alongside his Ford. Entering the eatery, the vanquished removed his hat while meekly approaching his conqueror (and unlikely hot rodder).

"Ex, excu, excuse me, sir," he stammered in transparent admiration, "but your hood, what ever do you have under it?"

*　*　*

Please Pay or Leave

For many years my brother Jim ran a Chevron station as a franchise. In good times and bad he always managed to pay Chevron promptly for his monthly rent, franchise fees and purchases of Chevron products. His work was taxing and he put in long hours.

To help make ends meet, during football season he would earn extra money by using all available station space for parking cars of the fans who would then only have a short walk to San Francisco's nearby Kezar Stadium.

He developed a system of squeezing the vehicles in so close to each other, that oftentimes to get to a particular one it would be necessary to crawl through the windows of several cars in the same lateral row.

One football afternoon as Jim and his men were busy parking cars a limousine pulled up. The tinted back window rolled down and a well-dressed executive type leaned out the window. Jim addressed him, "That will be $2.00 please."

"Son, do you realize that I am a Chevron vice president?" he retorted condescendingly, clearly anticipating his intimidating tactic would earn him free parking.

Jim's rejoinder, without a moment's hesitation, "Sir, I work long hours at this station so that I can pay Chevron promptly each month. So that will be $2.00 please or else I would ask you to move on so I can attend to the cars lined up behind you."

The wealthy but suddenly humbled would be free-loader paid his $2.00.

*   *   *

TAIL WAGS DOG

We were doing a major remodel and expansion to our home. During this work it was necessary for us to store temporarily a good part of our personal things out in the backyard stable.

One night our son, Frank Jr., met my wife and me as we were coming into the driveway. "Be calm" he said, "no one is hurt but there has just been a fire and the stable has burned down."

The next morning, as we stood surveying the smoldering ruins, a man walked up and offered his company's services which, as independent insurance adjusters, he claimed would optimize the recovery we could expect from our own insurance company. Their fee would be 10% of the settlement.

He seemed knowledgeable and honest. And besides we, as with so many of our friends, wasted no special love on insurance companies in general who may cancel your policy if late on a payment, yet either squawk over settling a legitimate claim or else drag their feet in paying out.

Thus we figured there was little to lose so we signed up this fire truck chaser.

When our own insurance company, a nationally-known underwriter, was told that we had hired these independent adjusters, they were quite upset and indignantly asked, "What's the matter? Don't you trust us?" Our response was studied, if eloquent, silence.

These newly-found independent adjusters were real pros and worked as a superb, well-oiled team. Their first specialist met with us and helped organize our thinking. Amazingly, through a series of well planned family brainstorming sessions, it was not long before we had virtually a complete list of all the items lost or badly burned; and this, despite our having begun this exercise without an inventory of any kind.

Then a second specialist arrived and led us through the complicated task of pricing out each item, with the evaluation of family heirlooms being among his distinct skills. He also carefully arranged the sequence of items to follow a bargaining strategy.

A third man scheduled a bargaining session with our insurance company to be held at our home.

"I want you and your wife to make yourselves scarce once you have shown your insurance agent in and introduced me. That way we can avoid any discussion you might otherwise have with him that might inadvertently derail my bargaining strategy," he cautioned.

So we dutifully greeted our agent, a young, spry, alert person, and ushered him into our family room where our adjuster (an extremely smooth New York Jew) was waiting, spider-like, for the fly. His left arm was badly deformed and almost useless as a result of a bad hunting accident. Thus the uninitiated might erroneously conclude that his brain was as useless as his arm, a dangerous assumption as will soon become apparent.

We then left the two alone.

About two hours later we were summoned to bid the insurance agent goodbye. The latter, who earlier had seemed sharp, calm and composed, now was discernibly flustered. We shook his hand. He then told us he knew the way out, whereupon he promptly mistook our hall closet door for the front door and walked right into our clothes.

After his departure, we turned to the adjuster. "How did it go?" we asked, our intense interest clearly showing. His response: "Remember when you told us what you would find to be an acceptable settlement?" We nodded.

"Well," he continued through a triumphant smile, "after deducting our 10% you will be left with exactly twice the figure you gave me."

"My heavens," I gasped, "how in the world did you do it?"

"Easy," he said. "You will recall the long list of items we had you prepare. Well, we rearranged them in a sequence to conform to a negotiating strategy, and it worked.

"For example, I would say to him, 'Do you see here where the Walkers want $15 for this high chair? Well, I think it should be cut to $5.' At once he would respond, 'Yeah, I agree.'

"'And this toaster they think is worth $10, I feel is 8 bucks too high.

"'Yeah, I agree,' the agent once again would quickly agree, pleased over what he thought was an ally helping him to make out like a bandit at claimants' expense.

"Well, after about four or five, 'Yeah, I agrees,' in a row on this inexpensive stuff, I would then slip in a morsel like:

"'However, Walker has an item here, imported English fishing flies, he thinks would cost $800 to replace. I think this is reasonable.

"'Yeah, I agree,' our by then programmed friend would automatically nod.

"So, by giving in on the cheap articles and holding firm on the costly ones, we were able to maximize your settlement," purred our newly-acquired fast friend.

Needless to say we wrote them a glowing letter of recommendation, for this was one time when the huge insurance company dog had had its tail wagged.

*   *   *

VOSS AND HIS GUN

Back in the fifties I worked under a delightful boss. He was George Voss.

George, a kind man, was the perfect extrovert besides being blessed with a steel trap memory. A born salesman, he was also a leader of men. Not surprisingly, therefore, his great giftings allowed him ultimately to retire with a pension that would have turned many an active executive emerald green.

This particular vignette took place in Louisiana earlier in Voss' career.

His work, requiring as it did that he be on the road much of the time, was an understandable cause for concern for him over leaving his wife alone back home without protection.

So on one of his trips he purchased Jeanne a handgun and promptly stashed it under his car seat.

En route home a weary George pulled up to a roadside café, trudged in and ordered a coffee. As he was sipping his drink, his tired eyes gazing unfocused, a couple was dancing on the floor to the tune of a jukebox piece.

Presently George rose, left his coffee money and a tip on the table and made his way to his car, a low-slung open topped Corvette.

No sooner had he inserted his key in the ignition when a ham-size hand plopped down on his window sill. Looking up, George saw a hulk, the same guy who had been dancing minutes earlier in the café.

"I don't like the way you looked at my gal, buddy. Step out please so I can punch your lights out," he leveled in measured tones at Voss, while his lady friend, dutifully impressed, tittered in the background.

Remembering the small arm he was taking back to Jeanne, George reached below his seat and then with gun aimed at the bully's midriff, inquired, "Excuse me, you were saying?"

Quickly raising his hands defensively, Mr. Macho backed away stammering, "Oh, n-n-nothing at all, sir!"

ABOUT AUTHOR FRANK BANCROFT WALKER

PERSONAL:

Born San Francisco in 1924; married 58 years; 5 children; wife Peruvian, European educated, multi-lingual

SCHOOLING: (1940-1949)

St. Ignatius H.S., San Francisco* (degree)

Univ. San Francisco (engineering, Navy V-1 program)*

Gonzaga Univ. (engineering, Navy V-12)*

Cornell Univ. (Navy midshipman's school) (degree)

North Carolina State Univ. (Naval officer's diesel engineering school) (degree)

Georgetown Univ. School of Foreign Service* (degree)

———

* Jesuit Institution

YWAM Missionary School including Malaysia outreach (degree)

JOB HISTORY: (1949-1989)

Commercial sword fishing and boat construction, Peru (where resided)

Farm chemical market development all Latin America (resided Mexico, Brazil and Coral Gables)

Professional tennis teacher and California board member of U.S. Professional Tennis Assn. Wrote for national tennis magazines. Staff, advanced tennis instructor as assistant professor at California State University Northridge.

Licensed California general building contractor

SINCE RETIREMENT: (1991-Present)

Newspaper columnist and feature writer for the Mariposa Gazette and later the Mariposa Tribune

Volunteer Gideon speaking at churches

Volunteer food for the poor work at Manna House, Mariposa

Volunteer jail chaplain, Mariposa Co. California Jail (18 years)

Professional award winning scenic photographer (over 100 ribbons)

Semi-professional harmonica soloist (classical and modern). Schooled in Brazil under Brazil's leading harmonica player. Have done many hundreds of gigs.

MISCELLANEOUS:
National H.S. ROTC small bore rifle marksman champion
College handball doubles champion
Fluent in Spanish and Portuguese
The above events pale alongside the greatest of all, viz. when, at age 47, I asked Jesus Christ into my heart, thereby assuring my eternal salvation.

CPSIA information can be obtained at www.ICGtesting.com
Printed in the USA
BVOW020304130213

313125BV00009B/394/P